Appleton Morgan

The Shakespearean Myth

William Shakespeare and circumstantial Evidence

Appleton Morgan

The Shakespearean Myth
William Shakespeare and circumstantial Evidence

ISBN/EAN: 9783337081263

Printed in Europe, USA, Canada, Australia, Japan

Cover: Foto ©ninafisch / pixelio.de

More available books at **www.hansebooks.com**

THE

SHAKESPEAREAN MYTH

WILLIAM SHAKESPEARE

AND

CIRCUMSTANTIAL EVIDENCE

BY

APPLETON MORGAN, A. M., LL. B.

AUTHOR OF "THE LAW OF LITERATURE," "NOTES TO BEST'S PRINCIPLES
OF EVIDENCE," ETC., ETC

Sic vos non vobis nidificatis aves;
Sic vos non vobis vellera fertis oves;
Sic vos non vobis mellificatus apes;
Sic vos non vobis fertis aratra boves.
—*P. Virgil. Maro*

CINCINNATI
ROBERT CLARKE & CO
1881

PREFACE.

M. GUIZOT, in his History of England, states the
Shakespearean problem in a few words, when he says:
"Let us finally mention the great comedian, the
great tragedian, the great philosopher, the great poet,
who was in his lifetime butcher's apprentice, poacher,
actor, theatrical manager, and whose name is William
Shakespeare. In twenty years, amid the duties of
his profession, the care of mounting his pieces, of instructing his actors, he composed the thirty-two tragedies and comedies, in verse and prose, rich with an
incomparable knowledge of human nature, and an un-
equaled power of imagination, terrible and comic by
turns, profound and delicate, homely and touching,
responding to every emotion of the soul, divining all
that was beyond the range of his experience and for
ever remaining the treasure of the age—all this being
accomplished, Shakespeare left the theater and the
busy world, at the age of forty-five, to return to Stratford-on-Avon, where lived peacefully in the most
modest retirement, writing nothing and never return-

ing to the stage—ignored and unknown if his works had not forever marked out his place in the world—a strange example of an imagination so powerful, suddenly ceasing to produce, and closing, once for all, the door to the efforts of genius."

But M. Guizot is very far from suggesting any prima facie inconsistency in this statement as it stands.

Since every man reads the Shakespearean pages for himself and between the lines, much of what we are expected to accept as Shakespearean criticism must fail of universal appreciation and sympathy. But none who read the English tongue can well be unconcerned with the question as to WHO WROTE those pages; and it would be affectation to deny that the intense realism of our day is offering some startling contributions to the solution of that question.

For instance, the gentlemen of the "New Shakespeare Society" (whom Mr. Swinburne rather mercilessly burlesques in his recent "*Studies of Shakespeare*") submit these dramas to a quantitative analysis; and, by deliberately counting the "male," "female," "weak," and "stopped" endings, and the Alexandrines and catalectics (just as a mineralogist counts the degrees and minutes in the angles of his crystals), insist on their ability to pronounce didatically and infallibly WHAT was written by William Shakespeare, and at what age; WHAT was composed by Dekker, Fletcher, Marlowe, or

anybody else; what was originally theirs, touched up
by William Shakespeare or *vice versa*, etc. It is curious to observe how this process invariably gives all the
admirable sentiments to William Shakespeare, and all
the questionable ones to somebody else; but at least
these New Shakespearean gentlemen have surrendered
somewhat of the "cast-iron" theory of our childhood—
that every page, line, and word of the immortal
Shakespearean Drama was written by William
Shakespeare demi-god, and by none other—perhaps,
even opened a path through which the unbelievers
may become, in due time, orthodox.

There are still, however, a great many persons who
are disposed to wave the whole question behind them,
much as Mr. Podsnap disposed of the social evil or
a famine in India. It is only a "Historic Doubt,"
they say, and "Historic Doubts" are not rare, are
mainly contrived to exhibit syllogistic ingenuity in the
teeth of facts, etc., etc. The French, they say, have
the same set of problems about Molière. Was he a
lawyer? was he a doctor? etc.—and they all find their
material in INTERNAL evidence—e. g., an accurate
handling of the technique of this or that profession
or science : parallelism, practical coincidence, or something of that sort.

The present work is an attempt to examine, for the
benefit of these latter, from purely EXTERNAL evidence,
a question which, dating only within the current quar-

ter century, is constantly recurring to confront investigation, and, like Banquo's troublesome shade, seems
altogether indisposed to " down."

I have to add my acknowledgments to Mr. Julian
Norris, for his careful preparation of the Index to
these pages.

GRANDVIEW-ON-HUDSON, *October* 2, 1881.

THE SHAKESPEAREAN MYTH.

PART I

THE MYSTERY.

THE thirty-seven plays called, collectively, "Shakespeare," are a phenomenon, not only in English letters, but in human experience. The literature of the country to which they belong, had, up to the date of their appearance, failed to furnish, and has been utterly powerless since, to produce any type, likeness, or formative trace of them; while the literature of other nations possesses not even a corresponding type. The history of a century on either side of their era discloses, within the precints of their birth, no resources upon which levy could have been made for their creation. They came and went like a meteor; neither borrowing of what they found, nor loaning to what they left, their own peculiar and unapproachable magnificence.

The unremitting researches of two centuries have only been able to assign their authorship (where it rested at first) to an hiatus in the life of a wayward village lad named William Shakespeare—who fled his native town penniless and before the constable, to return, in a few years, a well-to-do esquire—with a coat of arms and money in his pocket.

(9)

We have the history of the boy, and certain items as to the wealthy squire, who left behind him two or three exceedingly common-place and conventional epitaphs (said to be his handiwork) and a remarkable WILL; but, between them, no hint of history, chronicle, or record. Still, within this unknown period of this man's career, these matchless dramas came from somewhere, and passed current under his name.

The death of their reputed author attracted no contemporary attention, and for many years thereafter the dramas remained unnoticed. Although written in an idiom singularly open to the comprehension of all classes and periods of English-speaking men, no sooner did they begin to be remarked, than a cloud of what are politely called "commentators" bore down upon them; any one who could spell feeling at liberty to furnish a "reading;" and any one who supposed himself able to understand one of these "readings," to add a barnacle in the shape of a "note." From these "commentators" the stately text is even now in peril, and rarely, even to-day, can it be perused, except one line at a time, across the top of a dreary page of microscopic and exasperating annotation. But, up to within a very few years, hardly a handful of Shakespearean students had arisen with courage to admit— what scarcely any one of the "commentators" even, could have failed to perceive—the utterly inadequate source ascribed to the plays themselves.

It is not yet thirty years since an American lady was supposed to have gone crazy because she declared that William Shakespeare, of the Globe and Blackfriars theaters in London, in the days of Elizabeth, was not the author of these certain dramas and poems for which—for almost three hundred years—he has stood sponsor.

Miss Bacon's " madness," indeed, has been rapidly contageous. Now-a-days, men make books to prove, not that William Shakespeare did not write these works, but that Francis Bacon, Walter Raleigh, or some other Elizabethan, did not. And we even find, now and then, a treatise written to prove that William Shakespeare was, after all, their author ; an admission, at least, that the ancient presumption to that effect no longer covers the case. And, doubtless, the correct view is within this admission. For, probably, if permitted to examine this presumption by the tests which would be applied to any other question of fact, namely, the tests of contemporary history, muniments, and circumstantial evidence, it will be found to be quite as well established and proved that William Shakespeare was not the author of the plays that go by his name, as any other fact, occurring in London between the years 1585 and 1616, not recorded in history or handed down by tradition, could be established and proved in 1881.

If a doubt as to the authorship of the plays had arisen at any time during or between those years, and had been kept open thereafter, the probability is that it would have been settled by this time. But, as it is, we may be pretty certain that no such doubt did arise, and that no such question was asked, during the years when those who could have dispelled the doubt or answered the question were living. When we are about to visit a theater in these days, what we ask and concern ourselves with is : Is the play entertaining? Does it " draw ?" And, when we wit-

ness it, the question is: Do we enjoy it—or does
it bore us? Will we recommend our friends to
come that they may be entertained, too, and
that we may discuss it with them? or will we warn
them to keep away? We very speedily settle these
questions for ourselves. Doubtless we may and do inquire who the author is. But we do not enter into
any discussion upon the subject, or charge our minds
enough with the matter to doubt it when we are told.
The author's name is, not unusually, printed on the
play-bill before us; we glance at it indifferently, take
what is told us for granted, and think no more about
it. If the name happens to be assumed, we may possibly see its identity discussed in the dramatic columns
of our newspapers next morning, or we may not. If
the play entertains us, we commend it. If it drags,
we sneer at it, get up and go off. That is all the concern we give it. The evening has slipped away; and,
with it, any idle speculations as to the playwright who
has essayed to amuse us for an hour.

If, three hundred years hence, a question as to who
wrote the play we saw at Mr. Daly's theater or Mr.
Wallack's theater last evening should come up, there
would be very little evidence, not any records, and
scarcely an exhibit to refer to in the matter. Copies
of the play-bill or the newspapers of the day might
chance to be discovered; but these—the internal testimony of the play itself, if any, and a sort of tacit
presumption growing out of a statement it was nobody's cue to inquire into at the time it was made, and
had been nobody's business to scrutinize since—would
constitute all the evidence at hand. Now this supposititious case is precisely all-fours with the facts

in the matter of the dramatic works which we call, collectively, Shakespeare's. Precisely: except that, on the evenings when those plays were acted, there were no play-bills, and, on the succeeding morning, no daily newspaper. We have, therefore, in 1881, much fewer facilities for setting ourselves right as to their authorship than those living three hundred years after us could possess in the case we have supposed. The audiences who witnessed a certain class of plays at Shakespeare's theaters, in the years between 1585 and 1606, were entertained. The plays "drew." People talked of them about town, and they become valuable to their proprietors. The mimic lords and ladies were acceptable to the best seats; the rabble loved the show and glitter and the alarum of drums; and all were Britons who gloated over rehearsal of the prowess of their own kings and heroes, and to be told that their countrymen at Agincourt had slain ten thousand Frenchmen at an expense of but five and twenty of themselves. But, if M. Taine's description of the Shakespearean theaters and the audience therein wont to assemble may be relied upon, we can pretty safely conclude that they troubled themselves very little as to who fashioned the dialogue the counterfeit kings and queens, soldiers, lords, and ladies spoke; or that they saw any thing in that dialogue to make such speculation appear worth their while. Nor can we discover any evidence, even among the cultured courtiers who listened to them—or in the case of Elizabeth herself, who is said to have loved them (which we may as well admit for the argument's sake)—that any recognition of the plays as works worthy of any other than a stage-manager, occurred.

Even if it should appear that these plays thus performed were the plays we now call Shakespeare's; had any of this audience suspected that these plays were not written for them, but for all time; that, three hundred years later—when the plays should not only be extant, but more loved and admired than ever—the thinking world should set itself seriously to probe the mystery of their origin; there might have been some interest as to their producer manifested, and we might have had some testimony competent to the exact point to-day.

But it is evident enough that no such prophetic vision was vouchsafed to them, and no such prophetic judgment passed. Nor is the phenomenon exceptional. The critic does not live, even to-day, however learned or cultured or shrewd, who would take the responsibility of affirming upon his own judgment, or even upon the universal judgment of his age and race, that any literary composition would be, after a lapse of three hundred years, not only extant, but immortal, hugged as its birthright by a whole world. Such a statement would have been contrary to experience, beyond the prophecy of criticism, and therefore only to be known—if known at all—as a Fact. Moreover, it could only be known as a fact at the expiration of the three hundred years. Doubtless, few critics would care, in any case, to commit themselves upon record one way or the other in a matter so hypothetical and speculative as the judgment of posterity upon a literary performance, and certainly nothing of the sort occurred in Shakespeare's day, even if there were any dramatic or literary critics to speculate upon the subject. There can be no doubt—and it must be conceded

—that certain acted plays *did* pass with their first audiences, and that certain printed plays, both contemporaneously and for years thereafter, did pass with the
public who read them, as the compositions of Mr.
Manager Shakespeare; and that probably even the
manager's pot companions, who had better call to
know him than any others, saw nothing to shake their
heads at in his claim to be their author (provided he
ever made any such claim; which, by the way, does
not appear from any record of his life, and which nobody ever asserted as a fact). If they did—with the
exception only of Robert Greene—they certainly kept
their own counsel. On the one hand, then, the question of the authorship was never raised, and, on the
other hand, if it had been, the scholars and critics who
studied the plays (supposing that there were any such
in those days) could not possibly have recognized them
as immortal. If they had so recognized them, they
would doubtless have left us something more satisfactory as to the authorship of the compositions than the
mere "impression that they were informed" that the
manager of the theater where they were produced
wrote them; that they supposed he was clever enough
to have done so, and they therefore took it for granted
that he did. That is all there is of the evidence of
Shakespeare's own day, as to the question—if it still
is a question—before us.

But how about the presumption—the legal presumption, arising from such lapse of time as that the memory of man runneth not to the contrary—the presumption springing from tradition and common report—that
William Shakespeare composed the Shakespearean
plays? It is, of course, understood that one presump-

tion is as good as another until it is disturbed. It is
never safe to underrate an existing presumption; as
long as it stands at all, it stands as conclusive; once
overthrown, however, it is as if it had never existed.

A presumption three hundred years old may be a
strong one to overthrow. But if its AGE is all there is
of it—if it be only strong in years—it can yet be top-
pled over. Once overthrown, it is no more venerable
because it is three hundred years old than if it were
only three. An egg-shell will toss upon the crest of
an angry surf, and, for very frailty, outride breakers
when the mightiest ship man ever framed could not
survive an instant. But it is only an egg-shell, for all
that, and a touch of the finger will crush and destroy
it. And so, formidable as it was in age, the presumption as to William Shakespeare's authorship of
the great dramas which for three hundred years had
gone by his name, had only to be touched by the thumb
and finger of common sense to crackle and shrivel like
the egg that sat on the wall in the Kindergarten rhyme,
which all the king's army and all the king's men could
not set up again, once it had tumbled over.

But as the world advanced and culture increased,
why did not the question arise before? Simply because the times were not ripe for it. This is the age
and generation for the explosion of myths, and, as one
after another of them falls to pieces and disappears,
who does not wonder that they have not fallen sooner?
For how many years has the myth of William Tell been
cherished as history! And yet there is no element of
absolute impossibility or even of improbability—much
less of miracle—in the story of an archer with a sure
eye and a steady aim. Or, in the case of physical

myths—which only required an exploration by physical sense for their explosion—the maps of two centuries or so ago represented all inaccessible seas as swarming with krakens and ship-devouring reptiles. And it is not twenty years since children were taught in their geographies that upon the coast of Norway there was a whirlpool which sucked down ships prow foremost. And here, in our midst, a cannon-shot from where we sit and write these lines, there was believed to be and exist a Hell Gate which was a very portal of death and slaughter to hapless mariners. But there are no krakens, and not much of a Maelstrom; and, for twenty years before General Newton blew up a few rocks at Hell Gate, people had laughed at the myth of its ferocity. And again: nothing is easier than to invent a story so utterly unimportant and immaterial that it will be taken for granted, without controversy, and circulate with absolute immunity from examination, simply because worth nobody's while to contradict it. For example, it is likely enough that Demosthenes, in practicing oratory, stood on a sea-beach and drilled his voice to outroar the waves. The story is always told, however, with the rider, that Demosthenes did this with his mouth filled with pebble-stones; and, as nobody cares whether he did or not, nobody troubles himself to ascertain by experiment that the thing is impossible, and that nobody can roar with a mouth full of pebble-stones. And not even then would he succeed in removing the impression obtaining with the great mass of the world, that a thing is proven sufficiently if it gets into "print." Charles II. set the Royal Society of his day at work to

2

find the reason why a dead fish weighed more than a
live one—and it was only when they gave it up, that
the playful monarch assured them that the fact they
were searching for the reason of was not a fact at all.
It is not impossible to demonstrate from experience,
that the human mind will be found—as a rule—to
prefer wasting laborious days in accounting for, rather
than take the very simplest pains to verify even a
proposition or alleged fact, which, if a fact at all, is of
value beyond itself. It was objected to the system of
Copernicus, when first brought forward, that, if the
earth turned on its axis as he represented, a stone
dropped from the summit of a tower would not fall at
the foot of it, but at a great distance to the west, in
the same manner that a stone dropped from the mast-
head of a ship in full sail does not fall at the foot of
the mast, but toward the stern. To this it was answered that a stone, being a part of the earth, obeys
the same laws and moves with it, whereas it is no part
of the ship, of which, consequently, its motion is inde-
pendent. This solution was admitted by some and
opposed by others, and the controversy went on with
spirit; nor was it till one hundred years after the death
of Copernicus that, the experiment being tried, it was
ascertained that the stone thus dropped from the head
of the mast does fall at the foot of it. And so, if, in
the case of the Shakespearean authorship, the day
has come for truth to dispel fiction, and reason to scout
organic miracle, why should we decline to look into
an alleged Shakespearean myth simply because it happens to be a little tardy in coming to the surface?

But, most of all, it is to be remembered that it is,
practically, only our own century that has compre-

hended the masterliness and matchlessness of the
"Hamlet" and " Macbeth," and the rest of those transcripts of nature, the prophetic insight of whose
author "spanned the ages that were to roll up after
him, mastered the highest wave of modern learning and discovery, and touched the heart of all time,
not through the breathing of living characters, but
by lifting mankind up out of the loud kingdom of
earth into the silent realm of infinity; who so wrote
that to his all-seeing vision schools and libraries,
sciences and philosophies, were unnecessary, because
his own marvelous intuition had grasped all the past
and seen through all his present and all his future, and
because, before his superhuman power, time and space
had vanished and disappeared."[1] The age for which
the dramas were written had not come, in that ·Eliza-
bethan era. The tongues of the actors were tied, the
ears of the audience were deaf to syllables whose burden was for the centuries that were to come after.
The time for the question, " Who wrote them?" was
not yet. For two hundred years more—from the day
of William Shakespeare's death down to years within
the memory of those now living—down to at least the
date of Lord Byron (who admits that it is the perfectly
correct thing to call Shakespeare "god-like," "mighty,"
and the like, but very unfashionable to read him),—
we may ransack the records of scholarship and criticism, and unearth scarcely a hint of what is now their
every-where conceded superiority, to say nothing of
their immortality. In short, we can not rise from
such a search without understanding, very clearly in-

---

[1] Jean Paul Frederich Richter.

deed, why our question did not arise sooner. Nobody
asked, " Who wrote Shakespeare?" because nobody
seemed to consider " Shakespeare " as any thing worth
speculating about.   Let us pause right here to demonstrate this.

Fuller, in 1622, chronicles that William Shakespeare's " genius was jocular," his comedies merry, and
his tragedies wonderful; his wit quick, but that his
learning was very little.   Evelyn notes that, in 1661,
he saw " Hamlet, Prince of Denmark," played : "but
now the old plays begin to disgust this refined age,
since His Majesty has been so long abroad." [1]   Pepys,
his contemporary, says that the " Midsummer-Night's
Dream " " was the most insipid, ridiculous play he
had ever seen   .   .   .   .   and, but having lately
read the ' Adventures of Five Hours,' ' Othello '
seemed a mean thing," though he liked Davenant's
opera of " Macbeth," with its music and dancing.[2]
When spending some money in books he looks
over Shakespeare, but chooses " ' Hudibras,' the book
now in the greatest fashion for drollery," instead.   It is
doubtful if Milton ever read the Shakespearean plays,
in spite of the eloquent verses, " What needs my
Shakespeare," etc.; since, in " L'Allegro," he speaks of
his (Shakespeare's) " native wood-notes wild." [3]   Surely
if there is any thing in letters that is not " native wood-
notes," it is the stately Shakespearean verse, full of
camps and courts, but very rarely of woodlands and

---

[1] "Amenities of Authors—Shakespeare," p. 210.

[2] Ibid., p. 211.

[3] Dr. Maginn, in his Shakespearean papers ("Learning of
Shakespeare"), endeavors to explain what Milton meant by
" native wood-notes wild."

pastures ; besides, whatever Milton might say of the book called "Shakespeare" in poetry—like Ben Jonson—he showed unmitigated contempt for its writer in prose : about the worst thing he could say about his king in " The Iconoclast," was that Charles I. kept an edition of Shakespeare for his closet companion.[1] " Other stuff of this sort," cries the blind poet, " may be read throughout the whole tragedy, wherein the poet used much license in departing from the truth of history."[2]

In 1681, one Nahum Tate, supposed to be a poet (a delusion so widespread that he was actually created " poet laureate") stumbled upon " a thing called Lear," assigned to one William Shakespeare, and, after much labor, congratulated himself upon having "been able to make a play out of it."[3] John Dryden, in or about 1700, in his " Defence of the Epilogue," a postscript to his tragedy " The Conquest of Granada," says : "Let any man who understands English, read diligently the works of Shakespeare and Fletcher, and I dare undertake that he will find in every page either some solecism of speech, or some notorious flaw in sense; and yet these men are reverenced, when we are not forgiven." He denounces " the lameness of their plots," made up of some " ridiculous incoherent story, . . . either grounded on impossibilities, or, at least,

---

[1] "Amenities of Authors—Shakespeare," vol. ii, p. 208. Ibid., p. 209, note.

[2] It is fair to say that "stuff" may only have meant "matter," but it is indisputable that the passage was meant as a slur on one who would read "Shakespeare."

[3] The "play" he did make out of it is to be found in W. H. Smith's " Bacon and Shakespeare," p. 129.

so meanly written that the comedy neither caused your mirth nor the serious part your concernment. . . . he writes, in many places, below the dullest writers of our own or any precedent age." Of the audiences who could tolerate such matter, he says: " They knew no better, and therefore were satisfied with what they brought. Those who call theirs the ' Golden Age of Poetry,' have only this reason for it: that they were then content with acorns before they knew the use of bread," etc.[1]   To show the world how William Shakespeare *should* have written, Mr. Dryden publishes his own improved version of "Troilus and Cressida," " with an abjectly fulsome dedication to the Earl of Sunderland, and a Preface,"[2] in which he is obliging enough to say that the style of Shakespeare being "so pestered with figurative expressions that it is as affected as it is obscure;" that, though "the author seems to have began it with some fire, the characters of ' Pandarus' and ' Troilus' are promising enough, but, as if he grew weary of his task, after an entrance or two, he lets 'em fall, and the latter part of the tragedy is nothing but a confusion of drums and trumpets, excursions and alarms. The chief persons who give name to the tragedy are left alive. ' Cressida' is left alive and is not punished." " I have undertaken to remove that heap of rubbish. . . . I new-modelled the plot; threw out many unnecessary persons, improved

---

[1] "Works," edited by Malone, vol. ii, p. 252.

[2] " Troilus and Cressida, or Truth Found Too Late." Written by John Dryden, servant to his Majesty, London (4to) printed for Abel Small, at the Unicorn at the West End of St. Paul's, and Jacob Tonson, at the Judge's Head, in Chancery Lane, near Fleet street. 1679.

those characters which were begun and left unfinished,
. . . made, with no small trouble, an order and
connection of the scenes, and . . . so ordered
them that there is a coherence of 'em with one another, . . . a due proportion of time allowed for
every motion, . . . have refined the language, etc."

The same thing was done in 1672, by Ravenscroft,
who produced an adaptation of "Titus Andronicus,"
and boasted "that none in all the author's works ever
received greater alterations or additions; the language
not only refined, but many scenes entirely new, besides
most of the principal characters heightened, and the
plot much increased." John Dennis, a critic of that
day, declares that Shakespeare "knew nothing about
the ancients, set all propriety at defiance, . . . was
neither master of time enough to consider, correct, and
polish what he had written, . . . his lines are utterly void of celestial fire," and his verses "frequently
harsh and unmusical." He was, however, so interested
in the erratic and friendless poet that he kindly altered
"The Merry Wives of Windsor," and touched up
"Coriolanus," which he brought out in 1720, under the
title of "The Invader of his Country, or the Fatal Re-
sentment." The play, however, did not prosper, and
he attributed it to the fact that it was played on a
Wednesday. Dean Swift, in his "The Narrative of
Dr. Robert Norris, concerning the Strange and Deplor-
able Frenzy of John Dennis," relates how the said Dennis, being in company with Lintot, the bookseller, and
Shakespeare being mentioned as of a contrary opinion
to Mr. Dennis, the latter "swore the said Shakespeare
was a rascal, with other defamatory expressions, which
gave Mr. Lintot a very ill opinion of the said Shake-

speare." Lord Shaftesbury complains, at about the
same date, of Shakespeare's "rude and unpolished
style and antiquated phrase and wit."[1]   Thomas
Rymer knows exactly how Othello, which he calls
"a bloody farce, the tragedy of the pocket-hand-
kerchief," ought to have been done.   In the first
place, he is angry that the hero should be a black-a-
moor, and that the army should be insulted by his being a soldier.   Of "Desdemona" he says: "There is
nothing in her which is not below any country kitchen-
maid—no woman bred out of a pigstye could talk so
meanly."   Speaking of expression, he writes that "in
the neighing of a horse or in the growling of a mastiff
there is a meaning, there is as lively expression, and,
I may say, more humanity, than in the tragical flights
of Shakespeare."   He is indignant that the catastrophe of the play should turn on a handkerchief.   He
would have liked it to have been folded neatly on the
bridal couch, and, when Othello was killing Desdemona, "the fairy napkin might have started up to dis-
arm his fury and stop his ungracious mouth.   Then
might she, in a trance of fear, have lain for dead; then
might he, believing her dead, and touched with remorse, have honestly cut his own throat, by the good
leave and with the applause of all the spectators, who
might thereupon have gone home with a quiet mind,
and admiring the beauty of Providence freely and
truly represented in the theater.   Then for the un-
raveling of the plot, as they call it, never was old

---

[1] Mr. De Quincy's painful effort to demonstrate that neither
Dryden nor Shaftesbury meant what he said is amusing reading.
See his "Shakespeare" in the "Encyclopædia Britannica."   Also
Knight, "Studies of Shakespeare," p. 510, as to Dr. Johnson.

deputy recorder in a country town, with his spectacles on, summing up the evidence, at such a puzzle, so blundered and bedoltified as is our poet to have a good riddance and get the catastrophe off his hands. What can remain with the audience to carry home with them? How can it work but to delude our senses, disorder our thoughts, scare our imaginations, corrupt our appetite, and fill our head with vanity, confusion, tintamarre and jingle-jangle, beyond what all the parish clerks in London could ever pretend to?" He then hopes the audience will go to the play as they go to church, namely, "sit still, look on one another, make no reflection, nor mind the play more than they would a sermon." With regard to "Julius Cæsar," he is displeased that Shakespeare should have meddled with the Romans. He might be "familiar with Othello and Iago as his own natural acquaintances, but Cæsar and Brutus were above his conversation." To put them "in gulls' coats and make them Jack-puddens," is more than public decency should tolerate —in Mr. Rymer's eyes. Of the well-known scene between Brutus and Cassius, this critic remarks: "They are put there to play the bully and the buffoon, to show their activity of face and muscles. They are to play for a prize, a trial of skill and hugging and swaggering like two drunken Hectors for a twopenny reckoning." Rymer calls his book "A Short View of Tragedy, with Some Reflections on Shakespeare and Other Practitioners for the Stage." Hume thought that both Bacon and Shakespeare showed "a want of simplicity and purity of diction with defective taste and elegance," and that "a reasonable propriety of

3

thoughts he (Shakespeare) can not at any time up-
hold." Voltaire thought the Shakespearean kings
"not completely royal." Pope (who declared that
Rymer, just quoted, was "a learned and strict critic"),
to show that he was not insensible to the occasional
merits of the plays, was good enough to distinguish,
by inverted commas, such passages as he thought
might be safely admired by the rest of mankind; while
. Richard Steele, in "The Tatler,"[1] borrows the story
of the "Taming of the Shrew," and narrates it as
"an incident occurring in Lincolnshire," feeling, no
doubt, that he did a good deed in rescuing whatever
was worth preserving from the clutches of such obscure and obsolete literature!

And then came the period when scholars and men
of taste were ravished with Addison's stilted rhymes,
and the six-footed platitudes of Pope, and the sesque-
pedalian derivatives dealt out by old Samuel Johnson.
The Shakespearean plays are pronounced by Mr. Addison[2] "very faulty in hard metaphors and forced
expressions," and he joins them with "Nat. Lee," as
"instances of the false sublime. Samuel Johnson is
reported as saying that William Shakespeare never
wrote six consecutive lines (he subsequently made it
seven) without "making an ass of himself," (in which
speech he seems to have followed his namesake without the "h," old Ben, in the "Discoveries")—backing
up his assertion with some very choice specimens of
literary criticism. Let any one, interested enough in

---

[1] Vol. vi, No. 31. He complains, in number 42, that the female
characters in the play make "so small a figure."

[2] Spectator, 39; p. 235.

the matter to see for himself, take down Dr. Johnson's own edition of Shakespeare, and read his commentaries on the Shakespearean text. Let him turn, for example, to where he says of " Hamlet ":

We must allow to the tragedy of " Hamlet" the praise of variety. The incidents are so numerous that the argument of the play would make a long tale. The scenes are interchangeably diversified with merriment and solemnity, . . . that includes judicious and instructive observations. . . . New characters appear from time to time in continual succession, exhibiting various forms of life and particular modes of conversation. The pretended madness of Hamlet causes much mirth; . . . the catastrophe is not very happily produced; the exchange of weapons is rather an expedient of necessity than a stroke of art. A scheme might easily be formed to kill Hamlet with the dagger and Laertes with the bowl.

Again, of " Macbeth :"

This play is deservedly celebrated for the propriety of its fiction, and solemnity, grandeur, and variety of its action, but it has no nice discriminations of character. . . . I know not whether it may not be said in defense of some parts which now seem improbable, that in Shakespeare's time it was necessary to warn credulity against vain and illusive predictions.

Again, of " Julius Cæsar :"

Of this tragedy, many particular passages deserve regard, and the contention and reconcilement of Brutus and Cassius is universally celebrated. But I have never been strongly agitated in perusing it, and think it somewhat cold and unaffecting, etc.

Was " Hamlet " a low comedy part, in the days when all England bowed at the feet of an unkempt and mannerless old man, awed by the brilliancy of his literary judgment? And did Hamlet's " pretended madness " cause " much mirth " to the age, or only to

Samuel Johnson? People now-a-days do not sit and giggle over "the pretended madness of Hamlet." But, waiving these questions, let him turn to the "Rambler,"[1] of this excellent lexicographer, and read him (patiently, if he can), citing the magnificent lines—

> Come thick night
> And pall thee in the dunnest smoke of hell;
> That my keen knife see not the wound it makes,
> Nor heaven peep through the blanket of the dark
> To cry "hold, hold!"

as an example of "poetry debased by mean expressions;" because "dun" is a "low" expression, "seldom heard but in the stable;" "knife" an instrument used by butchers and cooks in the meanest employment;" and asking "who, without some relaxation of his gravity, can hear of the avengers of guilt *peeping* through the blanket of the dark!" Let the reader look on a little further, and find this fossil-scanning machine telling off the spondees and dactyls in the dramas (to ascertain if the cæsura was exactly in the middle) on his fingers and thumbs, and counting the unities up to three, to see if he could approve of what the ages after him were to worship! if, haply, this Shakespeare (although he *might* have devised a scheme to kill Laertes with the bowl and Hamlet with the dagger, or *might* have thrown a little more fire into the quarrel with Brutus and Cassius) could be admitted to sit at the feet of Addison, with his sleepy and dreary "Campaign;" or Pope, with his metrical proverbs about "Man;" or even the aforesaid Samuel Johnson himself, with his rhymed dic-

---

[1] No. 168.

tionaries about the "vanity of human wishes," and
so on. Let him find the old lexicographer admitting,
in his gracious condescension, that " The Tempest" "is
sufficiently regular ;" of " Measure for Measure" that
" the unities are sufficiently preserved ;" that the " Midsummer Night's Dream" was " well written ;" that the
style of the "Merchant of Venice" was "easy ;" but
that in "As you Like It" "an opportunity of exhibiting a moral lesson" is unhappily lost. The " Winter's Tale" is " entertaining ;" in " King John " he finds
" a pleasing interchange of incidents and characters,"
remarking that "the lady's grief is very affecting."
Of "Troilus and Cressida" the old formalist says, that it
"is one of the most correctly written of Shakespeare's
plays ;" of " Coriolanus," that it " is one of the most
amusing." But, he says, that "Antony and Cleopatra"
is " low " and " without any art of connection or care of
disposition." He dismisses " Cymbeline" with the remark that he does not care " to waste criticism upon
unresisting imbecility ; upon faults too evident for de-
tection and too gross for aggravation." He is pleased to
approve of " Romeo and Juliet," because " the incidents
are numerous and important, the catastrophe irresistibly affecting, and the process of the action carried on
with such probability, at least with such congruity to
popular opinions, as tragedy requires" and, while on
the whole, approving of " Othello," he can not help remarking that, " had the scene opened in Cyprus, and
the preceding incidents been occasionally related, there
had been little wanting to a drama of the most exact
and scrupulous regularity." And so on every-where !
Let the reader imagine one thus patronizing these
mighty and deathless monographs to-day ! Let him

imagine a better illustration, if he can, of what our Johnson's friend Pope called—in long meter—"fools rushing in where angels feared to tread!" And let him confess to himself that these were not the times nor the men to raise the question.

Is it not the fact that, until our own century, the eyes of the world were darkened, and men saw in these Shakespearean dramas only such stage plays, satisfying the acting necessities of almost any theater, as might have been written—not by "the soul" of any age; not by a man "myriad-minded;" not by a "morning-star of song," or a "dear son of memory," but—by a clever playwright? The sort of days when an Addison could have been pensioned for his dreary and innocent "Campaign," and a Mr. Pye made poet-laureate of the land where an unknown pen had once written "Hamlet;" were, consequently, *not* the days for the discovery with which this century has crowned itself—namely, the discovery that the great first of poets lived in the age when England and America were one world by themselves, and that they must now draw together again to search for the master "who came"—to use, with all reverence, the words of Judge Holmes—"upon our earth, knowing all past, all present, and all future, to be leader, guide, and second gospel of mankind." But the fullness of time has come, and we now know that, whoever was the poet that he "kept," he was of quite another kidney than the manager of the theater. William Shakespeare, who employed him to write Plays, and who wrote Revelations and Gospels instead.

If we were interested to inquire what manner of man Mr. Manager Shakespeare was, we have only to

look about us among the managers of theaters in this
latter half of our nineteenth century. Let us take
Mr. Wallack or Mr. Daly, both of whom arrange plays
for the stages of their own theaters, for example; or,
better yet, take Mr. Dion Boucicault, who is an actor
as well as a manager, and is, moreover, as successful
in his day as was William Shakespeare in his. Mr.
Boucicault has, so far, produced about one hundred and
thirty-seven successful plays. Mr. William Shakespeare produced about a hundred less. All of Mr. Boucicault's plays show that gentleman's skillful hand in
cutting, expanding, arranging, and setting for the
stage; and in the representation of them, Mr. Boucicault has himself often participated. In like manner,
Mr. Shakespeare, the manager, we are told by tradition, often assisted at the representation of the dramas
produced on his boards, playing the Ghost in "Hamlet,"[1] and the King in "Henry VI," which indicate
very readily that his place in the "stock" was that of
a "walking (or utility) gentleman." We happen to
know, also, that Mr. Shakespeare rewrote for the stage
what his unknown poet, poets, or friends composed,
from the tolerable hearsay testimony of his fellow

---

[1] And played it, it is thought by some, so wretchedly that he
made "the gods" hoot. At any rate, in a pamphlet published
by Lodge, in 159 3, "Witt's Miserie and the World's Madness;
Discovering the Devil's Incarnate of this age," a devil named
"Hate-Vertue" is described as looking "as pale as the vizard of
the ghost, which cried so miserably at the theatre like an oister-
wife, 'Hamlet—Revenge.'" But perhaps Shakespeare did not
play the ghost that night. Shakespeare also played "Old
Knowell," Jonson's "Every Man in his Humor," "Adam," in
"As You Like It," and, according to Jonson, a part in the latter's
"Legacies," in 1603.

actor, Ben Jonson, who tells us that he remembers
to have heard the players say that the stage copies of
the plays were written in Shakespeare's autograph,
and were all the more available on that account, because he (Shakespeare), was a good penman, in that
"whatever he penned, he never blotted line."[1]   Mr.
Boucicault, while claiming the full credit to which he
is entitled, is quite too clever, as well as too conscientious
to set up for an original author or a poet, as well as a
playwright. Neither does Shakespeare (as we have
already said), anywhere appear to have ever claimed
to be a poet, or even to have taken to himself—what
we may, however, venture to ascribe to him—the merit
of the stage-setting of the dramatic works, which,
having been played at his theater, we collectively call
the "Shakespearean plays" to-day. Why, then, to
begin with, should we not conceive of Mr. Manager
Shakespeare discharging the same duties as Mr. Wallack, Mr. Daly, or Mr. Boucicault? as very much—
from the necessities of his vocation—the same sort of
man as either of them?

There is scarcely any evidence either way; but the
fact that the actors were in the habit of receiving their
fair copy of these plays from the manager's—William
Shakespeare's—own hand, seems to make it evident
that he did not originally compose them. Indeed, if
Shakespeare had been their author, well-to-do and
bustling manager as he was, he would probably have
intrusted their transcription to some subordinate or supernumerary; or, better yet, would have kept a playwright of experience to set his compositions for the

---

[1] See Post, part III, the Jonsonian Testimony.

stage, to put in the necessary localisms, "gags," and allusions to catch the ear of the penny seats. Such a division of labor is imperative to-day, and was imperative then—or at least to suppose that it was not, is to suppose that of his dozen or so of co-managers, William Shakespeare was the one who did all the work, while the others looked on.

But, it is surmised that Shakespeare was his own playwright; took the dramas and rewrote them for the actors; he inserted the requisite business, the exits, and entrances, and—when necessary—suited the reading to the actor who was to pronounce the dialogue, according as he happened to be fat or lean.[1] Such was

---

[1] It may be noted that the line, "He's fat and scant of breath," does not occur in the early and imperfect edition of "Hamlet" of 1603. Was it added to suit Burbadge? And was there a further change made also to suit Mr. Burbadge, the leading tragedian of the time? In the edition of 1603, the grave-digger says of Yorick's skull:

Looke you, here's a skull hath bin here this dozen year,
Let me see, ever since our last King Hamlet
Slew Fortenbrasse in combat, young Hamlet's father,
He that's mad.

But in all subsequent editions, the grave-digger says: "Here's a skull now; this skull has lain i' the earth three and twenty years." The effect of this alteration is to add considerably to Hamlet's age. "Alas, poor Yorick!" he says, "I knew him, Horatio; a fellow of infinite jest, of most excellent fancy. He hath borne me on his back a thousand times; and now how abhorred in my imagination it is! My gorge rises at it. Here hung those lips that I have kissed, I know not how oft," etc. How old, then, was Hamlet when Yorick died? But Hamlet's age is even more distinctly fixed by other lines which do not occur in the early edition of 1603:

Hamlet.—How long hast thou been a grave-maker?

the employment which fell to the part of William Shakespeare, in the division of labor among the management in which he was a partner, and the resulting manuscript was what Ben Jonson's friends told him of. For nobody, we fancy, quite supposes that the poet, whoever he was, produced "Hamlet" one evening, "Macbeth" on another, and "Julius Cæsar" on another, without blotting or erasing, changing, pruning or filing a line, and then handed his original drafts to the players next morning to learn their parts from! This is not the way that poems are written (nor, we may add, the way theaters are managed). The greater the geniuses, the more they blotch and blot and dash their pens over the paper when the frenzy is in possession of them. And besides, the fact that there exist to-day, and always have existed, numerous and diverse readings of the Shakespearean text, does very clearly show that their author or authors did, at different times, vary and alter the construction of the text

First Clown.—Of all the days i' the year, I came to't that day that our last King Hamlet o'ercame Fortenbras.

Hamlet.—How long is that since?

First Clown.—Can not tell that? Every fool can tell that; it was the very day that young Hamlet was born; he that is mad and sent to England.

And presently he adds:

I have been sexton here, man and boy, thirty years.

Mr. Marshall writes: "It would appear that Shakespeare added these details, which tend to prove Hamlet to have been thirty years old, for much the same reason as he inserted the line, 'He's fat and scant of breath,' namely, in order to render Hamlet's age and personal appearance more in accordance with those of the great actor, Burbadge, who personated him." The edition of 1603 is generally accounted a piratical copy of the first sketch of the play.—*All the Year Round.*

as taste or fancy dictated, and, therefore, that the manuscripts Ben Jonson's friends saw and told him of (and Heminges & Condell, as far as their testimony is of any value, confirm Jonson, for they assert that " what he thought, he uttered with that easiness that we have received from him scarce a blot in his papers"), were the acting copies, and not the original manuscripts of the Shakespearean plays.

With the exception of Ben Jonson (to whose panegyric we devote a chapter in its place further on), the contemporaries of William Shakespeare, who celebrated his death in verse, nowhere assert him to have been the myriad-minded Oceanic (to use Coleridge's adjectives) genius which we conceive him now-a-days— which he *must* have been to have written the works now assigned to him. Let any one doubting this statement open the pages of Dr. Ingleby's " Shakespeare's Centurie of Prayse," a work claimed by its compiler to be inclusive of every allusion to, comment or criticism on Shakespeare, which Dr. Ingleby has been able to unearth in print, dating anywhere within one hundred years of Shakespeare's death. We have industriously turned every page of this work, and will submit to any other who will do the same, the question whether it contains a line which exhibits William Shakespeare as any other than a wit, a successful actor, a poet of the day, a genial and generous friend, a writer of plays, or whether—when eulogistic of the plays called his seven years after his death (a very different list, by the way, than the one assigned him during his life), rather than biographical as to the man, they are of any more value as *evidence* than Gray's or Milton's magnificent apostrophes to a genius with whom their only familiarity was through report, rumor, or impression derived from the ever immortal works. For, like Gray, Coleridge, Emerson—all that John Milton knew about William Shakespeare was pure hearsay, derived from local report or perusal of the Shakespearean plays ("a book invalued," he calls them). Even if we were called upon to do so, we could hardly conceive Milton—a Puritan, and a blind Puritan at that —as much of a play-goer or boon companion of actors and managers. But we are not called upon to imagine any thing of the sort; for, as a matter of fact, John Milton was exactly seven years and four months old when William Shakespeare died. And so, what is called "the Milton testimony," upon examination, proves to be no testimony at all, but only hearsay— venerable, perhaps—but hearsay, nevertheless;[1] as utterly immaterial as his "warbling his native wood notes wild"—a line that might be, not inaptly, applied to Robert Burns, but which suggests almost any thing except the stately and splendid pages of the Shakespearean opera—to which we have before alluded as justifying us, indeed, in wondering if the Puritan poet had ever gone so far, before formulating his opinion, as to open the book assigned to the Shakespeare he wrote of. And so, in the first place, there was no great call or occasion for discussion as to the authorship of the Shakespearean dramas in the days when they first began to be known by the public; and, as for Mr. Manager Shakespeare's friends, and the actors of his company,

---

[1] Milton was the enemy of all the ilk. "This would make them soon perceive what despicable creatures our common rimers and playwriters be," he says in his essays "of Education," in 1634.

they testified to what they had heard, and, if they knew any thing to the contrary, they kept it to themselves. If his friends, jealous of his reputation, they were not solicitous of heralding him a fraud; and if the "stock" upon his pay-roll, they held their bread at his hand, and were not eager to offend him. If—as we shall notice further on—a wise few did suspect the harmless imposition, either they had grounds for not mentioning it, or there were reasons why people did not credit them. And so, in the second place, the times were not ripe for the truth to be known, because there was nobody who cared about knowing it, and nobody to whom it could be a revelation.

To suppose that William Shakespeare wrote the plays which we call his, is to suppose that a miracle was vouchsafed to the race of man in London in the course of certain years of the reign of Elizabeth. If, however, instead of probing for miracles, we come to consider that men and managers and theaters in the age of Elizabeth were very much the same sort of creatures and places that we find them now; that, among the habitues of the Globe and Blackfriars Theaters in that reign, were certain young gentlemen of abundant leisure and elegant education who admitted managers into their acquaintance by way of exchange for the entre of the green-room; and that managers in those days as in these, were always on the alert for novelties, and drew their material—in the crude, if necessary, to be dressed up, or ready made, if they were so fortunate—from wherever they could find it; if, in short, we find that among the curled darlings who frequented Master William Shakespeare's side doors there was at least one poet, and, in their vicinity,

at least one ready writer who was so placed as to be
eager to write anonymously-for bread (and who, moreover, had access to the otherwise sealed and occult
knowledge, philosophy, and reading, of which the
giants of his day—to say nothing of the theater-man-
agers—did not and could not dream)—if, we say, we
consider all this, we need pin our faith to no miracles,
but expect only the ordinary course of human events.

If William Shakespeare were an unknown quantity,
like Homer, to be estimated only by certain masterly
works assigned to him, this answer might, indeed, be
different. For, just as Homer's writings are so magnificent as to justify ascribing to him—so far as mere
power to produce them goes—any other contemporary
literature to be discovered, so the works attributed to
William Shakespeare are splendid enough to safely
credit him with the compositions of any body else; of
even so great a man as Bacon, for example. But
William Shakespeare is no unknown quantity—
except that we lose sight of him for the few years
between his leaving Stratford, and (as part proprietor
of the largest London play-house) accepting Ben Jonson's play of "Every Man in His Humour"—we know
pretty well all about him. There are half a hundred
biographies extant—new ones being written every day
—and any one of them may be consulted as to the
manner of life William Shakespeare's was. The
breakneck marriage bond, which waived all for-
malities, the consent of any body's parents, justifi-
cation of sureties, three askings of banns, etc., so he
could only be fast married; the beer-bouts, youthful
and harmless enough; the poaching, enough worse,
Sir Thomas Lucy thought, to justify instructing a War-

wick attorney to prosecute the lad before the law: all
these are matter of record, amply photographing for
us William Shakespeare in Stratford. Then the hiatus
—and this same lad appears, prosperous, and in the great
town; sending home money to his impoverished family
—part proprietor of a theater, purchasing freehold estates in London—a grant of arms for his father—the
great house in his native village for his own homestead; investing in the tithings of his county, and beginning a chancery suit to recover lands which his
father—in his poverty—had allowed himself to forfeit
by foreclosure. Surely we will not go far astray if
we set it down that some pretty hard work at what
this rising lad found to do in London, and learned to
do best, has filled up those unrecorded years! Was
all this money made by writing plays for the Globe,
or by working on Bacon's Novum Organum, or by
other literary labor? Was THAT the hard work William Shakespeare found to do, and laid up money at,
in the interval between his last crop of wild oats at
Stratford, and the condescension of the man of affairs
in London? If it were, it is curious that no rumor or
tradition of it comes from Stratford. Nothing travels
quite so fast in rural neighborhoods as a reputation
for " book learning," while the local worthy, who has
actually written a book of his own, is a landmark in
his vicinage. Now, William Shakespeare died one of
the richest men—if not the richest—in all Stratford. It
is strange that the gossip and goodwives, who so loaded
themselves with his boyish freaks and frailties, should
never have troubled themselves about his manly pursuits and accomplishments. The only English compositions he is credited with in Stratford gossip are one

or two excessively conventional epitaphs on Elias
James, John á Coombe, and others—the latter of
which is only to be appreciated by a familiarity with
Warwickshire patois. He sprang from a family so illiterate that they could not write their own name; and,
moreover, lived and died utterly indifferent as to how
anybody else wrote it—whether with an "x" or a "g,"
a "c" or a "ks." And as he found them, so he left
them. For, although William Shakespeare enjoyed an
income of $25,000 (present value of money) at his
death, he never had his own children taught to read
and write, and his daughter Judith signed her mark
to her marriage bond.

That the rustic youth, whom local traditions variously represent as a scapegrace, a poacher, a butcher's
apprentice, and the like, but never as a school-boy, a
student, a reader, a poet—as ever having been seen
with a book in his hand—driven by poverty to shift
for himself, should at once (for the dates, as variously
given by Mr. Malone and Mr. Grant White, are exceedingly suggestive) become the alter ego of that
most lax, opulent, courtly, and noble young gentleman
about town, Southampton, is almost incredible. But,
it is no more incredible than that this ill-assorted
friendship can be accounted for by the lad's superhuman literary talents. Southampton never was suspected, during his lifetime, of a devotion to literature,
much less of an admiration for letters so rapt as to
make him forget the gulf between his nobility and
that of a peasant lad—who (even if we disbelieve his
earliest biographers as to the holding horses and carrying links) must necessarily have been employed in
the humblest pursuits at the outset of his London

career. But yet, according to the various " chronologies " (which, in the endeavor to crowd these works into William Shakespeare's short life, so as to tally with the dates—when known—of their production, only vary inconsiderably after all), the Stratford boy hardly puts in his appearance in London before he presents Lord Southampton, as the " first heir of his invention," with—if not the most mature—at least the most carefully polished production that William Shakespeare's name was ever signed to; and, moreover, as polished, elegant, and sumptuous a piece of rhetoric as English letters has ever produced down to this very day.

Now, even if, in Stratford, the lad had mastered all the Latin and Greek extant; this poem, dedicated to Southampton, coming from his pen, is a mystery, if not a miracle. The genius of Robert Burns found its expression in the *idiom* of his father and his mother, in the dialect he heard around him, and into which he was born. When *he* came to London, and tried to warble in urban English, his genius dwindled into formal commonplace. But William Shakespeare, a peasant, born in the heart of Warwickshire; without schooling or practice, pours forth the purest and most sumptuous of English, unmixed with the faintest trace· of that Warwickshire patois, that his neighbors and coetaneans spoke—the language of his own fireside! As a matter of fact, *English* was a much rarer accomplishment in the days when Thomas Jenkins and Thomas Hunt were masters of Stratford Grammar School, than Greek and Latin. Children, in those days, were put at their hic, hæc, hoc at an age when we

4

send them to kindergartens. But no master dreamed
of drilling them in their own vernacular. Admitting
William Shakespeare to have been born a poet, he
must also have been born a master of the arbitrary
rules of English rhetoric, etymology, syntax, and prosody, as well, to have written that one poem. But, say
the Shakespeareans, even if William did not study
English at the Stratford Grammar School, or read it
in those crowded days when earning his bread by
menial employment in stranger London, he had an
opportunity to study Lyly, Nash, Greene, Peele, Chettle, and the rest. But the Shakespearean vocabulary
—like the whole canon of the plays—is a thing apart
—unborrowed, unimitated, and unlearned from any
of these. *These* were satisfied to write for the stages
of the barns called "play-houses," and for their audiences, which—according to all reports—were decidedly
indifferent as to scholarship. *These* might introduce
a Frenchman, but they never troubled themselves to
make him French; or a Scotchman, but they never
stopped to make him Scotch. But even if William
Shakespeare, in the immersions of the management,
was author of that intellectual Dane, over-refined in a
German university of metaphysics, he called Hamlet;
or of that crafty Italian, named Iago; or of that Roman
iceberg, Brutus—it is quite as difficult to conceive
either the skylarking boy in Stratford, where there
were no libraries, and his father too poor (not
daring to stir beyond his threshold for fear of arrest
for debt) to buy books; or the self-made man toiling
from the bottom rung of poverty to the top of fortune—with leisure to study the characteristics of race
and nationality—as acquiring all the grandeur of dic-

tion, insight into the human heart (which, at least, is not guess-work), knowledge and philosophy, we call his to-day. Even if we go no further than the "Venus and Adonis"—appearing at a date preluding a drill that, for the sake of the argument, we might even assume—how could that poem have been written by the peasant who only knew his native dialect, or the penniless lad earning his bread in stranger London, at the first shift at hand—with no entre to the great libraries, and no leisure to use one if he had it? Ben Jonson spent some years at Cambridge before he was taken away and set at brickmaking—he is said to have been a very studious brickmaker, working, according to Fuller, with a trowel in one hand and a book in the other. As to his career as a soldier—a soldier, when not actually in the field or on the march, may find considerable opportunity for rumination; and, when lying in jail, he would certainly have ample leisure for his Greek and Roman. But Jonson wrote for the Elizabethan theaters; he lived and died hungry and poor, a borrower, over his ears in debt to the last. William Shakespeare, his contemporary, loaned Ben Jonson money; rose rapidly from penury to affluence; made his father rich, and a gentleman with an escutcheon; bought himself the most splendid house in Stratford (so splendid as to be deemed worthy a royal residence by Queen Henrietta); invested in outlying lands; speculated in tithes, and lived, until his death—according to Dominic Ward—at the rate of $25,000 a year. We are familiar enough with these stories of self-made men (so-called) in our daily newspapers. Let those who will, believe that William Shakespeare accumulated this splendid fortune, *not* by the success-

ful management of the best appointed and affected
theater in London, but by writing plays for its stage!
and—at the same time—conceived, evolved from his
own inner consciousness, all the learning which other
playwrights (like Ben Jonson and the rest) were
obliged—like ordinary mortals—to get out of books!

The only efforts made to account for this wealth
flowing into the coffers of a poet, have been mere surmises, like the story of Southampton's munificence,
and of the royal favor of King James, who wrote the
manager a letter with his own hand. But neither of
these stories happens to be contemporary with William Shakespeare himself. The first was an after-
thought of Davenant, who was ten years old when
Shakespeare died; and who is not accepted as an authority, even as to his own pedigree, by the very commentators who most eagerly seize upon and swear to
his Southampton fiction. The other is not even hearsay, but the bold invention of Bernard Lintot, who
published an edition of the plays in 1710. Doubtless,
as has been the ambition of all the commentators, before Mr. Collier and since, Lintot was bound to be at
least one fact ahead of his rivals, even if he had to invent that fact himself. He vouchsafes, as authority
for this tale of the royal letter, however, the statement
of "a credible person now living," who saw the letter
itself in the possession of Davenant: in the teeth of
the certainty that, had Davenant ever possessed such
a letter, Davenant would have taken good care that
the world should never hear the last of it: and coyly
preserves the incognito of the "credible person,"
whom, however, Oldys conjectures must have been,
if any body, the Duke of Buckingham.

But, miracles aside, to consider William Shakespeare as the author of the Shakespearean drama—for that he has christened it, and that it will go forever by his name, we concede—involves us in certain difficulties that seem altogether insurmountable. In the first place, scholars and thinkers, whose hearts have been open to the matchless message of the Shakespearean text, and who found themselves drawn to conclude that such a man as William Shakespeare once lived, were amazed to discover that the very evidence which forced them to that conclusion, also proved conclusively that that individual *could not* have written the dramas since known by his name. Coleridge, Schlegel, Goethe, Jean Paul Richter, Carlyle, Palmerston, Emerson, Hallam, Delia Bacon, Gervinus, and, doubtless, many more, clearly saw that the real Shakespeare was not the Shakespeare we have described. "In spite of all the biographies, 'ask your own hearts,' says Coleridge —'ask your own common sense to conceive the possibility of this man being . . . the anomalous, the wild, the irregular genius of our daily criticism. What! are we to have miracles in sport? or (I speak reverently) does God choose idiots by whom to convey divine truths to man?'"[1] "If there was a Shakespeare of earth, as I suspect," says Hallam—alluding to the fact that all the commentators told him of the man Shakespeare, inferred him as any thing but the master he was cited—"there was also one of heaven, and it is of him we desire to learn more."[2]

---

[1] "Notes to Shakespeare's Works," iv., 56.—Holmes "Authorship of Shakespeare," 598.

[2] "Bacon and Shakespeare," by W. H. Smith, p. 26.

This evidence was of three sorts: 1. Official records and documents; 2. The testimony of contemporaries; and, 3. That general belief, reputation, and tradition, which, left to itself in the manner we have indicated, has grown into the presumption of nearly three hundred years. We will not recapitulate the well-thumbed records, nor recite the dog's-eared testimony, which together gave rise to the presumption. But the dilemma presented to the student was in this wise: By the parish records it appeared that a man child was christened in Stratford Church April 26th, (old style) 1564, by the name William. He was the son of one John Shakespeare, a worthy man, who lived by either, or all, the trades of butcher, wool-comber, or glover—three not incompatible pursuits variously assigned him—was, at different times, a man of some means, even of local importance, (becoming, on one occasion, even ale-taster for the town,) and, at his son's birth, owner in freehold of two plots of ground in Stratford village, on one of which plots a low-raftered house now stands, which has come to be a Mecca to which pilgrims from the whole world reverently repair. The next official record of the son so born to John Shakespeare is the marriage-bond to the Bishop of Worcester; enabling this son to wed one Anne Hathaway, his senior in years, which bond remains to this day on file in the office of the Prerogative Court of Canterbury.

Later on, the son, having become a person of means, purchases for his father a grant of arms; and (the name being Shakespeare) the heralds allot him an escutcheon on which is represented a shaking spear (symbolically treated)—a device which, under the circumstances, did not tax the heralds' ingenuity, or commit them to any theory about ancestors at Hastings or among the Saracens. The increasing wealth of the son leaves its traces in the title-deeds to and records of purchase of freehold and leasehold possessions, of the investment in meadow-lands, and tithes, and of sundry law suits incidental to these. Local tradition—which in like cases is perforce admitted as evidence—supplements all this record, and, so far as it can, confirms it, until we have an all but complete biography.

This biography the world knows by heart. It does not esteem the boy William Shakespeare the less because he was a boy—because—in the age and period reserved for that crop—he sowed and garnered his "wild oats." It has reason to believe him to have been much more than a mere wayward youth. Aubrey ("old Aubrey," "arch-gossip Aubrey," the Shakespeareans call him, probably because he wrote his sketch fifty years after his subject's death, instead of two hundred and fifty), says that he was the village prodigy, that "he exercised his father's trade—but, when he killed a calf he would do it in high style and make a speech," etc., etc. Nor is there anything in the record of his mature and latter years—of his investments in tithes, and messuages, and homesteads—of his foreclosures and suits for money loaned and malt delivered—of his begetting children and dying; leaving—still with finical detail and nice and exact economy—an elaborate testament, in which he disposes, item by item, of each worldly thing and chattel, down to the second-best bedstead in his chambers, which he tenderly bestows upon the wife of his youth and the

mother of his children—any thing at which the world
should sneer.

If he has done any thing worthy of posterity, he
shows no especial anxiety that posterity shall hear of
it. Besides such contracts and business papers as he
must sign in the course of his lesseeship at the theaters,
and in the investment of his savings, he leaves his
name to nothing except a declaration of debt against
a poor neighbor who is behind-hand with his account,
footed at one pound fifteen shillings and sixpence, and
a not over-creditable last Will and Testament. This
is his own business, and who has any thing to say?
But, when our biographers go a step further and demand that we shall accept this as the record of a demi-
god; of the creator of a "Hamlet" and an "Othello;"
and this practical and thrifty soul, who ran away to
London—worked himself up (as he must have worked
himself up) to the proprietorship of a theater; and, in
that business and calling earned money and kept it—
as the identical man who singly and alone wrote the
"Hamlet," the "Julius Cæsar," the "Othello," and
all the splendid pages of the Shakespearean drama—
some of us have been heard to demur! The scholar's
dilemma is how to reconcile the internal evidence of
the plays, which is spread before them undimmed by
age, with these records, which are as authentic and beyond question as the internal evidence itself. And,
once stated, the dilemma of the scholar becomes the
dilemma of the whole world. Let any one try to conceive of the busy manager of a theater (an employment to-day—when the theater is at its best, and half
the world play-goers—precarious for capital and industry; but in those days an experiment, in every

sense of the word), who succeeded by vigilance, exact accounting, business sagacity, and prudence, in securing and saving not only a competency, but a fair fortune; in the mean time—while engaged in this engrossment of business—writing Isabella's magnificent appeal to the duke's deputy, Angelo; or Cardinal Wolsey's last soliloquy! Or conceive of the man who gave the wife of his youth an old bedstead, and sued a neighbor for malt delivered, penning Antony's oration above Cæsar, or the soliloquy of Macbeth debating the murder of Duncan, the invocation to sleep in "King Henry IV.," or the speech of Prospero, or the myriad sweet, or noble, or tender passages that nothing but a human heart could utter! Let him try to conceive this, we say, and his eyes will open to the absurdity of the belief that these lines were written by the lessee and joint-manager of a theater, and he will examine the evidence thereafter for corroboration, and not for conviction; satisfied in his own mind, at least, that no such phenomenon is reasonable, probable, or safe to have presented itself.

Then, last and greatest difficulty of all, is the Will. This is by far the completest and best authenticated record we have of the man William Shakespeare, testifying not only to his undoubtedly having lived, but to his character as a man; and—most important of all to our investigation—to his exact worldly condition. Here we have his own careful and ante-mortem schedule of his possessions, his chattels real and chattels personal, down to the oldest and most rickety bedstead under his roof. And we may be pretty sure that it is an accurate and exhaustive list. But if he

5

were—as well as a late theater-manager and country
gentleman—an author and the proprietor of dramas
that had been produced and found valuable, how about
these plays? Were they not of as much value, to say
the least, as a damaged bedstead? Were they not, as
a matter of fact, not only invaluable, but the actual
source of his wealth? How does he dispose of them?
Does our thrifty Shakespeare forget that he has written them? Is it not the fact, and is it not reason and
common sense to conceive, that, *not* having written
them, they have passed out of his possession along
with the rest of his theatrical property, along with
the theater whose copyrights they were, and into the
hands of others? This is the greatest difficulty and
stumbling-block for the Shakespeareans. If their hero
had written these plays, of which the age of Elizabeth was so fond, and in whose production he had
amassed a fortune—that he should have left a will, in
items, in which absolutely no mention or hint of them
whatever should be made, even their most zealous
pundits can not step over, and so are scrupulous not
to allude to it at all. This piece of evidence is unim-
peachable and conclusive as to what worldly goods,
chattels, chattel-interests, or things in action, William
Shakespeare supposed that he would die possessed of.
Tradition is gossip. Records are scant and niggardly.
Contemporary testimony is conflicting and shallow,
but here, attested in due and sacred form, clothed with
the foreshadowed solemnity of another world, is the
calm, deliberate, ante mortem statement of the man
himself. We perceive what becomes of his second-
hand bedstead. What becomes of his plays? Is it
possible that, after all these years' experience of their

value—in the disposition of a fortune of which they had been the source and foundation—he should have forgotten their very existence?

But if, diverging from the scanty records, we go to the testimony of contemporaries, what do we find there? Very little more of the man William Shakespeare, but precisely the same dilemma as to his alleged authorship of the plays. We find that the country lad William, the village prodigy with whom the gossips concerned themselves, was no milksop and no Joseph; that he was hail-fellow with his fellows of equal age; that he poached—shot his neighbors' deer; lampooned their owner when punished for the offense; went on drinking-bouts with his equals of the neighboring villages; and, finally—just as any clever, country lad, who had made his fellows merry with mock eulogies over the calves he slaughtered might and probably would do to-day, and which is precisely what his earliest and, therefore, safest biographer, Rowe, asserts that he did do—wound up with following a company of strolling players to the metropolis; where he began his prosperous career by holding gentlemen's horses at the theater door, while the gentlemen themselves went inside to witness the performance. We turn to the stories of the poaching, the deer-shooting, and the beer-drinking, with relief. It is pleasant to think that the pennywise old man was—at least in his youth—human. A little poaching and a little beer do nobody any harm, and it is, at all events, more cheerful reading than the record of a parsimonious freeholder taking the law of his poorer neighbor who defaults in the payment of a few shillings for a handful of malt.

There is a village school in Stratford, and Mr. De-Quincy, and all his predecessors and successors who have preferred to construct pretty romances, and call them "lives of William Shakespeare," rather than to accept his known and recorded youth, boldly unite in making their hero attend its sessions. Their assertions are bravely seconded by the cicerones and local guides of Stratford, who, for a sixpence, will show you the identical desk which Shakespeare, the lad, occupied at that grammar school; and at Shottery, the same guides show us the chair in which our hero sat while courting Mistress Anne; just as, in Wittemburg, these same gentry point out the house where Hamlet lived when a student in the University there; or, in Scotland, the spot where Fitz-James and Roderick Dhu fought. But, William could not have attended this school very perseveringly, since he turns up in London at about the age that country lads first go to school. In London, he seems to have risen from nothing at all to the position (such as it is) of co-manager, along with a dozen others, of a theater. Here, just as young lords and swells take theater managers into their acquaintance to-day, he became intimate with greater men than himself, and so enlarged his skirts and his patronage, as it was the part of a thrifty man to do. At this time there were no circulating libraries in London, no libraries, accessible to the general public, of any sort, in fact; no booksellers at every corner, no magazines or reviews; no public educators, and no schools or colleges swarming with needy students; even the literature of the age was a bound-up book to all except professional readers. But, for all that, this William Shakes-

peare—this vagrom runaway youth, who, after a
term at Stratford school (admitting that he went
where the romancers put him), cuts off to London at
the heels of a crew of strolling players—who begins
business for himself somewhere (perhaps as "link-
boy" at a theater door, but we may be sure, at an
humble end of some employment) and, by saving his
pence, works up to be actually a part-proprietor in
two theaters, and ultimately a rich man—begins to
possess himself of a lore and knowledge of the Past
which, even to-day, with all our libraries, lyceums,
serials, and booksellers, it would need a lifetime to
acquire.

He did the work of a lifetime. Like Mr. Stewart,
in New York, he began penniless, and by vigilance,
shrewdness, and economy, rose to respectability, affluence, and fortune.

But, as we could not imagine Mr. Stewart, gentleman as he was, writing all the tags and labels on his
goods or making with his own hand every pen-stroke
necessary in the carrying on of his immense trade; or
poems or philosophical essays on the manufacture of
the silks and linens and cottons he handled while slow-
ly coining his fortune, and revolving poetry in his over-
worked brain while overseeing the business that was
evolving that fortune; so do we fail to conceive of
William Shakespeare doing all the pen-work on the
dramas he coins his money by producing on his boards.
How much less can we conceive of this man composing, not only poems of his own, but a Literature of his
own—drawing his material from the classic writers
(and notably from those Greek plays not at that time
translated, and only accessible in the originals and in

manuscript), from legal works, "caviare to the general;" from philosophical treatises not known to have been available even for reference; writing of the circulation of the blood in the human system—a fact not discovered until years after his own death! Let us find him, too, setting down, in writing, epitomes of all known wisdom; ascertaining the past, prophesying of the future; laying down off-hand the philosopher's, the lawyer's, the leech's, the soldier's, the scholar's craft and art, which only these themselves, by long years of study, might attain to—and all this while coining a fortune in the management of two theaters; to have solved, in short, the riddle of the sphinx and all the as yet unspinning whirligigs of time! Verily, a greater riddle than the sphinx's is this the riddle of the boy —Master Shakespeare. Thomas Chatterton found his wealth in a musty chest in an old muniment room. But here the chest and muniment room were not in existence till years after the boy Shakespeare has been a man, and traveled on to his grave. It is no solution of this riddle to say the lad was a genius, and that genius is that which soars, while education plods.[1] Genius itself can not account for the Shakespearean plays. Genius may portray, but here is a genius that not only portrayed that which after his death became fact, but related other facts which men had forgotten; the actors in which had lain in the dust for centuries, and whose records had slept sealed in dead languages, in manuscripts beyond his reach! Genius, intuition,

---

[1] This class of evidence can not be recapitulated in the space of a foot note, but the curious reader will do well to refer to the chapter on the attainments of the author of Shakespeare, at pages 56–65 Holmes's "Authorship of Shakespeare," third edition.

is beyond education indeed. It may prophesy of the future or conceive of the eternal; but only knowledge can draw record of the past. If the author of Shakespeare had been a genius only, his "Julius Cæsar" might have been a masterpiece of tragedy, or pathos, or of rage; but it would have portrayed an ideal Rome, not the real one. His "Comedy of Errors" might have been matchless in humor and sparkling in contretemps, but, three years afterward, on translating a hidden manuscript of Plautus, the comedies would not have been found quite identical in argument.[1]

The precocity of a child may be intuitive. But no babe learns its alphabet spontaneously or by means of its genius; but out of a book, because the characters are arbitrary. Pascal, when a child, discovered the eternal principles of geometry, and marked them out in chalk upon the floor; but he did not know that the curved figures he drew were called "circles," or that the straight ones were called "lines;" so he named them "rounds" and "bars." He discovered what was immutable and could be found by the searcher, but his genius could not reinvent arbitrary language that had been invented before his birth. In short, to have possessed and to have written down, in advance, the learning and philosophy of three centuries to come,

---

[1] Viz: with the Menæchmi of Plautus. In "Pericles," allusion is made to a custom obtaining among a certain undiscussable class of Cyprians, which it is fair to say could not be found mentioned in a dozen books of which we know the names to-day, and which, from its very nature, is treated of in no encyclopædia or manual of information, or of popular antiquities. How could any one but an antiquarian scholar, in those days, have possessed himself —not in this alone, but in a thousand similar instances— of such minute, accurate, and occult information?

might have been the gift of Prophecy (such a gift as
has ere this fallen from we know not where upon the
sons of men) descending into the soul of a conceivable
genius. But who can tell of more than he knows? Second sight is not retrospective. And to have testified
of the forgotten past, without access to its record, was
as beyond the possibilities of genius as the glowing
wealth of the Shakespearean page is above the creation of an unlettered man of business in the age of
Elizabeth or of Victoria.

Here is the dilemma with which the Shakespeareans struggle: that in those years the man William
Shakespeare *did* live, and was a theatrical manager
and actor in London; and precisely the same evidence which convinces us that this man did live in
those days, convinces the world to-day—or must con-
vince it, if it will only consent to look at it—that the
dramas we call Shakespearean were so called because
they were first published from the stage of William
Shakespeare's theaters in London, just as we call certain readings of the classics the "Delphin classics,"
because brought together for a Dauphin of France;
or certain paintings "Düsseldorf paintings," because
produced in the Düsseldorf school. If, however, in
the course of ages it should come to be believed that
the Dauphin wrote the classics, or that a man named
Düsseldorf painted the pictures, even then the time
would come to set the world right. If there had been no
Dauphin and no Düsseldorf, we might have assigned
those names to a power which might have produced
the poems or the pictures. If there had been no
William Shakespeare, we might easily have idealized
one who could have written the plays. But, unhap-

pily, there was the actual, living, breathing man in possession of that name, who declines to assign it to another, and who is any thing but the sort of man the Shakespeareans want. And, moreover, once the presumption is waived and the question is opened again; there is a mass of evidence in the possession of this century, which, taken piecemeal, can be separately waived aside, but which, when cumulated and heaped together, is a mountain over which the airiest skeptic can not vault.

But did none of William Shakespeare's contemporaries suspect the harmless deception? There is no proof at hand, nor any evidence at all positive, that the intimates of the manager understood him to be, or to have ever pretended to have been, the original author of the text of the plays he gave to his players. Let us hasten to do William Shakespeare the justice to say that we can find nowhere any testimony to his having asserted a falsehood. But, if he did so pretend to his intimates, and if the dramas we now call "Shakespearean" were actually produced, in those days, on William Shakespeare's own stage, under that pretension, certainly some of them must have wagged their heads in secret. Surely, Ben Johnson, who bears testimony that his friend Shakespeare had "small Latin and less Greek," must have queried a little within himself as to where certain things he read in the text of his friend's plays came from, always supposing that he did not know perfectly well where they *did* come from. It seems more than probable, as we have already said, that, whoever suspected or knew the source of the plays, and who also knew, if such was the fact, that they were claimed as Shakespeare's compositions

—had more cue to wink at than to expose the humbug. We find, indeed, that one, Robert Greene, by name, did protest against "an upstart crow, beautified with our feathers," (i. e. a borrower and adapter of other men's work, pretending to be a dramatist when he was not), "that, with his tygres heart wrapt in a player's hyde, supposes he is as well able to bombast out a blank verse as the best of you; and, beeing an absolute *Johannes Factotum*, is in his owne conceyt the only Shake-scene in a countrey." That is to say, in language more intelligible at this day, that, being a sort of Jack-of-all-trades around the theater—holding horses, taking tickets, acting a little, putting pieces on the stage, and writing out their parts for the actors—he (Shakespeare) came in time to consider himself a dramatist, a manager, and a tragedian, all in one. Doubtless Greene was inspired by jealousy—for he was a writer of plays for the stage himself—in making and publishing this sneer. But, as he was endeavoring to make his remarks so personal to Shakespeare as to be readily recognized, he would not have alluded to him except by some well-known characteristic. So he calls him a "Jack-of-all-trades," that is, a man who did a little of every thing. Is a Jack-of-all-trades about a theater the ideal poet, philosopher, and seer, who wrote the Shakespearean drama—the ideal of the Shakespeareans?

According to the chronicles and the record, then, one William Shakespeare, a "general utility" actor, and *Johannes Factotum*, lived and thrived in London, some two hundred and fifty odd years ago. At about that date a book is likewise written. Who are these who find this book, and make this man to fit it?

Verily, there are none so blind as those who are determined not to see! To have written that book one must needs have been, let us say—for he was at least all these—a philosopher, a poet, a lawyer, a leech, a naturalist, a traveler, a student of Bible history! Strange to say, at the time this book—in portions—is making its appearance, there are two men living, each of whom is a poet, a philosopher, a student of laws and of physics, and a traveler over the by-ways of many lands beside his own. One of them is known to have read the Bible, then what we understand to-day by a " current work." Together, these two men possess in themselves about all of their age with which subsequent ages care to connect themselves. But it is not suggested that these two men, Bacon and Raleigh, might have written the book for which an author is wanted. We are to pass them by, and sift the dust at their illustrious feet, if haply we may find a fetich to fall down before and worship!

Must the man that wrote the dramas have visited Italy? Mr. Halliwell and others inform us of Shakespeare's visit to Verona, Venice, and Florence. Must Shakespeare have been at the bar? My Lord Campbell writes us a book to show his familiarity with the science of jurisprudence. (That book has traveled far upon a lordly name. It is an authority until it happens to be read. Once we open it, it is only to find that, the passages of the Shakespearean dramas which stamp their author's knowledge of the common law are the passages his lordship does not cite, while over the slang and dialect which any smatterer might have memorized from turning the pages of an attorney's hornbook, his lordship gloats and postulates and relapses into ecstasy). Must Shakespeare have been a physician? There have not been wanting the books to prove him that.[1] And, crowning this long misrule of absurdity, comes an authority out of Philadelphia, to assure us that the youth Shakespeare, on quitting his virgin Stratford for the metropolis, was scrupulous to avoid the glittering temptations of London; that he eschewed wine and women; that he avoided the paths of vice and immorality, and piously kept himself at home, his only companion being the family Bible, which he read most ardently and vigorously![2] It is to be hoped, for charity's sweet sake, that his latest authority has truth for his color and testimony

---

[1] "The Medical Acquirement of Shakespeare." By C. W. Stearns, M. D. New York, 1865. Shakespeare's Medical Knowledge. By Dr. Bucknill. London. 1860.

[2] "Shakespeare and the Bible." By John Rees, etc., etc. Philadelphia: Claxton, Remsen & Haffelfinger, 1876.

We commend to readers of this paper this latest authority, and can not forbear noting a few of his "discoveries." Mr. Rees has found out (p. 37) not only that William Shakespeare wrote the lines—

> "——— Not a hair perished,
> On their sustaining garments not a blemish,
> But fresher than before." ("The Tempest," i. 2)

But that he took them from Deuteronomy viii. 4.
And in Acts xxvii. 34:

> There shall not a hair fall from the head of any of you.

In which the parallelism is in the word *hair !!!*
Or, again (p. 36) that the lines:

> Though they are of monstrous shape, . . .
> Their manners are more gentle, kind, than of
> Our human generation you shall find
> Many, nay, almost any ("The Tempest," iii. 3),

for his oil. The picture has at least the freshness and charm of utter novelty!

The work of Shakespeare-making goes on. The facts are of record. We may run as we read them! But rather let us, out of reverence for the errors of our fathers, refuse to read at all, and accept the ideal of Malone, of Halliwell and De Quincey, of Grant White, and of ten thousand more, who prefer to write their biographies of William Shakespeare, not in the first person, like Baron Münchhausen, nor in the second person, like the memoirs of Sully, but in the probable and supposititious person of "it is possible he did *this*," and "it is likely he did *that*."

Let those who will, disparage the boy and man William Shakespeare, who married and made an honest woman of Anne Hathaway of Shottery; left home to earn his own living rather than be a drain on the slender household store; used his first wealth to make a gentleman of his father; and who, with what followed, purchased himself a home on his boyhood's

---

are taken from the following:

In the same quarters were possessions of the chief man of the island, whose name was Publius; who received us, and lodged us three days courteously, . . . who also honored us with many honors; and when we departed, they laded us with such things as were necessary.—(Acts xxviii. 7-10.

In which—unless it be in the fact that one of these passages is in *an act* and the other in *Acts*—the reader must find the parallelism for himself, without assistance from Mr. Rees.

Shakespeare, Mr. Rees tells us, never neglected his Bible, because (p. 28) "he was indebted to one whose love added a bright charm to the holy passages she taught him to read and study—to his mother was Shakespeare indebted for early lessons of piety, and a reverence for a book from whose passages in after-life he wove himself a mantle of undying fame!"

banks, where—"procul negotiis"—in the evening of
life he might enjoy the well-won fruits of early toil.
But that he ever claimed, much less wrote, what we
call the Shakespearean drama, let those bring proof
who can.

PART II.

THE APPEAL TO HISTORY.

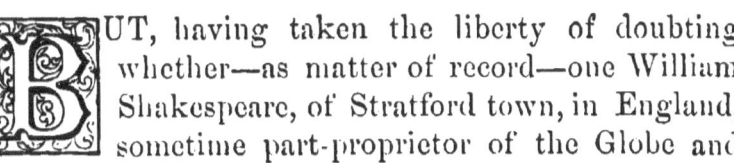UT, having taken the liberty of doubting whether—as matter of record—one William Shakespeare, of Stratford town, in England, sometime part-proprietor of the Globe and Blackfriars Theaters in London, could have very well been himself and the author of what are known popularly to-day as "the plays of Shakespeare," although there seemed to be ground for supposing that he might have cast them into something of the acting form they possess as preserved to us; and having come to the conclusion that—once this presumption is lifted—all the evidence procurable as to the life and times of the actual William Shakespeare is actually evidence cumulative to the truth of the proposition as to the record: let us proceed to inquire whether—on review—a case rested on this evidence can be rebutted by those certain considerations and matters, by way of rejoinder, which are stereotype and safe to come to the surface whenever these waters are troubled—which whoever ventures to canvass the possibilities of an extra Shakesperean authorship of the dramas can so infallibly anticipate.

Granted that the Shakespeare Will does not prove the testator oblivious of his own copyrights or rights in the nature of copyrights; granted that the story of the deer-stealing was actual invention and not merely rejected by the Shakespereans, because conceived to be unworthy of the image they set up; granted that the fact of the circulation of the blood was a familiar fact in the days of William Shakespeare; that the "Menæchmi" of Plautus; that Iago's speech in "Othello" and the stanza of Berni's *Orlando Innamorato* were mere coincidences; or, better yet, admit that there was an English version of the Italian poem in Shakespeare's day[1]—admit, if required—that the "Hamlet" of Saxo, had been translated;[2] that the law in "The

---

[1] When Iago utters the often quoted lines, "who steals my purse steals trash, etc.," he but repeats, with little variation, this stanza of the *Orlando Innamorato* of which poem, to this day, there is no English version.

> " Chi ruba un corno nn cavallo, un anello
> E simil cose, ha qualcha discrezione,
> E patrebbe chimarsi ladroncello ;
> Ma quel che ruba la reputazione
> E de l'altrai patiche si fa bello,
> Si puo chiamare assassino e ladrone ;
> E tanto piu del dover trapassa il segno ? "

As no English translation has been made of the Orlando Innamorato, I must ask the reader who can not command the original to be content with this rendering of the above stanza:

> "The man who steals a horn, a horse, a ring,
> Or such a trifle, thieves with moderation,
> And may be justly called a robberling ;
> But he who takes away a reputation
> And pranks in feathers from another's wing
> His deed is robbery—assassination,
> And merits punishment so much the greater
> As he to right and truth is more a traitor."

Shakespeare, by R. G. White, vol. I, p. 23.

[2] Of Saxo Grammaticus, the Danish historian from whom the plot of the "Hamlet" was taken, Whalley says, writing in 1748, that "no translation hath yet been made," must have been read by the writer of "Hamlet" in the original. "An Enquiry into the Learning of Shakespeare," etc. By Peter Whalley, A. B.,

Merchant of Venice" was "Venetian" instead of
"crowner's quest" law; admit that William Shakespeare "had the advantages in school of something
more than the mere rudiments of learning;" admit
that "his devotion to his family drove him forth from
the rural seclusion of Stratford into the battle of the
great world;" that the immortal gift of the second-
best bed was, (we quote from Mr. Grant White, who
is apparently willing to sacrifice anybody's reputation
if he can thereby prove his William to have been a
prodigy of virtue no less than of genius), explained by
the fact that, at the time of the hurried marriage,
a husband had to be provided for Mistress Hathaway
without loss of time, and that little Susannah was as
much of a surprise to William as to anybody—in
other words, that Anne was "no better than she
should be," (oblivious of the fact that "the prema-
ture Susannah" was William Shakespeare's favorite
child; that he, at least, never doubted her paternity,
for he left her the bulk of his fortune in his will); or
even that—according to Steevens, that testamentary
second thought was actually "a mark of rare confidence and devotion;" granted all these—if they have
anything to do with the question—and a dozen more,
and we only attenuate, by the exact value of these,

Fellow of St. John's College, London. Printed for J. Waller at
the Crown and Mitre, 1748—And see a suggestion that the
"Hamlet" came from Germany, in a pamphlet "On the Double
Personality of the Hamlet of Saxo Grammaticus, the Hamlet of
Shakespeare. Its Relation to the German Hamlet." By Dr.
Latham, Royal Society of Literature Transactions. 1878. Also,
"Shakespeare in Germany. Alfred Cohn. Berlin and London.
1874.

6

the mountain of probability, nothing less than the complete dilapidation and disappearance of which could leave room for substitution, in the stead of the probability, the *possibility* of such a suspension of the laws of nature as is required by the Shakespearean theorists. For, as we have said, the evidence is CUMULATIVE, and, therefore, no more to be waived or disposed of by doubts as to, or even the dispelment of, this or that or the other item—or disintegration of this or that or the other block—of evidence than the Coliseum has been wiped away and disposed of because its coping has crumbled, or because, for some centuries, the petty Roman princes built their palaces from its débris.

And we may as well remark that, just here, it is always in order to mention Archbishop Whately's "Historic Doubts." We wish some of the gentlemen who cite it so glibly, would take the trouble to read that clever little book. It is a logical, not a whimsical effort. It was intended by its author as an answer to "Hume's Essay on Miracles." Hume's argument being, in the opinion of the Archbishop, reducible to the proposition that miracles were impossible because they were improbable, his lordship wrote his little work to show that the history of Napoleon was actually most improbable, and, written of feigned characters, would read like the most extravagant fable. Surely it can not be necessary to reiterate the difference between the Archbishop's brochure and the proposition of "The Shakspearean Myth!" The one was the argument from improbability, applied to facts in order to show its dangerous and altogether vicious character. The other is the demonstration

that history—that the record—when consulted, is directly fatal to a popular impression, and directly con-
tradictory of a presumption, born of mere carelessness
and accident, and allowed to gather weight by mere
years and lapse of time.

But, for the sake of the argument, let us leave the
discussion, for the moment, just where it stands, and
take still bolder ground. Instead of sifting evidence
and counting witnesses, let us assume that, when we
painted William Shakspeare—who lived between the
years 1564 and 1616—as an easy-going rural wag,
with a rural wit, thereafter to be sharpened by
catering to the "gods" of a city theater; a poacher
on occasion, and scapegrace generally in his youth,
who chose the life of "a vagabond by statute"—
i. e. a strolling player—but who turned up in London, and found his way into more profitable connection with a permanent play-house; and, in his
advancing years, became thrifty, finally sordid—we
had only taken the liberty of conceiving, like
every other who ever wrote on a Shakespearean
theme, yet one more William Shakespeare; so that,
instead of ten thousand William Shakespeares, no
two of which were identical, there were now ten
thousand and one! Admitting *that*, the next question
would of necessity be—and such an investigation as
the present must become utterly valueless if prose-
cuted with bias or with substitution of personal opinion for historical fact—whose William Shakespeare is
probably most a likeness of the true William Shakespeare, who *did* wander from Stratford to London,
who *did* sojourn there, and who *did* wander back

again to Stratford, and there was gathered to his fathers, in the year 1616?

The popular William Shakespeare, built to fit the plays, is a masterless philosopher, a matchless poet, a student of Greek manuscripts and classic manners, of southern romance and northern sagas, a traveler and a citizen of the world, a scientist, a moralist, a master of statecraft, and skilled in all the graces and amenities of courtly society! Which of these two portraits is nearest to the life? Let us take an appeal to History.

There appears to be but one way to go about to discover; that way is to appeal to the truth of history; to go as nearly back as we can get to the lifetime of the actual man we are after, and inquire, wherever a trace of him can be touched, what manner of man he was. Now, it happens that the very nearest we can come to an eye-witness as to the personnel of William Shakespeare is the Reverend John Ward, Vicar of Stratford, who wrote in that town a diary or memoranda, between February, 1662, and April, 1663, say forty-seven years after William Shakespeare's death. The following meager references to his late fellow-townsman are all (except an entry to the effect that he had two daughters, etc.; and another memorandum, "Remember to peruse Shakespeare's plays, etc.,) thought worth while by Dominie Ward, viz:

"I have heard that Mr. Shakespeare was a natural wit, without any art at all; he frequented the plays all his younger time, but in his elder days he lived at Stratford, and supplied the stage with two plays every year, and for that he had an allowance so large that he spent at the rate of £1,000 a year, as I have heard."

.   .   .   .

"Shakespeare, Drayton, and Ben Jonson had a merrie meeting, and, it seems, drank too hard, for Shakespeare died of a feaver there contracted."

Next, chronologically, we come to a gentleman named Aubrey. This Mr. Aubrey was himself a native of Warwickshire; was born in 1627—that is, eleven years after Shakespeare died. He entered gentleman commoner of Trinity College, Oxford, and so, presumably, was no Puritan. He was considerable of a scholar himself, and was esteemed, we are told, a Latin poet of no mean abilities. He was admitted a barrister of the Inner Temple in 1646; and so, a scholar, a poet, and a lawyer, might presumably know the difference between a wag and a genius. His manuscripts are preserved in the Ashmolean Museum. He gives an account of his fellow-countyman, and, coming as it does, next to Dominie Ward's, nearer to the lifetime of William Shakespeare than any chronicle extant, (Malone admits it was not written later than 1680), we give it entire:

"Mr. William Shakespeare was born at Stratford-upon-Avon, in the county of Warwick. His father was a butcher, and I have been told heretofore by some of his neighbours that, when he was a boy, he exercised his father's trade; but when he killed a calfe he would doe it in a high style, and make a speech. There was, at this time, another butcher's son in that towne, that was held not at all inferior to him for a natural witt, his acquaintance and coetanean, but died young. This Wm. being inclined naturally to poetry and acting, came to London, I guess about eighteen, and was an actor at one of the play-houses, and did act exceedingly well. (Now B. Jonson never was a good actor, but an excellent instructor.) He began early to make essays at dramatic poetry, which at that time was very lowe, and his plays took well. He was a handsome, well-shaped man, very good company, and of a verie redie and pleasant smooth witt. The humour of the Constable in 'A Midsummer Night's Dream,' he happened to take at Grendon, in Bucks,¹ which is the road from London to Stratford, and there was living that Constable, about 1642, when I first came to Oxon. Mr. Jos. Howe is of that parish, and knew him. Ben Jonson and he did gather humours of men dayly, wherever they came. One time, as he was at Stratford-upon-Avon, one Combes, an old rich usurer, was to be buryed; he makes there this extemporary epitaph :

> Ten in the hundred the Devil allows,
> But Combes will have twelve, he swears and vows.
> If any one asks who lies in this tomb,
> " Hoh," quoth the Devil, " 'tis my John a Combe! "

He was wont to go to his native country once a year. I think I have been told that he left £200 or £300 a year, or thereabouts, to a sister. I have heard Sir William Davenant and Mr. Thomas Shadwell (who is counted the best comedian we have now) say that he had a most prodigious witt, and did admire his natural parts beyond all other dramaticall writers. He was

---

¹Aubrey says, in a note at this place : " I think it was a midsummer's night that he happened there. But there is no Constable in 'Midsummer Night's Dream.'" Aubrey probably intended reference to Dogberry, in the " Much Ado."

wont to say that he never blotted out a line in his life; says Ben Jonson, 'I wish he had blotted out a thousand.' His comedies will remain witt as long as the English tongue is understood, for that he handles *mores hominum:* Now our present writers reflect much upon particular persons and coxcombites that twenty years hence they will not be understood. Though, as Ben Jonson says of him, that he had but little Latin and less Greek, he understood Latin pretty well, for he had been, in his younger days, a school-master in the country." [1]

Imagine this as the record of a real "Shakespeare!" Could we imagine it as the record of a Milton? Let us conceive of a fellow-countryman of John Milton's, a college-bred man and a Latin poet, saying of the author of " Paradise Lost;" " He was a goodish-looking sort of man, wore his hair long, was a clerk, or secretary, or something to Cromwell, or some of his gang; had some trouble with his wife; was blind, as I have heard; or, perhaps, it was deaf he was." And conceive of this, a few years after Milton's death being

---

[1] Aubrey's MSS. was called " Minutes of Lives," and was addressed to his " worthy friend Mr. Anthony Wood, Antiquary of Oxford." A letter to Wood, dated June 15, 1680, accompanied it, in which Aubrey says: " 'T is a task that I never thought to have undertaken till you imposed it upon me, saying that I was fit for it by reason of my general acquaintance, having now not only lived above half a century of years in the world, but have also been much tumbled up and down in it, which hath made me so well known. Besides the modern advantage of coffee-houses, before which men knew not how to be acquainted but with their own relations or societies, I might add that I come of a long-aevious race, by which means I have wiped some feathers off the wings of time for several generations, which does reach high."

actually all the information accessible concerning
him!

But to continue our search in the vicinage. On the
10th day of April, 1693 (thirteen years later), a visitor
to Warwickshire wrote a letter to his cousin, describing, among other points of interest, the village and
church of Stratford-upon-Avon. And, as the letter
was discovered among the papers of a well-known
nobleman, addressed to a person known to have lived,
and indorsed by this latter, " From Mr. Dowdall; description of several places in Warwickshire "—as it
bears on its face evidence of its genuineness, and, above
all, mentions William Shakespeare, precisely in the
same strain that it alludes to other worthies of the
county—the Beauchamps, the Nevilles, etc.—it has always been accepted as authentic. After a description
of the tomb and resting place of " our English tragedian, Mr. Shakespeare," the writer continues :

" The clerk that showed me this church was above
eighty years old.¹ He says that this Shakespeare was
formerly of this town, bound apprentice to a butcher;
but that he ran from his master to London, and there

¹ *I.e.* (more than "above" three years old when s. died.) This
letter was among the papers of Lord DeClifford, which were sold
by auction—and was purchased by Mr. Rodd, a well-known antiquarian bookseller, of Great Newport Street, London, in 1834.
Mr. Rodd printed it in pamphlet form in 1838 (at least the copy
we have bears imprint of that year). It is dated "Butler's Mer-
ston in Warwickshire, April, the 10th, 1693;" is signed, "Your
very faithful kinsman and most aff'te humble serv't till death,
JOHN AT STILES," and is addressed, "These for Mr. Southwell, pr.
serv't." This is Mr. Edward Southwell, and the letter is indorsed
in his handwriting, " From Mr. Dowdall. Description of several
places in Warwickshire." Mr. Rodd says that the writer was
" an Inns'-of-Court-Man."

was received into the play-house as a servitour, and
by this means had an opportunity to be what he afterwards proved. He was the best of his family, but the
male line is extinguished. Not one, for fear of the
curse abovesaid, dare touch his gravestone, though his
wife and daughters did earnestly desire to be laid in
the same grave with him."

Next, chronologically, comes the contribution preserved to us by a Reverend Richard Davies, Rector of
Sapperton,[1] in Gloucestershire. The Reverend William
Fulman, who died in 1688, bequeathed certain of his
biographical collections to this Reverend Davies.
Davies died in 1708, leaving many annotations to
his friend's manuscripts. Among these annotations
he writes the following of William Shakespeare:
"William Shakespeare was born at Stratford upon
Avon, in Warwickshire, about 1563–4, much given
to all unluckiness in stealing venison and rabbits,
particularly from Sir Lucy, who had him oft whipt,
and some times imprisoned, and at last made him
fly his native country to his great advancement.
But his revenge was so great that he is his 'Justice
Clodpate'[2] and calls him a great man, and that, in allusion to his name, bore three lowses rampant for his
arms. From an actor he became a composer. He died
April 23, 1616, aetat fifty-three, probably at Stratford
—for there he is buried, and hath a monument (Dugd.

---

[1] His MS. additions to the MSS. of the Rev. William Fulman
(in which the allusion to Shakespeare is made) are all in the library of Corpus Christi College, Oxford.

[2] Probably a reference to Justice Shallow, in " Merry Wives of
Windsor."

p. 520) on which he lays a heavy curse upon any one who shall remove his bones. He died a papist."

Whatever these may be worth—for, of course, like the rest, they are mere second-hand and hearsay—it is fair to include them in a collection of what the law calls "general reputation," "general report," or "common fame," and it is fair to offset this collection, at least, against that "common fame" and "common reputation" which has grown up during the last hundred years or so concerning William Shakespeare, which is so unboundedly to his glory and renown. Much later along, we are made acquainted, too, with a tradition, related by one John Jordan, a townsman of Stratford, (who was known in the days of Malone and the Ireland forgeries as "the Stratford poet,") who claimed to have succeeded in the line of descent to a tradition of an alleged drinking-bout of Shakespeare and others (as representing Stratford) against the champions of Pebworth, Marston, Hillborough, Grafton, Wixford, Broom, and Bidford, in which William was so worsted that his legs refused to carry him farther homeward than a certain thorn-tree, thereafter to come in for its share of worshipful adoration from the Shakespearean sticklers. But the tradition is of no value except as additional testimony to the impression of his boon companions, associates, and contemporaries, that William Shakespeare was a jolly dog who loved his frolic, his pot of ale, and his wench—was almost any thing, in short, except the student of history, antiquity, and classic manners, no less than the scholar of his own times, that he has been created since by those who knew him not. Nothing travels faster in rural communities, as we have remarked, than a reputation for "book-learning;" let us continue our search for Shakespeare's.

When an interest in the Shakespearean drama began to assert itself, and people began to inquire who wrote it, not a step could they get beyond the Rev. John Ward, Richard Davies, and Aubrey. At the outset they ran full against this village "ne'er-do-weel" and rustic wag, who worked down into a man of thrift, made money off his theatrical shares and properties in London, and spent it royally in Stratford, drinking himself into his grave some seven years before the first collection of what the world in time was to credit him with, (but improved and enlarged beyond what it ever was in his day) the Shakesperean drama—first saw the light. Perhaps Dominie Ward may have been dazzled by the open house of the richest man in town. A thousand pounds a year is an income very rarely enjoyed by poets, and, we think, more easily accounted for by interests in tithes and outlying lands in Stratford, than by the "two plays a year," in and about the days when from four to eight pounds was the price of an acting play (according to Philip Henslow, a sort of stage pawnbroker and padrone of those days, who kept many actors in his pay, and whose diary or cash book, in which he entered his disbursements and receipts, is still extant), and twenty pounds a sum commanded only by masters. The prodigality which dazed the simple Stratford dominie was easily paid for, no doubt, by something less than the income named; and such an income, too, would tally with William Shakespeare's own estimate of his wordly goods in his Will.

But the statement is the nearest and best evidence

we have at hand, and so let it be accepted. And so, running up against this William Shakespeare, these commentators were obliged to stop. But there were the dramas, and there was the name " William Shakespeare " tacked to them ; it was William Shakespeare they were searching for; and, since the William Shakespeare they had found, was evidently not the one they wanted, they straightway began to construct one more suitable. The marvelous silence of history and local tradition only stimulated them. They must either confess that there was no such man, or make one ; they preferred to make one.

First (for Rowe has only—in his eight honest pages of biographical notice—narrated certain gossip or facts, on the authority, perhaps, of Betterton, and does not claim to be an explorer, and Heminges and Condell, who edited the first folio, made no biographical allusion whatever) came Edmund Malone. With the nicest and most painstaking care he sifted every morsel and grain of testimony, overturned histories, chronicles, itineraries, local tradition, and report— but in vain. The nearer he came to the Stratford " Shaughraun," the further away he got from a matchless poet and an all-mastering student. But, like those that were to come after him, instead of accepting the situation, and confessing the William Shakespeare who lived at Stratford not mentionable in the same breath with the producer of the august text which had inspired his search, he preferred to rail and marvel at the stupidity of the neighborhood, and the sins of the chroniclers who could so overlook prodigies. Far from concluding that—because he finds no such name as William Shakespeare in the national Walhalla—

therefore no such name belonged there, he assumes, rather, that the Walhalla builders do not understand their business. He says:

" That almost a century should have elapsed from the time of his [William Shakespeare's] death, without a single attempt having been made to discover any circumstance which could throw a light on the history of his life or literary career, . . are circumstances which can not be contemplated without astonishment.[1] . . Sir William Dugdale, born in 1605, and educated at the school of Coventry, twenty miles from Stratford-upon-Avon, and whose work, ' The Antiquities of Warwickshire,' appeared in 1646, only thirty years after the death of our poet, we might have expected to give some curious memorials of his illustrious countryman. But he has not given us a single particular of his private life, contenting himself with a very slight mention of him in his account of the church and tombs of Stratford-upon-Avon. The next biographical printed notice that I have found is in Fuller's ' Worthies,' folio, 1662; in ' Warwickshire,' page 116—where there is a short account of our poet, furnishing very little information concerning him. And again, neither Winstanley, in his ' Lives of the Poets,' 8vo, 1687; Langbaine in 1691; Blount in 1694; Gibbon in 1699—add any thing to the meager accounts of Dugdale and Fuller. That Anthony Wood, who was himself a native of Oxford, and was born but fourteen years after the death of our author, should not

---

[1] Malone's " Life:" " Plays and Poems," London, 1821, vol. ii, p. 4.

[2] Ibid., p. 5.

have collected any anecdotes of Shakespeare, has
always appeared to me extraordinary. Though
Shakespeare has no direct title to a place in the
'Athenæ Oxoniensis,' that diligent antiquary could
easily have found a niche for his life as he has done
for many others not bred at Oxford. The Life of
Davenant afforded him a very fair opportunity for
such an insertion."

The difficulty was, that Mr. Malone was searching
among the poets for one by the name of William
Shakespeare, when there was no such name among
the poets. He found him not, because he was not
there. He might with as much propriety have
searched for the name of Grimaldi in the Poets'
Corner, or for Homer's on the books of the Worshipful Society of Patten-makers. To be sure, in
writing up Stratford Church, Sir William Dugdale
can not very well omit mention of the tomb of Shakespeare, any more than a writer who should set out to
make a guide-book of Westminster Abbey could
omit description of the magnificent tomb of John
Smith. But in neither the case of Dugdale nor in
that of the cicerone of the Abbey is the merit of the
tomb a warrant for the immortality of the entombed.
It is, possibly, worth our while to pause just here,
and contemplate the anomaly the Shakespeareans
would have us accept—would have us to swallow, or
rather bolt, with our eyes shut—namely, the spectacle
(to mix the metaphor) of the mightiest genius the
world has ever borne upon its surface, living utterly
unappreciated and unsuspected, going in and out
among his fellows in a crowded city of some two
hundred thousand inhabitants, among whom were

certain master spirits whose history we have intact to-day, and whose record we can possess ourselves of with no difficulty—without making any impression on them, or imprint on the chronicles of the time, except as a clever fellow, a fair actor (with a knack, besides, at a little of every thing), so that in a dozen years he is forgotten as if he had never been; and—except that a tourist, stumbling upon a village church, finds his name on a stone—passed beyond the memory of a man in less than the years of a babe! The blind old Homer at least was known as a poet where he was known at all; the seven cities which competed for the tradition of his birth when criticism revealed the merit of his song—though he might have begged his bread in their streets—at least did not take him for a tinker! It is not that the Shakespearean dramas were not recognized as immortal by the generation of their composer that is the miracle; neither were the songs of Homer. Perhaps, so far as experience goes, this is rather the rule than the exception. The miracle is, that in all the world of London and of England nobody knew that there *was* any Shakespeare, in the very days when the Drama we hold so priceless now was being publicly rendered in a play-house, and printed—as we shall come to consider further on—for the benefit of non-theater-goers!

But, it is said, the great fire of London intervened and burned up all the records—that is how we happen to have no records of the immortal Shakespeare. Then, again, there is the lapse of time—the ordinary wear and tear of centuries, and the physical changes of the commercial center of the world. But how

about Edmund Spenser? That we have his poetry
and the record of his life, is certain. Or, how about
Chaucer? Did the great fire of London affect his
chronicle and his labors? The records of Horace,
and Maro, of Lucretius, of Juvenal, and Terence, had
more than a great fire of London to contend with.
But they have survived the ruin of empires and the
crash of thrones, the conflagrations of libraries and
the scraping of palimpsests. And yet the majesty and
might of the Shakespearean page, how greater than
Horatius or Maro, than Juvenal and Terence! If it
all were a riddle, we could not read it. But it is not
a riddle. It is the simplest of facts—the simple fact
that the compilers of the Shakespearean pages worked
anonymously, and concealed their identity so successfully that it lay hidden for three hundred years, and
defies even the critical acumen, the learning and the
research of this nineteenth century.

But to return to Edmund Malone. He is not deterred by his failure to find a poet of the name of
Shakespeare. Determined that a poet of that name
there shall be, and not being at hand, he proceeds—
and he has the credit of being the first to undertake
the task—to construct an immortal bard. And a very
pretty sort of fellow he turns out, too!—one that,
with such minor variations as have, from time to time,
suggested themselves to gentlemen of a speculative
turn of mind, has been a standard immortal William
all along. For they who seek will find. Had Mr.
Malone searched for the Stratford "shaughraun," who
ran off and became an actor (as capably respectable a
profession as any other, for the man makes the profession, and not the profession the man); who revis-

ited his native haunts—on the lookout, not for kings and cardinals, not for dukes and thanes and princes—but for clowns and drunkards and misers to dovetail in among the Hamlets and Othellos that passed under his adapting pen;[1] had he searched for the

---

[1] It is as curious as suggestive to find that the prologue and choruses of the "Henry V." and "Henry VIII." are apologies for the imperfections of the plots, and the folly of the multitude they catered to. As to the internal testimony of the authorship of these compositions, any reader can judge for himself. We have expressed our own opinion as being that William Shakespeare might be credited with the characters of Nym and Bardolph; especially of the Corporal, whose part consists of the phrase, "There's the humor of it," intruded at each convenient interval; and it is possible that Shakespeare, in fitting up the matter in hand, interpolated this as the reigning by-word of the moment. There seems to be reason for believing that this expression *did* happen to be a favorite at about that time; and that Shakespeare was not the only one who rang the changes on it as a season to stage material. Witness the following:

Cob. Nay, I have my rheum, and I can be angry as well as another, sir!
Cash. Thy rheum, Cob? Thy humor, thy humor! Thou mistak'st.
Cob. Humor? Mack, I think it be so indeed! What is that humor? Some rare thing, I warrant.
Cash. Marry, I tell thee, Cob, it is a gentlemanlike monster, bred in the special gallantry of our time by affectation, and fed by folly.
Cob. How must it be fed?
Cash. Oh, aye; humor is nothing if it be not fed. Didst thou never hear that? It's a common phrase, "Feed thy humor."
　　　　　　　　　　　　　　　Every Man in his Humor, iii. 4.

　　Couldst thou not but arrive most acceptable
　　Chiefly to such as had the happiness
　　Daily to see how the poor innocent word
　　Was racked and tortured.
　　　　　　　　　　　　　　　Every Man Out of his Humor.

"Humor" was, it would seem by this, the over-used and abused word of these times; just as for example "awful" might be said to be an over-used and abused word during our own times.

Stratford butcher's son, who was the Stratford wag as well, and who never slaughtered a sheep without making a speech to his admiring fellow-villagers, here he was at his hand. But he was searching, not for a butcher's son, but for a poet—for a " courtier's, soldier's, scholar's eye, tongue, sword,

> The expectancy and rose of the fair state,
> The glass of fashion and the mold of form,
> The observed of all observers "—

for " an amazing genius which could pervade all nature at a glance, and to whom nothing within the limits of the universe appeared to be unknown;"[1] and his instinct should have assured him that—however the works which such a genius had left behind him might travel under the name of the butcher's boy—it was not the pen of the butcher-boy that had written them; that the composer of pages " from which, were all the arts and sciences lost, they might be recovered,"[2] was

---

[1] Whalley.

[2] Ibid. A curious instance of this familiarity—to be found in the Shakespearean dramas—with the least noticed facts of science, and which, so far as we know, has escaped the critics, we might allude to here: In one of Jules Verne's realistic stories wherein he springs his romantic catastrophes upon scientific phenomena—" Michael Strogoff"—he makes Michael fall among enemies who sentence him to be blinded. The blinding is to be accomplished with a heated iron, but Michael sees his mother at his side, and, tears suffusing his eyes, the heat of the iron is neutralized, and fails to destroy the sight. So, in " King John," Act IV., Scene 1, Arthur says to Hubert:

> The iron of itself, though heat red-hot,
> Approaching near these eyes would drink my tears
> And quench his fiery indignation.

This may be mere coincidence, but the dramas are crowded with

no "jack-of-all-trades," and could not have lived and publicly presented his compositions nightly, year in and year out, in the glare of a metropolis crowded with courtiers, play-goers, and students—in the age and days of Bacon and Raleigh and Elizabeth—unknown save to a handful of his pot-fellows, and faded out of the world, unknown and unnoticed, fading from the memory of men, without the passing of an item in their mouths!

Most wonderful of all, this utter ignoring of William Shakespeare among the poets, if unjust, provoked no remonstrance from the immediate family or any kin of the Stratford lad. Either the Shakespeares, Ardens, and Hathaways were wonderfully destitute of family pride, or else the obscurity accorded their connection was perfectly just and proper. No voice of kin or affinity of William Shakespeare (at least we may say this with confidence) ever claimed immortality for him; although it can not be said that they had no opportunity, had they wished to do so, for William Shakespeare's granddaughter, Lady Barnard, was alive until 1670; his sister, Joan Hart, till 1646; and his daughters, Susannah Hall and Judith Queeny, until 1662. So that Dugdale, at least, if not Wood and the rest of them, would not have had to go far to confirm any rumors they might have stumbled upon as to the

such coincidences, and for that, if for that only, are marvelous. In either case, according to the Shakespereans, we have only to go on, for the rest of time, in discovering new truths in nature and facts in science, only to find that the Stratford butcher's boy knew all about them three hundred years ago—was familiar with all that we have yet to learn, and that to his unlettered genius our wisdom was to be sheer foolishness.

acquirements and accomplishments of the man Shakespeare; but it seems that not even the partiality of his own kin, nor family fame, nor pride of ancestry, ever conceived the idea of palming off their progenitor upon futurity as a giant of any build. If there is any exception to this statement, it would appear to be as follows:　　　　　　　·

I. It is recorded by Oldys that, one of his (Shakespeare's) "younger brothers, who lived to a great age, when questioned, in his last days, about William, said he could remember nothing of his performance but seeing him ' act a part in one of his own comedies, wherein, being to personate a decrepit old man, he wore a long beard, and appeared so weak and drooping and unable to walk, that he was forced to be supported and carried to a table at which he was seated among some company, and one of them sang a song.'" Mr. Fullom has demonstrated from the Shakespeare family records, that Oldys must have been mistaken as to any brother of William Shakespeare's having furnished this reminiscence; but, admitting it as the statement of a surviving brother, it stands for what it is, and it certainly IS NOT the record or tradition of one whose popular memory in men's minds was that of an immortal prodigy.[1]

---

[1] We take this quotation from Mr. Grant White's article on Shakespeare in Appleton's " American Cyclopœdia." Mr. White's admirable contributions to our Shakespearean literature entitle his opinion to great weight in any mooted question as to William Shakespeare; and we must confess that in some portions, his paper we have just mentioned almost suggests him as agreeing with us as to his subject. Mr. White says, in another place: " Young lawyers and poets produced plays rapidly. Each

II. An epitaph was placed over the remains of Susannah Hall, presumably by one of the family, which
read:

> " Witty above her sex, but that's not all:
> Wise to salvation was good Mistress Hall.
> Something of Shakespeare was in that, but this
> Wholly of him with whom she's now in bliss."

Whether the writer of this mortuary eulogy meant
that either William Shakespeare or Mistress Hall, or
both, were " witty above their sex " or " wise to sal-
vation," cannot, at this date, be determined : but it
would seem that this is all the immediate family of
William Shakespeare have ever contributed to our
knowledge of him, and that their estimate of him
was not unlike that of his chroniclers and contemporaries.

But Mr. Malone—and, being the first investigator,
he would, doubtless, have been followed, as he has
been, whatever the result of his inquiries—Mr. Malone, in spite of the silence of the authorities to whose

---

theatrical company not only ' kept a poet,' but had three or four,
in its pay.   At the time of his leaving Stratford the drama was
rising rapidly in favor with all classes in London, where actors
were made much of in a certain way.   And where there was a
constant demand for new plays, ill-provided younger sons of the
gentry, and others who had been bred at the universities and the
inns-of-court, sought to mend their fortunes by supplying this
demand."   And again: " We are tolerably well informed by
contemporary writers as to the performances of the eminent actors of that time, but of Shakespeare's we read nothing."   Mr.
White admits, a few lines below the sentence just quoted, that
Shakespeare's position in the stock at the Blackfriars was " general utility."   We should rather call it, from the evidence, " first
old man."

pages he had recourse, not only assumed all he could
not find authority for, but undertook to tell us the
precise dates at which his Stratford lad composed the
plays themselves. Among other achievements he constructed an admirable "chronology" of the Shakespearean plays; which—with such fanciful variations
as have been made to it from time to time since—is an
authority with the Shakespeareans even to this day.
To be sure, Mr. Malone did not rely entirely upon external evidence for this apochrypha. He often appeals
to the text, as when, for example, he settles the date
at which the "Merchant of Venice" was composed—
as 1594, because Portia says:

> " Even as a flourish when true subjects bow
> To a new crowned monarch,"

referring of course, says Mr. Malone, (and this guess-
work he not only called "commentary," but has actually succeeded in making all his successor "commentators" accept him as final) to the coronation of
Henry IV., of France! Again, in the "Merry Wives
of Windsor" he finds the words, (Act I, scene iii)
"Sail like my pinnace to these golden shores." "This
shows," says Mr. Malone, "that this comedy must
have been written after Sir Walter Raleigh's return
from Guinia, in 1696. And so on."

We will not rehearse the scope and burden of Mr.
Malone's painstaking and wonderful labors, but, from
one instance of the credulity which, once it has over-
mastered the ablest mind, can suppress and subordinate
reason, judgment, and common sense to a zealous and
silly search, we can judge of the calm historical value
of his "discoveries." In 1808, Mr. Malone published

a pamphlet—"An Account of the Incidents from which the Title and Part of the Story of 'The Tempest' were derived, and the Date ascertained."[1] It seems that Mr. Malone finds reference to a hurricane that once dispersed a certain fleet of a certain nobleman, one Sir George Somers, in July, 1609, on a passage, with provisions, for the Virginia Colony; the above nobleman, and a Sir Thomas Gates, having been wrecked on the island of Bermuda. This discovery is warranty enough for Mr. Malone, and he goes on gravely to argue that William Shakespeare not only wrote his "Tempest" to commemorate this particular

[1] By Edmond Malone. London: printed by C. & R. Baldwin, Newbridge street, 1808.

The "Tempest" is the most purely fanciful and poetical of the Shakespearean plays, but the commentators determined to show that there is nothing fanciful or poetical about it; that it is all real: the "Magic Island," a real island; the magician Prospero, a real portrait; the "monster," a real, living curiosity, which happened to be on exhibition in England in the days when the play either was written or about to be written, (it makes no difference to these gentlemen which) and the storm at sea— as if the brain which conceived the play could not have conceived—what is not, now-a-days, at least, the most uncommon thing in the world—a storm at sea!—a real historical hurricane!

In 1839, the Reverend Joseph Hunter, following in the Malone footsteps, published "A Disquisition on the Scene, Origin. Date, etc., of Shakespeare's Tempest," in which the Magic Island is the island of Lampedusa: first, because it is uninhabited; secondly, because it is small; thirdly, because it lies on the route between Naples and the coast of Africa, so that had a prince been traveling from one to the other, and wrecked on an island between, he could have been conveniently wrecked on this one without going out of his course; fourthly, because it bore the reputation (Mr. Hunter does not say with whom) of being

tempest—and, as will be seen by an examination of the premises, the relation between the occurrence and the play is confined merely to the word "tempest" and goes no further—but that he (Shakespeare) DID NOT place the scene of his shipwreck on the Bermudas, " because he could spread a greater glamour over the whole by not alluding to so well-known islands as the Bermudas." Mr. Malone further remarks naively that, " without having read Tacitus, he (Shakespeare) well knew that 'omne ignotum pro magnifico est'!" Without pausing to wonder how Mr. Malone knew that Shakespeare of Stratford had never read Tacitus —(a slander, by the way, on the omniscient Shakespeare, too—the man who studied Plautus in Greek manuscript, the author of " Julius Cæsar"—that he had not read a simple Latin historian !)—or to dwell on the most marvelous coincidence between the wreck of Sir George Somers and that of Prince Ferdinand

---

haunted; fifthly, because there was a cell upon it, which Prospero might have found most opportune for his ghostly residence; and sixthly, that the island of Malta gets fire-wood from it. This last fact being strongest in the way of proof, because we are told that Prospero impressed Ferdinand into his service and kept him piling logs of wood.

But it was reserved for Mr. Edward Dowden, in 1881, to locate the island beyond the necessity of further conjecture, and to give us accurate sailing directions for reaching it. " Prospero's Island," he tells us, " was imagined by Shakespeare as within two days' quick sail of Naples," for " Ariel is promised his freedom after two days" (Act I, scene ii). " Why two days? The time of the entire action of *the Tempest* is only three hours. What was to be the employment of Ariel during two days? To make the winds and seas favorable during the voyage." (Dowden's Shakespeare's Mind and Art. New York : Harper & Brothers. 1881. p. 373.)

(the coincidence, according to Malone, being, that one
was wrecked on the Bermuda and the other wasn't);
or ask if a storm at sea was so rare an occurrence as
to be easily identified; or to note that "the tempest"
in the play of that name is an episode which covers
only about a dozen lines of text, and which has absolutely nothing to do with the rest of the argument—
without pausing for this, or to remark that Mr. Malone
might have taken to himself the 'omne ignotum pro
magnifico est" of Tacitus more appositely than he applied it either to Sir George Somers or the Bermudas,
had he reflected as generously as he took it for granted
—it is as well to take our leave of Mr. Malone and his
labors at this point, with a compliment to their zeal
and impressment which must be withheld from their
results.[1]

And the world would doubtless be as well off could
we also here take leave of the rest of the Shakespeare-
makers. But we are not allowed to do so. From the
time of Malone onward, the Shakespeare-making,
Shakespeare-mending, and Shakespeare-cobbling have
gone on without relaxation. Each fresh rencontre
with an emergency in the Shakespearean text has ne-
cessitated at least one and often several new Shakespeares. And they have been prepared and forthcom-
ing as fast as wanted. Was it found that the bard had,
of all his worldly goods, left the wife of his bosom no
recognition save the devise of a ramshackle old bedstead? A score of gentlemen hurried to the front to
prove that, by law, history, logic, custom, and every

---

[1] DeQuincy accepts this "origin" "with great alacrity."

8

thing else, in those days a "second-best bed" was really the most priceless of possessions; of fabulous value, and a fortune in itself; and that in no other way could her immortal husband have so testified his tender regard and appreciation of Mrs. Shakespeare— the sweet Ann Hathaway of old, who had thrown herself away on a scapegrace butcher's son! The fact (as it appears, on inspection of the instrument itself, to be) that Mrs. Shakespeare was not even alluded to in the first draft of the testament—her name and the complimentary devise of the precious husband's precious " second-best bed " having been written in as " a poet's after-thought," and not appearing in the first draft at all—does not affect their statements in the least! They have even gone so far as to ascertain that William was no truant lord to willingly desert his lonesome lady. According to the very latest authority we are able to cite, the fault of the separation was wholly her own. We are assured by a very recent explorer that Mrs. Shakespeare " did not accompany her husband to London, objecting to the noise and turmoil of that city."[1] Unless it be assumed, therefore, that investigation is reliable in proportion to the distance from its subject at which it works, it would seem to

---

[1] "Shakespeare and his Contemporaries." By William Tegg, F. R. H. S. London: William Tegg & Co., 1879. Chapter I., "Sketch of the Life of Shakespeare," p. 4. As every circumstance connected with William Shakespeare and Stratford is of interest in the connection, we may as well note that, according to Mr. Grant White, when William Shakespeare first went to London, he went into the office of a cousin of his, who was an attorney in that city. Like Mr. Tegg, Mr. White gives himself as an authority for this item. See his "Shakespeare" in Johnston's Encyclopædia.

appear that, even if the William Shakespeare we have
portrayed were our own creation, the creation is actually a nearer resemblance to the William Shakespeare
known to those nearest to him in residence and time;
than the inspired genius of the Shakespeareans, who,
from Malone downward, have rejected every shred of
fact they found at hand, and weaved, instead, their
warp and woof of fiction (and that it is charming and
absorbing fiction, we are eager to admit) around a
vision of their own.

Nor have the Shakespeareans rested their labors
here.   Having created a Shakespeare to fit the plays,
it was necessary to proceed to create a face to fit the
Shakespeare, and a cranial development wherein might
lodge and whence might spring the magic of the works
he ought to have written.   This may, very fairly, be
called " the young ladies' argument." [1]   " Look on his
portrait," say the Shakespeareans; "look at that magnificent head!"—and they point to the Chandos portrait—"is not that the head of a genius?"   " Was
there ever such a head?"   We should say, yes, there
might have been such another head created, even admitting the Chandos portrait to be the very counterfeit head of William Shakespeare.   But it does not
appear, on taking the trouble to look into the matter,
either that the Chandos picture is a portrait, or that
—with one exception—any other of the pictures, casts,
masks, busts, or statues of William Shakespeare are
any thing but works of art, embodying the individual

---

[1] So the young ladies of New York were of opinion that Stokes
should not be hanged for the murder of Fisk, " because he was
so awfully good-looking."

inspiration—the ideal of the artist, who conceives, in
every case, his own "Shakespeare;" (and if we were
called upon for proof that "Shakespeare" is quite as
much of an ideal to the most of us as a "Hamlet," or
a "Lear," we could cite, perhaps, nothing more convincing than the latitude which is allowed to artists
with any of the three—"Shakespeare," "Hamlet," or
"Lear," and the elaborate criticism to which a new
"portrait" of either of them is subjected—criticism,
which, in the case of a portrait of William Shakespeare,
in no case pretends to be historical, but is always romantic, or sentimental, or picturesque: as to the proper
pose of a poet, or the correct attitude for a man receiving efflatus directly from the gods; never as to the
stage manager of the Blackfriars, or the husband of
Anne Hathaway, or the son of John Shakespeare, of
Stratford.)

It appears that, as a matter of fact, there never was
but one picture of the Elizabethan Manager which
ever enjoyed any thing in the semblance of a certification to its authenticity; and that certification was in
the very unsatisfactory form of rhyme, in the shape of
a set of verses said to have been written by Ben Jonson (and, as we propose to show, are quite as likely to
have been placed under the particular picture without
Jonson's authority as with it); while, that they were
written to fit the particular picture in question (for they
are in the form of a sort of apostrophe to some picture
or portrait, and will be hereafter quoted), there seems
to be no information sufficient to form a belief either
way. If they were written for that particular picture,
and if that particular picture is a speaking likeness,
then the phrenological, or at least the physiognomical,

argument must droop away and die; for the person represented has as stupefied, stultified, and insignificant a human countenance as was ever put upon an engraver's surface; and, as a matter of fact, no Shakespearean has yet been found to admit it as the image of his dream. But, of course, this is mere matter of personal opinion, and entitled to no weight whatever in the discussion. The question is—Is there any authentic portrait of William Shakespeare, as there is of Elizabeth, Bacon, Raleigh, Southampton, and other more or less prominent characters of the age in which William Shakespeare is known to have lived and died? Let us do the best we can toward investigating this question.

We have before us a volume, "An Enquiry into the Authenticity of Various Pictures and Prints, which, from the Decease of the Poet to our own Times, have been offered to the Public as Portraits of Shakespeare. Containing a Careful Examination of the Evidence on which they claim to be received; by which the Pretended Portraits have been rejected, the Genuine confirmed and established," etc., etc. By James Boaden, Esq.[1] We must content ourselves with a simple review of Mr. Boaden's labors. He was a friend and disciple of Malone's, and a Shakespearean; a believer in the poet; and he writes under the shadow of the mighty name—the shadow ·out from under which we of this age have stepped, and so become able to inspect, not only the facts of history uncurtained by that shadow, but the shadow itself. But we will take every

---

[1] London. Printed for Robert Triphook, 23 Old Bond Street, 1824.

one of Mr. Boaden's statements for granted, nevertheless, and draw our opinions, when we venture on any,
from the portraits which he has given in his book.   At
least Mr. Boaden is not a "Baconian," and not a
"Raleigh man," and, whenever he finds it necessary
to speak of Shakespeare's history, he follows Malone's
own version.   For convenience, we will change Mr.
Boaden's numeration of the "portraits," preserving
the designation, however, which he assigns them.

No. 1. William Shakespeare dies in Stratford in
1616.   In 1623, appears, on the title-page of Heminges and Condell's first folio of the plays, the portrait
by Martin Droeshout.   It is an engraving, and, Mr.
Boaden believes, a good engraving, of some original
picture from which it must have been taken; "for,"
he says, "there were good engravers in those days;
for Chapman's 'Homer' was published in that year,
with a very fine engraving of Chapman."

Under this engraving is printed a copy of Jonson's
lines, as follows:

> TO THE READER.
>
> This figure that thou here seest put,
> It was for gentle Shakespeare cut;
> Wherein the graver had a strife [1]
> With nature to outdo the life:
> O, could he but have drawn his wit
> As well in brasse as he hath hit
> His face: the print would then surpasse
> All that was ever done in brasse.
> But, since he can not, reader, look,
> Not on his picture, but his booke.

---

(1) Look, when a painter would surpasse the life,
   His art's with nature's handiwork at strife.
                                        Venus and Adonis.

In this picture the head of the subject is represented as rising out of an horizontal plain of collar appalling to behold. The hair is straight, combed down the sides of the face and bunched over the ears; the forehead is disproportionately high; the top of the head bald; the face has the wooden expression familiar in the Scotchmen and Indians used as signs by tobacconists' shops, accompanied by an idiotic stare that would be but a sorry advertisement for the humblest establishment in that trade; and which we would be quite as unlikely to look for in the Stratford scapegrace as in the immortal bard of the Shakespeareans. It is of this picture that Boaden quotes somebody's remark that "it is lucky these metrical commendations are not required to be delivered on oath." And Steevens says, on the supposition that Ben Jonson, and not the engraver, put the copy of verses on the title-page beneath the effigy: "Ben Jonson might know little about art, care less about the resemblance, and, never having compared the engraving from the picture, have rested satisfied with the recollection that the original was a faithful resemblance; and that, no doubt, the engraver had achieved all that his art could perform."

No. 2. The edition of the plays of 1690 is accompanied with what is known as "Marshall's picture;" which so closely follows, as to face, forehead, hair, beard, and collar, the engraving above described, as to suggest that it was a copy either of that engraving, or of the unknown picture from which that was taken. But, if a copy, it is certainly, from a pictorial point of view, an improvement. It looks much more like a man. The simpleton stare around the eyes is toned down, and the wooden aspect is modified into something like life. Marshall has taken liberties with the dress of No. 1, throwing in a sort of tunic over the left shoulder, hitching on an arm with a gauntleted hand grasping a sprig of laurel, etc., etc.

No. 3. The Felton Head.—" In the catalogue of the fourth exhibition and sale by private contract," says Boaden,"(page 81),"at the European Museum, King Street, St. James Square, 1792," this picture was announced to the public in the following words:

" No. 359—a curious portrait of Shakespeare, painted in 1597."

On the 31st of May, 1792, a Mr. Felton bought it for five guineas, and, on requiring its credentials, received the following letter:

To Mr. S. Felton, Drayton, Shropshire—Sir: The head of Shakespeare was purchased out of an old house, known by the sign of " The Boar," in Eastcheap, London, where Shakespeare and his friends used to resort; and report says was painted by a player of that time, but whose name I have not been able to learn.

This letter was signed "J. Wilson," who was the conductor of the European Museum. This "J. Wilson" appears to have been the original Barnum. Although Prince Hal and Falstaff are said in the play to have affected "The Boar's head in Eastcheap," it does not appear, except from Mr. "J. Wilson," that " Shakespeare and his friends " ever resorted thither. There was an old inn in Eastcheap, but it was not called " The Boar's Head." There was an inn by that name, however, in Blackfriars, near the theater, from which the manager might have borrowed it. Then, again, Mr. "J. Wilson" seemed to have forgotten the great fire in London in 1666, which, "in a few hours, in a strong east wind, left the whole of Eastcheap a mass of smoking ruins, and the wretched inhabitants could think of saving nothing but their lives." Mr. Wilson subsequently amended his story so as to read that "it was found between four and five years ago at a broker's shop at the Minories by a man of fashion, whose name must be concealed," etc., etc. Mr. Steevens, who scouted the other pictures as spurious, accepted this picture, for a time, as the original of the engravings we have called No. 1 and No. 2; but finally, the whole thing exploded and was forgotten.

No. 4. The Bust in Stratford Church.—This was carved by nobody knows whom, from nobody knows what, nobody knows when; for the statement that it was cut by "Gerard Johnson," an Amsterdam "tombmaker," is invariably accepted, but can be traced to no historical source. Says Boaden (page 31), "The performance is not too good for a native sculptor." In 1623 Leonard Digges alludes to it in a few verses well known. It seems to have been originally colored, but there is no testimony as to the original colors. In 1748, one hundred and twenty-five years after Digges, John Hall, a Stratford artist, "restored" it, painting the eyes a light hazel, and the hair and beard auburn. This was "a good enough" Shakespeare for all practical purposes for the next half-hundred years or so. But in 1793 came Mr. Malone. He caused the bust —in deference, probably, to a purer taste and a sense of churchly propriety—to be covered completely with a thick coat of white paint.[1] From this bust, Mr.

---

[1] While these pages are going through the press (April, 1879), however, we find a statement that within a year or two (and

Boaden says, a Mr. Bullock once took a .cast, which is sometimes engraved as frontispiece to an edition of the plays, in which case it is entitled "Cast of the head of William Shakespeare, taken after death," which may or may not—for Mr. Boaden can not tell us who this "Mr. Bullock" was—be the German "Death Mask" noticed further on, (at any rate the statement "taken after death"—William Shakespeare being unquestionably dead at the time—is literally true.)

The bust represents its subject as possessing a magnificent head, admirably proportioned, with no protruding "bumps." The face is represented as breaking into a smile. According to this effigy, Shakespeare must have had an extraordinarily long upper lip, the distance between the base of the nose and the mouth being remarkably out of proportion with the other facial developments; there seems to be a little difficulty, too, about the chin, which is pulled out into what appears to be a sort of extra nose; but, nevertheless, the Stratford bust represents a fine, soldierly-looking man, with a fierce military mustache cocked up at the ends, and a goatee. If Ben Jonson—knowing his friend William Shakespeare to have been the martial and altogether elegant-looking gentleman the Stratford bust represents him—authorized the verses we have already quoted to be placed under the "Droeshout engraving," it was a deliberate libel on his part, and as gross as it was deliberate, and only perhaps to

since the writer of these pages visited it) one Simon Colling has applied a bath to the bust—removing Malone's whitewash, and revealing the identical auburn hair and hazel eyes which tradition had asserted to be underneath.

be explained by Jonson's alleged secret enmity to, or jealousy of, William Shakespeare, his rival playwright, which we shall be called to examine at length further on.[1]

No. 5. "The Chandos Portrait." This picture, so termed because once the property of the Duke of Chandos, is the best known of all the so-called portraits—being, in fact, the one from which the popular idea of Shakespeare is derived; therefore, when a man is said to resemble Shakespeare, it is meant to be conveyed that he bears a likeness to the Chandos picture. Mr. Malone announced that it was painted in 1607, but never gave any other authority than his own ipse dixit for the statement, not even taking the trouble to refer, like Mr. J. Wilson, to "a man of fashion, whose name must be concealed." Mr. Boaden says (page 42) that he once saw it, and compared it "with what had been termed a fine copy, I think by Piamberg, and found it utterly unlike." "Indeed," he continues, "I never saw anything that resembled it." He also says (pages 41-42) that "the copies by Sir Joshua Reynolds and Mr. Humphrey were not only unlike the original, but were unlike each other, one being smiling and the other grave." That is to say, that not only have the romancers constructed "biographies," but the artists have kept up with them; and we may, every one of us, select our own Shakespeare to-day—poet or potman, scholar or clown, tall or short, fair or dark; we may each suit our own tastes with a Shakespeare to our liking. Mr. Boaden continues (page 49): "It" (the Chandos) "was very probably painted by Burbage,

---

[1] Post Part III. The Jonsonian testimony.

the great tragedian, who is known to have handled the pencil; it is said to have been the property of Joseph Taylor, our poet's Hamlet, who, dying about 1653, at the advanced age of seventy, left the picture by will to Davenant. At the death of Davenant in 1663, it was bought by Betterton, the actor, and when he died Mr. Robert Keck, of the Inner Temple, gave Mrs. Barry, the actress, forty guineas for it. From Mr. Keck it passed to Mr. Nichol, of Southgate, whose daughter married the Marquis of Caernarvon.

Steevens, whom Boaden quotes (page 43), declined to be convinced by this genealogy, and said, " Gossip rumor had given out that Davenant was more than Shakespeare's godson.[1] What folly, therefore, to suppose that he should possess a genuine portrait of the poet, when his lawful daughters had not one! Mrs. Barry was an actress of acknowledged gallantry; as she received forty guineas for the picture, something more animated might have been included though not specified in the bargain," etc., etc. Steevens was fond of calling this picture " the Davenantico-Bet-

---

[1] There is a story that once, on the occasion of one of Shakespeare's visits to Stratford, a villager, meeting young Davenant in the street, asked him where he was going. " To the inn, to see my godfather Shakespeare," said the lad. " Beware how you take the name of God in vain, my lad," said the other. The allusions to William's gallantries are numerous. On the Stratford parish records there is entry of the birth of one " Thomas Green, *alias* Shakespeare." The tale of the interrupted amour, at the theater, of " Richard the Third " and " William the Conqueror," as is apt to be the case, is about the most widely familiar of the Shakespearean stories, and unnecessary to be repeated here. But Davenant was proud to claim the dishonor of his mother, and Shakespeare for his father, to his dying day.

tertono-Barryan-Keckian-Nicolsian-Chandosian portrait." "There are," says Boaden (page 53), "a few
circumstances relating to the picture of which some
notice should be taken in this examination. There is,
it seems, a tradition that, no original picture of
Shakespeare existing, Sir Thomas Clarges caused a"
(i. e., this) "portrait to be painted from a young man
who had the good fortune to resemble him" (i. e.,
Shakespeare. Query: How did Sir Thomas know that
the young man resembled Shakespeare?). Mr. Malone
traced this story to " The Gentleman's Magazine" for
August, 1759, and called on the writer for his authority;
but the writer, whoever he was, never gave it, any
more than Malone gave his authority for announcing
its date to be 1607; but Malone himself says that "most
reports of this kind are an adumbration of some fact,
and indication of something in kind or degree similar
or analogous."

No. 6. This is a portrait, so called, by Zuccharo, which
need not detain us, since Mr. Boaden himself demon-
strates very clearly that it was not in any event painted
from life, and, not improbably, did not originally claim
to have been intended for Shakespeare at all.

Mr. Boaden's No. 7 is the " Cornelius Jansen picture," and to this Mr. Boaden pins his earnest faith.
He says this " is now in the collection of the Duke of
Somerset;" but he appears to make no attempt to
connect it with William Shakespeare except as follows:
Cornelius Jansen is said to have painted the daughter
of Southampton—ergo, he might have been Southampton's family painter, and Southampton might have
been desirous to possess a portrait of his friend Shakespeare done by his own painter—ergo, Jansen might

have had William Shakespeare for a sitter! This is all the authority for the authenticity. But that it is—judging from the engraving in Mr. Boaden's book—a magnificent picture, we think there can be no question.

On the supposition that the Chandos is an authentic likeness of Shakespeare, this Jansen certainly bears a strong Shakespearean resemblance. In it the hair is curling, as in the Chandos, not straight, as in the Droeshout and the Marshall engravings. The mustache, which is cut tight to the face without being shaved, as in the Droeshout, and strong and heavy, as in the bust, is lighter than the Chandos, while the beard is fuller. There is nothing of the tremendous upper lip represented in the bust.

Mr. Boaden (page 195) describes it as an eye-witness, he having had access to it for the purposes of the book before us. He says: "It is an early picture by Cornelius Jansen, tenderly and beautifully painted. Time seems to have treated it with infinite kindness, for it is quite pure, and exhibits its original surface. . . . The portrait is on panel, and attention will be required to prevent a splitting of the oak, in two places, if my eyes have not deceived me."

As for Earlom, who copied the picture, Boaden says: " He had lessened the amplitude of the forehead; he had altered the form of the skull; he had falsified the character of the mouth; and, though his engraving was still beautiful, and the most agreeable exhibition of the poet, I found it would be absolutely necessary to draw the head again, as if he had never exercised his talent upon it" (page 195). Mr. Boaden specifies further the picture said to have once decorated the pair of bellows belonging to Queen Elizabeth's own private apartments, besides still one other, both of which he rejects as spurious.

Thus, it has taken an army of novelists, painters, engravers, and essayists to erect simple William Shakespeare of Stratford into the god he ought to have been; and, on the best examination we are enabled to make, and according to the Shakespeareans themselves, there is only one picture of William Shakespeare extant which has the even assumed advantage of having been pronounced a likeness by any one who ever saw William Shakespeare himself in his (William Shakespeare's) lifetime. Even if—as Mr. Steevens surmises —this eye witness never saw the engraving, but only the original portrait from which it was copied, the Droeshout still enjoys an authentication possessed by no other so-called likeness, and, if rejected—as it infallibly is by all devout Shakespeareans—there remains nothing of certitude, nothing even of the certitude of conjecture, as to the features of the Stratford boy, whoever he was, and whatever his works. One further effort was, however, made, so lately as 1849, to clinch this "young lady's argument," by yet one more genuine discovery. This time it was a "Becker 'death mask!'" A plaster mask of an anonymous dead face is found in a rubbish-shop in Mayence, in 1849. Regarded as a mask of William Shakespeare, it bears a certain resemblance to the Stratford bust; and, regarded as a mask of Count Bismarck (for example), it would be found to bear a very strong resemblance to Count Bismarck. (We write from an inspection of photographs only, never having seen the mask.) Having always been annoyed that a creature so immortal

as they had created their Shakespeare left no death-
mask, the Shakespeareans at once adopt this anonymous mask as taken from the face of the two-days de-
funct William Shakespeare, who died in 1616. *Credat
Judæus!* Either William Shakespeare, at his death,
was known to be an immortal bard or he was not. If
he was, how could the sole likeness moulded of departed greatness be smuggled away from the land that
was pious to claim him as its most distinguished son
and nobody miss it, or raise the hue and cry? If he
was not, to whose interest was it to steal the mask
from the family who cared enough about the dead
man's memory to go to the expense of it?   But, at
any rate, in 1849 it falls into the hands of jealous be-
lievers.   They search upon it for hairs of auburn hue,
and for the date of their hero's death, and they find
both.   Had they made up their minds to find a scrap
of Shakespearean cuticle, we may be sure it would have
been there.   Professor Owen, of the British Museum,
declared that, if the fact of the mask having originally come from England could be established, there
was "hardly any sum of money which the Museum
would not pay for the mask itself." But the missing
testimony has not been supplied, though doubtless it
is incubating.   For now and then we see a newspaper
paragraph to the effect that old paintings have turned
up (in pawn-shops invariably) which "resemble the
death-mask," thus accustoming us to the title, which,
in time, we shall doubtless come to accept—as we have
come to accept Shakespeare himself—from mere force
of habit.   The last of these discoveries is in Australia,
farther off than even Mayence, "said to resemble the

Becker death-mask."[1] The Stratford portrait of Shakespeare claims no authority further than a resemblance to the accepted ideal, and the terra-cotta bust in the possession of the Garrick club was "found to order," and represents a man who, it would seem, bore not even a resemblance to the accepted Shakespearean features.

We should, perhaps, mention that Mr. Boaden surmises that the Droeshout picture is a portrait of William Shakespeare the actor, in the character of " Old Knowell," and that the Stratford bust was caused to be executed by Dr. Hall, a son-in-law of its subject, and was the work of one Thomas Stanton, who followed a cast taken after death. But, as Mr. Boaden admits, this is his surmise only. However insuperable, therefore, in the run of cases, the "young ladies argument" to prove from the pictures that William Shakespeare WAS NOT author of the plays is quite weak enough; but, as an argument to prove that he WAS such author, it is weakness and impotence itself.

It now becomes necessary to ask the ordinary question which a court would be obliged to ask concerning any exhibit produced before it, and claimed as authentic or authoritative : namely, Where did the plays called Shakespeare's come from ? how did they get into print ? who, if anybody, delivered the "copy" to the printer, and vouched for its authorship ? It is manifest that we have no business here with any question of criticism, or as to an authenticity between different editions of the

---

[1] See the "Academy," London, May 31, 1879, p. 475. We understand that the mask is at present in possession of the British Museum.

same play; but the plays were written TO BE PLAYED; how did they come to be published so that millions of readers, who never entered a playhouse where they were performed, read and still read them?

In order to arrive at any supposition as to these considerations which would be of value to our purpose in these papers, it will be necessary to glance at the state of literary property in the days between 1585 and 1606. Now, in those days, there was absolutely no legal protection for an author's manuscript. Once it had strayed beyond the writer's hand it was practically "publici juris"—any body's property. The first law of copyright enacted in England was the act of Anne, of April 10, 1710, more than one hundred years after the last date at which commentators claim the production of a Shakespearean play. Even the first authoritative pronunciation of a competent tribunal as to literary property at common law (which preceded, of course, all literary property definable by statute) was not made until 1769, fifty-nine years later. But the Court of Star Chamber (of obscure origin, but known to have been of powerful jurisdiction in the time of Henry VII.) was in the height of its ancient omnipotence in those years. And of the various matters of which it took cognizance, one of the earliest was the publishing, printing, and even the keeping and reading of books. Under date of June 23, 1585—the year that many commentators assign as that in which William Shakespeare first turned up in London—this Star Chamber, which had already issued many such, issued a decree that none should "print any book, work, or copy, against the form or meaning of any restraint contained in any statute of laws of this realm," except,

etc., etc. Twenty-nine years before—in 1556—Philip
and Mary had erected ninety-seven booksellers into a
body called " The Stationers' Company," who were to
monopolize the printing of books, if they so chose.
They had given them power and authority—and their
second charter, in 1558, confirmed them in it—to print
such books as they obtained, either from authors' manuscripts or translations, and to see very carefully that
nobody else printed them. Their power was absolute
—they had their " privilegium ad imprimendum
solum," and in the pursuit of any body who interfered
with it they were empowered to "break locks, search,
seize," and, in short, to suppress any printed matter
they did not choose to license, wherever they pleased.
This the Worshipful Company of Stationers did not
fail to do; they pursued, and the Star Chamber con-
victed. The disgraceful record of infamous and inhu-
man prosecutions and punishments for reading, keeping, selling, or making books might well detain us
here, did our scope permit.[1] Whatever literature accomplished in those days it accomplished by stealth, in
defiance of the implacable and omnipotent Star Chamber and its bloodhound, the Stationers' Company, who
ran in its victims.

It can not, we think, be doubted, by a student of
those times,[2] that whatever literary property existed

[1] See "Omitted Chapters of the History of England," by Andrew
Basset, 1864

[2] "The person who first resolved on printing a book, and entered his design on that register, became thereby the legal proprietor of that work, and had the sole right of printing it."—
Carte, quoted in " Reasons for a Further Amendment of the Act
54, George III., c. 15," London, 1817.

John Camden Hotten, "Seven Letters, Etc., on Literary Prop-

at common law then existed in the shape of a license
TO PRINT a work under permission of the Stationers'
Company; that no estate or property obtained in anything except the types, ink, paper, in the license to use
them all together to make a book, and in the resulting
volume; and that what we understand by "copyright"
to-day—namely, an author's or a proprietor's right to
demand a royalty or percentage, or to exercise other
control over the work when once printed and published—was altogether unconceived and unclaimed.
Whatever compensation the author of a work was
able to obtain, he doubtless obtained beforehand, by
sale of his manuscript, and dreamed not of setting up
a tangible property as against any one who had obtained the Stationers' Company's license to print it.
The Stationers' Company, at the outset of their career,
opened a record, in which it entered the name of every
book it licensed—the date, and the name of the person
authorized to print it.[1]   It was not until 1644, twenty-
eight years after William Shakespeare's death (so far
as we can ever know) that John Milton, in his "Areopagitica"—the greatest state paper in the republic

---

erty," London, Hotten, 1871, describes the modern Stationers'
Company as entrusted with "a vested interest over somebody
else's property, a prescriptive right to interfere with the future
work of other people's hands."

[1] We are aware that this statement as to the condition of authors' rights in the days of Elizabeth will not pass unchallenged;
but a review of the reported cases, as well as the extant records
of the Stationers' Company, will, we think, support our conclusion.   The first reported case of piracy was in 1735, when the
Master of the Rolls enjoined publication of "The whole Duty of
Man" (Morgan's "Law of Literature," vol. ii., p. 672).

of letters, the declaration of independence, and the
bill of rights of the liberty of literature—asserted[1] for
the first time " the right of every man" to "his several
copy, which God forbid should be gainsayd."

Once in their hands, printers did what they pleased
with a manuscript; abridged it if they found it too
long, and lengthened it if they found it too short.
Thomas Nashe says, that, in a play of his, called " The
Isle of Dogs," four acts, without his consent " or the
least guesse of his drifte or scope," were added by the
printers.[2] The printers also assigned the authorship of
the work to any name they thought would help sell
the book, and dedicated it to whom they pleased.
(Just as the first printer of the sonnets we call Shakespeare's, dedicated them to " W. H.," which two
initials have supplied the Shakespeareans with an
excuse for at least as many dozen octavo volumes
of conjecture as to who " W. H." was.) Sometimes
the author thus despotically assigned to the work
rebelled.   Dr. Heywood recognized two of his own
compositions in a collection of verses called " The
Passionate Pilgrim," printed by one Jaggard, in 1599,
upon the title-page to which, this Jaggard had placed
the name of William Shakespeare as author.   Heywood publicly claimed his own, but William Shakespeare never denied or affirmed; his name, however,
was removed by the printer from the title-page of the

---

[1] For the text of the "Areopagitica" and copious notes as to the
history of the days which called it out, see edition of J. W.
Hale's, Clarendon Press Series, Macmillan & Co., Oxford, 1874.

[2] In a pamphlet, "The Prayse of the Red Herring" cited by
Farmer, in his " Learning of Shakespeare," page 45.

third edition of the book, in 1612.[1] But, as a rule, the Stationers' Company were too powerful, and the author too poor, to bring the trick to exposure.

It was under these circumstances, and in times like these, that the Shakespearean plays began to appear in print. Where did they come from? They were written to be played. According to all accounts they were very valuable to the theater which produced them. Every personal and selfish interest of the proprietors, whether of the theater or of the manuscript plays, dictated that they should be kept in secret—least of all that they should be printed and made accessible to the public outside of the theater, who otherwise, to see them, must become patrons of the house where they were performed. That the author or authors of the plays could have made them of more profit by selling them to the printers than to the players is doubtful; that they personally entered them—or such of them as were entered—on the books of the Stationers' Company, is certainly not the fact; the only persons to whose interest it was to print them were the printers themselves, and, in all probability, it was the printers who did cause them to be printed. But where did these printers procure the "copy" from which to set up the plays they printed? The question will never be answered. The manuscripts might have been procured by bribing individual actors, each of whom could have easily furnished a copy of his individual part, and so the whole be made up for the press. The fact that the plays never were printed without more or less of the stage directions or "business" included, lends probability to this theory:

---

[1] Shakespeare, by R. G. White. Vol. 1., page lxxvii.

but, as to whether a play made up in this fashion would
have resulted in any thing like what we possess to-day,
we have considered further on.   Mr. Grant White admits,[1] as must everybody who examines into the matter, that whatever the printers printed was unauthorized and surreptitious.   But, having admitted this
much, Mr. White is too ardent a Shakespearean not
to make some effort to throw a guise of authenticity
around the text he has so lovingly followed.   In the
article we have just quoted from in our foot-note, he
says, "It is not improbable that, in case of great and
injurious misrepresentation of the text of a play by"
this surreptitious method of publication, "fair copies
were furnished by the theatrical people at the author's
request in self-defence."   Perhaps these plays might
have found their way into print just as the comedy
of "Play" found its way into print in 1868,[2] or the
play of "Mary Warner,"[3] at about the same date.   At
any rate the editors of the first folio speak of the
"stolne and surreptitious copies" which had preceded
them.

---

[1] "Such of his plays as were published during his lifetime seem
to have been given to the press entirely without his agency; indeed, his interest was against their publication. . . . It was
the interest of all concerned, whether as proprietors, or only as
actors, or, like himself, as both, that the theaters should have the
entire benefit of whatever favor they enjoyed with the public.
But the publishers, or stationers, as they were then called, eagerly
sought copies of them for publication, and obtained them surreptitiously: sometimes, it would seem, by corrupting persons
connected with the theater, and sometimes, as the text which
they printed shows, by sending short-hand writers to the performance."

[2] Palmer v. DeWitt, 47 New York R. 532.

[3] Crowe v. Aiken. 2 Bissel R. 208.

The first and second editions of "Hamlet," says Mr. White, "in 1603 and 1604, might have been the result of such maneuvers on the part of the printers and the stenographers, or those who had access to the manuscripts of the author.   However this may be, twenty of Shakespeare's plays were published by various stationers during his lifetime; they are known as the quartos, from the form in which they are printed.   They are most of them full of errors. . . . Some of them seem to have been put in type from stage copies, or, not improbably, from an aggregation of the separate parts which were in the hands of the various actors."   In other words, Shakespeare's works were so imperfectly printed, against his will, during his lifetime, that he himself authorized *other imperfect*—Mr. White says they were imperfect—versions to be likewise printed!

Mr. White might have looked nearer home to more purpose. Nobody knows, nobody can know better than he, that what is called the "accepted" or "received" text of Shakespeare (if there is, to speak minutely, any such to-day) has been arrived at and made up piecemeal, and in the course of time, by the commentators selecting from the folios, and other original editions, such "readings" as the judgment of scholarship or the taste of criticism has, on the whole, adopted; and any body who cares to take the trouble to examine these original editions can see as much for himself. To suppose that this text, as it stands to-day, is the text as its author or authors wrote it, is, it seems to us, to suppose at least ten thousand coincidences, every one of which is, to say the least, improbable.

Before proceeding any further, let us recapitulate

the three historical certainties to which we have arrived. First, that the state of the law was favorable,
(indeed, it would be impossible to conceive of a state
more favorable), to literary imposture or incognito.
Second, that nobody stands on record as claiming to
know the authorship of these plays, except the printers, who were able to sell them by using the name of the
manager of a popular theater; and, therefore, whose
interest it was to affix that name to them ; and, Third,
that there was never a period in which it was so reasonably an author's interest to be anonymous, or preserve his incognito, as these very years covered by the
lifetime of William Shakespeare; when, between the
Stationers' Company and the Star Chamber, it was a
fortunate author, printer or reader, who escaped hanging, disemboweling, and quartering, with only the
loss of ears or liberty.

Who wrote these plays? London was full of playwrights, contemporary with William Shakespeare,
many of them his friends and familiars; possibly, all
of them submitting their manuscripts to his editorial
eye. We have their works extant to-day.

Ben Jonson was a poet and a pedant; Greene, a
university-bred man. And we may go through the list
and verify the records of them all, and find in each
some quality or training from which to reasonably expect fruitage. But nobody has ever ventured to haz-
ard so wild a theory as that any of them wrote the
anonymous immortal plays to which the best of their
own acknowledged masterpieces are mere rubbish.
But a butcher's boy, lately from Stratford, happens to
be manager of a contemporary theater. He, there-
10

fore, must be the writer, and there can not be the
slightest doubt of it. The story that this boy ever
stole deer is rejected as resting on insufficient evidence.
But no evidence is required to prove his authorship
of the topmost works in the history or the literature
of England. We have seen the monopoly that overruled
the press. We have seen that the Stationers' Company
insisted upon recording the name and ownership of
every printed thing; and their record-books are still extant, and bear no trace of any such claimant as William
Shakespeare. We have weighed the surmises of the
Shakespeareans as to these times, and seen their probable value; and have found it just as impossible to connect the immortal fragments we call the Shakespearean
plays to-day with William Shakespeare, of Stratford,
as we have already found it to imagine him as having
access to the material, the sealed records, and the hidden muniments employed in their construction. Is
there any more evidence to be examined?

But were these plays, so printed *outside*, the same
plays as those acted *inside* the theater? When we recall the style of audiences that assembled in those days
(M. Taine says the spectators caroused and sang songs
while the plays progressed; that they drank great
draughts of beer; and, if they drank too much, burned
juniper instead of retiring; anon, they would break
upon the stage, toss in a blanket such performers as
pleased them not, tear up the properties, etc., etc.)—
when we recall this, it is not the easiest thing in the
world to imagine this audience so very highly delighted, for instance, with Wolsey's long soliloquy
(which the actor of to-day delivers in a dignified, low,
and unimpassioned monotone, without gesture), or

Hamlet's philosophical monologues, or Isabella's pious strains. *Some* plays were highly popular inside those theaters. Were these the ones? Mr. Grant White has all reason, probability, and common sense on his side, when he insists that the theater most jealously guarded the manuscripts of the plays that were making its fortune; and that it would have been suicide in it to have circulated them outside, in print. But may not the echo of the popularity of certain plays called "Hamlet," "King John," "Macbeth," etc., have induced others, outside the theater, to have circulated plays, christened with these names (or with and under the popular name of Shakespeare), for gain among the "unco guid" who would not, or the impecunious who could not, enter the theater door? There is no need of opening up so hopeless a speculation—a speculation pure and simple, that can never, in the nature of things, be confronted by data either way. But the fact does remain that these marvelous plays appeared in print contemporaneously with the professional career of an actor named William Shakespeare, and in the same town where he acted; that, if they were his, it would have been to his interest to have kept them out of print; and that their appearance in print he most certainly did not authorize; and who can claim that one guess is not as good as another, where history is silent, and tradition askew, and the truth buried under the dust of centuries, overtopped by the rubbish of conjecture? We repeat, we have no warrant to intrude upon the domain of criticism. The Shakespearean text, as we possess it to-day, is too priceless, whatever its source, to be rudely touched. But, so far as is revealed by the record of its appearance

among printed literature, there is no evidence, internal
or external, as to William Shakespeare's production of
it, and as to its origin we are as hopelessly in the dark
as ever.

Dubious as is the chronicle of those days as to other
matters, it is singularly clear as to what was printed
and what was not. For those were the sort of days
when men whose names were not written in the books
of the Stationers' Company printed at the peril of
clipped ears and slit noses, or worse; and those books
are still extant. But, by the fatality which seems to
follow and pervade the name of William Shakespeare,
this record, like every other, national or local, yields
nothing to the probe but disappointment and silence
as to the man of Stratford and the actor of Blackfriars.

We will, presently, consider as to whether the same
intellect composed the " Hamlet " at one sitting, and
at another, located Bohemia on the sea-coast; and
whether, on inspection, it might not be strongly suggested that the two conceptions indicated geniuses of
quite different orders and not one and the same person ; that one showed the hand-marks of a poet and
the other the hand-marks of the stage-manager, etc.
If the limits of this work permitted, we believe the
same hand-marks might be collected from the treatment of the text of every play. For instance, the
" Comedy of Errors " is supposed to occur during the
days when Ephesus was ruled by a duke, and follows
—as we have already shown—the unities of the Menæchmi of Plautus. But the ignoramus who doctored
the paraphrase for the Blackfriars stage found it convenient, to bring on his stage effect, to introduce a
Christian monastery into Ephesus at about that time,

with a lady abbess who could refuse admission to the
duke himself, so inviolable and sacred was the sanc-
tuary of consecrated Christian walls!   The monastery
was as convenient to bringing all the befogged and
befooled and sadly mixed up personages of the comedy
face to face at the moment, as was the seashore and the
bear, in "A Winter's Tale," to account for the princess
Perdita among the shepherds, and so in they all go.
These, and the like brummagem and ruses de con-
venances, are simple enough to understand, and detract
in no degree whatever from the value of the plays:
they can be retired or retained at pleasure, and no
harm done, if we only remember to whom and to
what they are assignable.   But, if we forget that, and
insist that the very same pen which wrote the dialogue
wrote the setting—wrote every entrance, exit, and
direction to the scene-shifters and stage-carpenters,
and, therefore, that every dot and comma, every call and
cue, every "gag" and localism, is as sacred as holy
writ, no wonder the scholars of the text are puzzled!

For example, we find that Mr. Wilkes, and Mr.
Harper, in the "American Catholic Review" for
January, 1879—who otherwise believe the author
of the Shakespearean plays to have been a roman
catholic—are almost persuaded that he must have
been a protestant, because he finds occasion to make
mention of an "evening mass."   But let us assure
Messrs. Wilkes and Harper that they need neither
abandon nor adopt a theory on rencontre with so
trivial a phenomenon.   If William Shakespeare felt
the need of an "evening mass" at any time, we may
be fairly sure, from our experience of that worthy,
that he put one in.   He had bolted too many camels

in his day to hesitate at such a gnat as that! The creator of a convent in old Ephesus and of a sea-coast to Bohemia was not one to stick at a trifling "evening mass!"

The gentlemen above mentioned, believe the author of the plays to have been a romanist, not because the reverend Richard Davies, writing soon after 1685, distinctly says "he died a Papist," (for any statement made anywhere within a hundred years of William Shakespeare's lifetime is "mere gossip," and it is only the biographies we write now-a-days that are to be relied upon), but mainly because the liturgy and priesthood of that church are invariably treated with respect in the plays, while dissenting parsons are poked fun at without stint. Doubtless, in the modern drama the same rule will be perceived to obtain. The imperious liturgy and priesthood of the roman or of the stately anglican church appear to be beyond the attempts of travesty; while the snivel and preach of mere puritanism has always been too tempting an opportunity for "Aminadab Sleek" and his type—to be resisted, and such a fact would justify very little conclusion either way. Besides, there is no call to insist that the stage, in epitomizing life into the compass of an hour, shall preserve every detail; nothing less than a Chinese theater could answer a demand like that. There is a dramatic license even broader than the license accorded to poetry, and we would doubtless find the drama a sad bore if there were not. William Shakespeare, during his mana-gerial career, appears to have understood this as well as any body; nor have the liberties he took with facts and chronology befogged any body, except the daily lessening throng of investigators, who believe him to be the original of the masterpieces he cut into play-books for his stage.

But did William Shakespeare ever try his hand at verse-making? There is considerable rumor to the effect that, during the leisure of his later life, no less than in the lampooning efforts of his vagrom youth, he did turn his pen to rhymes. And the future may yet bring forth a Shakespearean honest enough to collect these verses—as they follow here—and to entitle them—

THE COMPLETE POETICAL WORKS

OF

WILLIAM SHAKESPEARE.

EPITAPH ON ELIAS JAMES.[1]

When God was pleased, the world unwilling yet,
Elias James to nature paid his debt,
And here reposeth; as he liv'd he dyde;
The saying in him strongly verified—
Such life, such death; then, the known truth to tell,
He lived a godly lyfe, and dyde as well.

EPITAPH ON SIR THOMAS STANLEY.[2]

Ask who lyes here, but do not weepe:
He is not dead, he doth but sleepe;
This stony register is for his bones,
His fame is more perpetual than these stones,

---

[1] On the authority of "a MS. volume of poems by Herrick and others, said to be in the handwriting of Charles I., in the Bodleian Library.

[2] On the authority of Sir William Dugdale ("Visitation Book"), who says, "The following verses were made by William Shakespeare, the late famous tragedian." This appears to be our author's longest and most ambitious work.

And his own goodness, with himself being gone,
Shall live when earthly monument is none.

Not monumental stone preserves our fame
Nor skye aspyring pyramids our name;
The memory of him for whom this stands
Shall outlive marble and defacer's hands,
When all to Time's consumption shall be given;
Stanley, for whom this stands, shall stand in heaven.

EPITAPH ON TOM-A-COMBE, OTHERWISE THINBEARD. [1]

Thin in beard and thick in purse,
Never man beloved worse;
He went to the grave with many a curse,
The Devil and he had both one nurse.

WHOM I HAVE DRUNKEN WITH. [2]

Piping Pebworth, dancing Marston,
Haunted Hillsborough and hungry Grafton;
With dancing Exhall, Papist Wixford,
Beggarly Bloom and drunken Bidford.

DAVID AND GOLIATH. [3]

Goliath comes with sword and spear,
  And David with a sling;
Although Goliath rage and swear
  Down David doth him bring.

ON JOHN COMBE, A COVETOUS RICH MAN, MR. WILLIAM SHAKE-SPEARE WRIGHT THIS ATT HIS REQUEST WHILE HEE WAS YETT LIVEING FOR HIS EPITAPHE. [4]

Ten in the hundred lies here engraved;
' Tis a hundred to ten his soul is not saved;

---

[1] On the authority of Peck, "Memoirs of Milton," 4to, 1740
[2] On the authority of John Jordan. There is a strong poetic license here—according to the well-known legend, William had really only drunk with Bidford; the quantrain is probably the work of Jordan and not Shakespeare.
[3] On the authority of Stratford local tradition.
[4] Ashmolean MS., cited by Halliwell. The pun is on the War-

If any one asks, " Who lies in this tomb?"
"Ho! ho!" quoth the Devil, "'tis my John a Combe."

BUT BEING DEAD, AND MAKING THE POOR HIS HEIRES, HEE AFTER
WRIGHTES THIS FOR HIS EPITAPHE.[1]

Howere he lived judge not,
John Combe shall never be forgott
While poor hathe memmorye, for he did gather
To make the poor his issue, he their father,
As record of his tilth and seedes,
Did crown him in his later needes.

FINIS.   W. SHAK.

LAMPOON ON SIR THOMAS LUCY.[2]

Sir Thomas was too covetous,
To covet so much deer,

---

wickshire pronunciation, " Ho! ho!" quoth the Devil, "'tis my
John HAS COME!" See Aubrey's version:

"Ten in the hundred the Devil allows,
But Coombs will have twelve he swears and vows," etc.

[1] Ashmolean MS. same as preceding.   Both the above are
given by Mr. Grant White.   Shakespeare, vol. I, p. ci.

[2] This is given to us by Mr. S. W. Fullom (History of William
Shakespeare, Player and Poet; with New Facts and Traditions.
London: Saunders, Oatley & Co., 1864, p. 133, with the following
note: "The manner in which this fragment was recovered is not
different from that to which we owe so many local ballads, known
only to the common people.   About 1690, Joshua Barnes, the
Greek Professor at Cambridge, was in an inn at Stratford, when
he heard an old woman singing these stanzas, and, discerning
the association with Shakespeare, offered her ten guineas to repeat the whole ballad.   This, however, she was unable to do,
having forgotten the remaining portion."   Mr. Fullom says these
verses "reveal the Shakespearean touch," and alludes to a scan-
dal touching Lady Lucy's infidelity to her husband.

The following additional verses were furnished by John Jordan, who altered the above stanza into the same meter, and as-

When horns enough upon his head
Most plainly do appear.

Had not his worship one deer left ?
What then ? he had a wife

---

serted the whole to be Shakespeare, as unearthed and restored
by himself:

> He's a haughty, proud, insolent knight of the shire
> At home nobody loves, yet there's many that fear;
> If Lucy is lowsie, as some volke miscall it—
> Synge lowsie Lucy, whatever befall it.
>
> To the Sessions he went, and did lowdly complain
> His park had been robbed and his deere they were slain;
> This Lucy is lowsie, as some volke miscall it—
> Synge lowsie Lucy, whatever befall it.
>
> He sayd 'twas a ryot, his men had been beat,
> His venison was stol'n and clandestinely eat:
> So Lucy is lowsie as some volke miscall it—
> Synge lowsie Lucy, whatever befall it.
>
> So haughty was he when the fact was confessed
> He sayd 'twas a wrong that could not be redressed;
> So Lucy is lowsie, as some volke miscall it—
> Synge lowsie Lucy, whatever befall it.
>
> Though luces a dozen he wear on his coat,
> His name it shall lowsie for Lucy be wrote;
> For Lucy is lowsie, as some volke miscall it—
> We'll sing lowsie Lucy, whatever befall it.
>
> If a juvenile frolic he can not forgive,
> We'll sing lowsie Lucy as long as we live;
> And Lucy the lowsie a libel may call it—
> We'll sing lowsie Lucy whatever befall it.

Mr. Collier (Shakespeare, R. G. White, Ed. 1854, p. cciii), gives
the following four verses as by William Shakespeare:

> ON THE KING.
> Crown have their compass, length of days their date,
> Triumphs their tomb, Felicity her fate;
> Of naught but earth can earth make us partaker,
> But knowledge makes a king most like his maker.

but gives no other authority for it than "a coeval manuscript."
The world has, very regrettingly, come to look with such suspicion on Mr. Collier's discoveries, that this relic, until confirmed,
will hardly be accepted as genuine.

Took pains enough to find him horns
Should last him all his life.

ANOTHER VERSION OF THE LAMPOON.[1]

A Parliament member, a justice of peace,
At home a poor scarecrow, at London an asse;
If lowsie is Lucy, as some volke miscalle it,
Then Lucy is lowsie, whatever befalle it.
  He thinks himself greate,
  Yet an asse is his state:
We allowe by his ears but with asses to mate.
If Lucy is lowsie, as some volke miscalle it,
Sing, O lowsie Lucy, whate'er befalle it.

Some lampoon was affixed by young William to
Sir Thomas Lucy's park gate, and enraged the baronet to such a degree that—according to Capell—he directed a lawyer at Warwick to commence a prosecu-
tion against the lad. The Lucy note, however, makes
no mention of the lawyer, only stating that young
Shakespeare deemed it prudent to quit Stratford,
"at least for a time." The long ballad of six stanzas
(which we give in the foot-note) was written by John
Jordan, a harmless rustic who lived at Stratford in
the days of Malone and Ireland, i. e. in the last years
of the eighteenth century, and went about claiming
to have inherited the mantle of Shakespeare. The
"Piping Pebworth" verses, and perhaps the whole
story was written by him. At any rate, he seems to
have succeeded in obtaining immortality by mixing
his own efforts so successfully with the Shakespearean

---

[1] According to Capell, Oldys, and Grant White. (See Mr.
White's Shakespeare, Vol. I. p. xxxviii.) Oldys leaves out the
"O" in the fourth and eighth lines. Mr. Fullom (cited above)
declares this version to be spurious. (See note 3, p. 121.)

remains as to make them all one in the local traditions. The above, with the

Good frend, for Jesvs' sake forbeare,
To digg y⁰ dust encloased here.
Blesse be y⁰ man y' spares thes stones,
And cvrst be he y' moves my bones.

(which was originally placed on the stone over William Shakespeare's vault in the chancel of Trinity
Church, Stratford—was recut in the new stone which
was found necessary fifty years ago, and now appears with the verbal contractions as given above)
are all the literary compositions which, according to
the local traditions of Stratford, his home, where he
was born, lived, and died—where alone, for a century
or more after his death his reputation was cherished—
William Shakespeare ever produced. There is nothing in them inconsistent with the record of the man
himself; and, so far as we know, have never been rejected by the Shakespeareans themselves. It certainly
would not be honest, in our present APPEAL TO HIS-
TORY, to insert in this edition—we may fairly call it
"The Stratford Edition"—of Master Shakespeare's
poetry, all that he edited for the stage; or, worse yet,
borrowed and dressed up, and—according to Robert
Greene—passed for his own.

We are very far from desiring even to do justice to
poor Robert Greene, if in so doing we shall detract a
hair's weight from the merits of William Shakespeare.
But it is not impossible to say a good word even for
Greene. Although his language is not within such
bounds of propriety as the Shakespeareans could wish,

modern research has amply proved that he told the
truth, and that William Shakespeare borrowed, or
rather seized upon and adopted, without compensation,
the work by which Greene earned his bread. For
Greene's language, Chettle, Greene's editor, makes
haste, sometime afterward, when William Shakespeare
had been taken up by "divers of worship" to apologize, as far as an editor can apologize for an author.
We shall see, further on, how William Shakespeare
was shrewd enough to make himself useful to these
"divers of worship," and in those days, and for a century after, no slavery was so abject as the slavery of
letters to patronage. So, of course, Chettle hastened
to make his peace with them too. But the truth
remains, nevertheless, that poor Greene told only
the truth. It is fashionable with the Shakespeareans
to sneer at Greene, because he was "jealous" of
Shakespeare. He appears to have had reason to
be jealous! But no name is bad enough to bestow
on him. Mr. Grant White says: "Robert Greene,
writing from the fitting deathbed of a groveling debauchee, warns three of his literary companions to
shun intercourse with," etc., "certain actors, Shakespeare among the rest." If Robert Greene died from
over-debauch, it is no more than Shakespeare himself
died of, according to the entry in the diary of the
Rev. John Ward. "It is not impossible," says Mr.
White, "even that this piece of gossiping tradition is
true." Mr. White is right to call it "gossiping tradition," for it is piece and parcel of all the other mention of William Shakespeare of Stratford. If it were
not for "gossiping tradition," we had never heard, and
Mr. White had never written, of that personage. But

Mr. White makes no reservation of "gossiping tradition" in the case of Robert Greene. Greene dies
"on the fitting deathbed of a groveling debauchee,"
because he was jealous of William Shakespeare, and
was so injudicious, and so far forgot himself as to
call that "jack of all trades" an " upstart crowe, beautified with our feathers," etc. It seems that poor
Robert Greene's dying words -if they were his dying
words—were his ante-mortem legacy of warning and
prophecy to the ages which were to follow him. But
they have not been heeded. His "upstart crowe"
has not only kept all his borrowed feathers, but is arrayed each passing day with somebody's richer and
brighter plumage. If Robert Greene could speak from
the dust, he doubtless could tell us—as Jonson and the
rest might have told us in their lifetimes, if they
only would—whose all this plumage really was and is.
But all are dust and ashes together now—dust and
ashes three centuries old—and, as Miss Bacon said,
"Who loses any thing that does not find" the secret of
that dust? However, not a Shakespearean stops to waste
a sigh over the memory of poor Robert Greene,[1] who
saw his bread snatched from his mouth by a scissorer
of other men's brains, and who was too human to see

---

[1] "Robert Greene was a clergyman, and with no less poetry or
rhetoric than his fellows (Nash, Peele, and William Shakespeare),
was, from his miscellaneous and discursive reading, a very useful
man in his coterie." Dr. Latham speaks of his book as " A
Groats Worth of REST, purchased with a Million of Repentance,"
which certainly makes better sense than " a groat's worth of
WIT," etc., as usually written. Which is right? Greene died
in 1592.

and hold his peace; but over the drunken grave of the Stratford pretender—who was vanquished in his cups at Bidford and Pebworth, and lay all night under the thorn-tree, but who died bravely in them at the last—they weep as for one cut off untimely, as Dame Quickly over the lazared and lecherous clay of Sir John Falstaff: "Nay, sure, he's in Arthur's bosom, if ever a man went to Arthur's bosom. 'A made a finer end, and went away an it had been any Christom child." But let us not assume the appearance of unkindness to William Shakespeare. He lived a merry life; and, so far as we can know, wronged nobody except his own wife, poor Robert Greene, and perhaps the delinquent for malt delivered. He loved his own, but that is no wrong. And, we must not forget that, so far as the world can ever know, he claimed not as his, save by his silence, the works a too flattering posterity has assigned him.

The appeal to history not only declines to set aside, but affirms, with costs, the verdict rendered upon the evidence. And the sum is briefly this: If William Shakespeare wrote the plays, it was a miracle; every thing else being equal, the presumption is against a miracle; but, here, every thing else is not equal, for all the facts of history are reconcilable with history and irreconcilable with the miracle; if history is history, then miracle there was none—in other words, if there were one miracle, then there must have been two. If there had lived no such man as William Shakespeare, that "William Shakespeare" would be as good a name as any other to designate the authorship of the Shakespearean page, who will consider it worth while to

question ?   But to credit the historical man with the
living page demands, in our estimation, either a willful
credulity, or an innocence that is almost physical blindness !

PART III.

THE JONSONIAN TESTIMONY.

UT what is the summing up on the other side?   Merely the following copy of verses:

TO THE MEMORY OF MY BELOVED, THE AUTHOR, MASTER WILLIAM SHAKESPEARE, AND WHAT HE HATH LEFT US.

To draw no envy, Shakespeare, on thy name
Am I thus ample to thy book and fame;
While I confess thy writings to be such
As neither man nor muse can praise too much.
'Tis true and all men's suffrage.   But these ways
Were not the paths I meant unto thy praise;
For seeliest ignorance on these may light,
Which, when it sounds at best, but echoes right;
Or blind affection, which doth ne'er advance
The truth, but gropes, and urgeth all by chance;
Or crafty malice might pretend this praise
And think to ruin where it seemed to raise.
These are as some infamous bawd or whore
Should praise a matron; what could hurt her more?
But thou art proof against them, and, indeed,
Above the ill fortune of them, or the need,
I, therefore, will begin: Soul of the age,
The applause, delight, and wonder of our stage!
My Shakespeare rise!   I will not lodge thee by
Chaucer, or Spenser, or bid Beaumont lie
A little further to make thee a room.
Thou art a monument without a tomb,
And art alive still while thy book doth live
And we have wits to read and praise to give.
That I not mix thee so, my brain excuses,
I mean with great but disproportioned muses.

For if I thought my judgment were of years,
I should commit thee surely with thy peers,
And tell how far thou didst our Lyly outshine,
Or sporting Kyd, or Marlowe's mighty line;
And though thou hadst small Latin and less Greek,
From thence to honor thee I would not seek
For names: but call forth thundering Æschylus,
Euripides and Sophocles to us.
Pacuvius, Accius, him of Cordova dead,
To life again to hear thy buskin tread
And shake a stage; or, when thy socks were on
Leave thee alone for the comparison
Of all that insolent Greece or haughty Rome
Sent forth, or since did from their ashes come.
Triumph, my Britain, thou hast one to show
To whom all scenes of Europe homage owe.
He was not of an age, but for all time!
And all the muses still were in their prime
When, like Apollo, he came forth to warm
Our ears; or like a Mercury to charm.
Nature herself was proud of his designs,
And joyed to wear the dressing of his lines!
Which were so richly spun and woven so fit
As, since she will vouchsafe no other wit,
The merry Greek, tart Aristophanes,
Neat Terence, witty Plautus, how not please,
But antiquated and deserted lie
As they were not of nature's family.
Yet must I not give nature all; thy Art,
My gentle Shakespeare, must enjoy a part;
For though the poets matter Nature be,
His art doth give the fashion; and that he
Who casts to write a living line must sweat
(Such as thine are), and strike the second heat
Upon the muse's anvil; turn the same
And himself with it, that he thinks to frame,
Or for the laurel he may gain a scorn,
For a good poet 's made, as well as born:
And such wert thou! Look how the father's face

Lives in his issue, even so the race
Of Shakespeare's mind and manners brightly shines
In his well-turned and true-filled lines:
In each of which he seems to shake a lance
As brandished at the eyes of Ignorance.
Sweet swan of Avon, what a sight it were
To see thee in our waters yet appear,
And make those flights upon the banks of Thames
That did so take Eliza and our James!
Shine forth, thou Star of Poets, and with rage
Or influence chide or cheer the drooping stage,
Which, since thy flight from hence, hath mourned like
night
And despairs day, but for thy volume's light.

This is all there is of Jonson's labored verses, of which very few Shakespeareans care to quote more than isolated passages of a line or two each. But taking them either as a whole (with their involved metaphors and most execrable and inapposite pun about Shakespeare's lines " shaking a lance at Ignorance ")— or in spots (whichever spots the Shakespeareans prefer), what sort of historical PROOF does this poem afford? What sort of testimony is this as to a FACT? Is it the sort we accept in our own personal affairs—in our business—in our courts of justice—in matters in which we have any thing at stake, or any living interest? Will any insurance company pay its risk on the ship DOLPHIN, on being furnished, by the DOLPHIN's owners, with a thrilling poem by Mr. Tennyson or Mr. Tupper, describing the dreadful shipwreck of the DOLPHIN, the thunderous tempest in which she went down—the sky-capping waves, rent sails, creaking cordage, etc., etc.? Will any jury of twelve men hang a thirteenth man for murder on production, by the State, of a harrowing copy of verses, dwelling on midnight assassination, stealthy stabs, shrieking victims, inconsolable widows, orphans, and the like?. And shall we require less or more proof, in proportion as the fact to be proved is nearer or more remote ?

However, since the Shakespeareans rest their case on these verses, (for any one who cares to examine for himself will find the residue of the so-called "contemporary testimony," which is usually in rhyme, to be rather CRITICISM—that is to say *eulogy*, for we find very little of any other sort of literary criticism in those days—as to the compositions than CHRONICLE as to the man) we can well afford to waive these questions, and cross-examine Ben Jonson and his verses without pressing any objection to their competency.

For criticism of the works is what Meres's[1] opinion that "the sweete wittie soul of Ovid lives in mellifluous and honey-tongued Shakespeare; witness his " Venus and Adonis," his "Lucrece," his sugared sonnets among his private friends. . . . "As Plautus and Seneca are accounted the best for comedy and tragedy among the Latines, so Shakespeare among the English is the most excellent in both kinds for the stage. . . As Epius Stolo said that the Muses would speake with Plautus' tongue, if they would speake Latin, so I say that the Muses would speake with Shakespeare's fine-filed phrase, if they would speake English," etc., etc., etc., amount to ; and so Weever's

> " Honey-tongued Shakespeare, when I saw thine issue,
>   I swore Apollo got them, and none other "—

probably means, if it means any thing, precisely what it says, namely, that when he read the PLAYS, he swore

---

[1] " Palladis Tamia."

that they were certainly Apollo's. And if the comments of Henry Chettle, Sir John Davies, Leonard Digges, Hugh Holland, and the rest, do not read to the same effect, they have a meaning beyond what they express. But panegyric is not history—at least it can not override history.

Between the affirmative theory of the Stratfordian authorship, then, and the demonstration of its utter impossibility and absurdity, there actually remains but the single barrier of the Jonsonian testimony, contained in the copy of verses entitled " To the Memory of my Beloved, the Author, Mr. William Shakespeare, and what he hath left us," written by Mr. Ben Jonson, and prefixed to the famous folio of 1623. If this testimony should ever be ruled out as incompetent, there would actually remain nothing except to lay the Shakespearean hoax away, as gently as might be, alongside its fellows in the populous limbo of exploded fallacies.

However, let it not be ruled out merely on the ground that it is in rhyme. We have no less an authority than Littleton—" auctoritas philosophorum, medicorum et poetarum sunt in causis allegandæ et tenendæ" [1]—to the effect that the testimony, even of poets, is sometimes to be received. It is to be ruled out rather by a process akin to impeachment of the witness—by its appearing that the witness, elsewhere in the same controversy, testifies to a state of facts exactly opposite. For the truth is that, whatever Ben Jonson felt moved to say about his " pal " William Shakespeare, whenever, " as a friend, he

---

[1] "Co. Lit.," 264 A.

dropped into poetry," he was considerably more
careful when he sat himself down to write "cold
prose." Just as "Bully Bottom," fearing lest a lion
should "fright the ladies," and "hang every mother's
son" of his troupe, devised a prologue to explain that
the lion was no lion, but only Snug the Joiner, "a
man as other men are," so Master Ben Jonson, however tropical and effusive as to his contemporary in
his prosody, in his prologue in *prose* was scrupulous
to leave only the truth behind him. Mountains—
Ossian piled on Pelion—of hearsay and lapse of time;
oceans of mere opinion and "gush" would, of course,
amount to precisely nothing at all when ranged alongside of the testimony of one single, competent, contemporary eye-witness. No wonder the Shakespeareans are eager to subpœna Ben Jonson's verses. But,
all the same, they are marvelously careful *not* to subpœna his prose.

And yet this prose is extant, and by no means inaccessible. When Jonson died, in 1637, he left behind
him certain memoranda which were published in 1640,
and are well-known as "Ben Jonson's Discoveries."
One of these memoranda—for the work is in the dis-
jointed form of a common-place book of occasional
entries—is devoted to the eminent men of letters in
the era spanned by its author's own acquaintance or
familiarity. It runs as follows:

Cicero is said to be the only wit that the people of Rome had
equaled to their empire. *Imperium par imperio.* We have had
many, and in their several ages (to take in the former sæculum),
Sir Thomas More, the elder Wiat, Henry, Earl of Surry, Chal-
oner, Smith, Eliot, B. Gardiner, were, for their times, admirable;
and the more because they began eloquence with us. Sir Nich-

olas Bacon was singular and almost alone in the beginning of
Elizabeth's time. Sir Philip Sidney and Mr. Hooker (in different matter) grew great masters of wit and language, and
in whom all vigour of invention and strength of judgment met.
The Earl of Essex, noble and high, and Sir Walter Raleigh not
to be contemned, either for judgment or style. Sir Henry Sa-
ville, grave and truly lettered. Sir Edwin Sandys, excellent
in both. Lord Egerton, a grave and great orator, and best when
he was provoked. *But his learned and able, but unfortunate successor, is he that hath filled up all numbers, and performed that in our tongue
which may be compared or preferred either to insolent Greece or haughty
Rome.*[1] In short, within this view, and about this time, were all
the wits born that could honour a language or help study. Now
things daily fall; wits grow downward and eloquence grows backward. So that he may be so named and stand as the mark and
ἀκμή of our language.[2]

Only fourteen years before, this Ben Jonson had
published the verses which *made* William Shakespeare.
Only fourteen years before he had asserted—what the
world has taken his word for, and never questioned
from that day to this—that his " best beloved" William Shakespeare had been the " soul of the age"—
" not for an age, but for all time"—and his works
" such as neither man nor muse can praise too much !"
We have no means of knowing the precise date at
which Ben Jonson's grief for his dead friend cooled,

---

[1] Judge Holmes ("Authorship of Shakespeare," third edition,
p. 650) italicises these words to point the allusion to Bacon, and
to notice that the passage in " The Discoveries," immediately preceding the above, is a direct allusion to Bacon, while the phrase
" insolent Greece and haughty Rome "occurs in line thirty-nine
of the verses eulogistic of William Shakespeare.

[2] " Timber, or Discoveries made upon Men and Matter: as they
have flowed out of his Daily Readings, or had their Reflux to his
Peculiar Notion of the Time." By Ben Jonson. " Works," by
Peter Whalley, vol. vii., p. 99.

and his feelings experienced a change. But he leaves behind him, at his death, this unembellished memoranda, this catalogue "of all the wits" living in his day, who, in his opinion, "could honour a language or help study," and in this catalogue he inserts no such name as William Shakespeare; William Shakespeare, the name—not only of the "soul" and epitome of all that —only. about fourteen years ago—he had deemed worth mentioning among men "born about this time;" but of his late most intimate and bosom friend! Had the "Discoveries" preserved an absolute silence concerning William Shakespeare, the passage we have quoted might, perhaps, have been considered a studied and deliberate slur on his dead friend's memory, on the part of Jonson, made for reasons best known to Jonson himself. But they are not silent. They devote a whole paragraph to William Shakespeare—but in the proper place; that is to say, not among "the wits who could honour a language or help study," but among the author's personal acquaintance. This is all there is of this paragraph as to the REAL William Shakespeare:

I remember the players have often mentioned it as an honor to Shakespeare, that in his writing (whatever he penned) he never blotted out a line. My answer hath been, "would he had blotted out a thousand!" which they thought a malevolent speech. I had not told posterity this but for their ignorance, who choose that circumstance to commend their friend by, wherein he most faulted. And to justify mine own candour (for I loved the man, and do honour his memory on this side idolatry, as much as any). He was (indeed) honest and of an open and free nature; had an excellent phantasie, brave notions, and gentle expressions: wherein he flowed with that facility that sometimes it was necessary he should be stopped. *Sufflaminan-*

dus crat, as Augustus said of Haterius. His wit was in his own power, would that the rule of it had been so too! Many times he fell into those things could not escape laughter; as when he said in the person of Cæsar—one speaking to him—"Cæsar, thou dost me wrong;" he replied, "Cæsar never did wrong, but with just cause," and such like; which were ridiculous. But he redeemed his vices with his virtues. There was ever more in him to be praised than pardoned.[1]

That is every word which a man who "loved him" could say of William Shakespeare!—that he was a skilled and careful penman, "never blotting out a line;" that he talked too fast, sometimes, and had to be checked; that, in playing the part of Cæsar on the stage, somebody interpolated the speech, "Cæsar, thou dost me wrong," and he made a bull in response;[2] and that he (Jonson) wished he (Shakespeare) had blotted out a thousand of his lines. Blot out a thousand Shakespearean lines!—a thousand of the priceless lines of the peerless book we call "Shakespeare!" Fancy the storm which would follow such a vandal proposition to-day! Ben Jonson does not specify *which* thousand he would have expurgated, but would be satisfied with any thousand, taken anywhere at random out of the writings of his "soul of the age," the man "not of an age, but for all time!" And yet it is on the uncorroborated word of this man Jonson that we build monuments to the Stratford lad, and make pilgrimages to his birthplace and worship his ashes, and quarrel about the spelling of his name! If there is not a

---

[1] "Works," cited *ante*, vol. vii., p. 91.

[2] Possibly this may have occurred in playing the very version of the "Cæsar" we now possess, though there are, of course, no such lines to be found there.

12

strong smack of patronage in this prose allusion to Shakespeare, we confess ourselves unable to detect its flavor. Very possibly the fact was that, so far from having been an admirer of William Shakespeare, Ben Jonson saw through his pretensions, and only through policy sang his praises against the stomach of his sense. For Ben Jonson, though one of the ripest scholars of the day (we have history as authority for that), was poor and a borrower, over head and ears in debt to Shakespeare; he was a stock actor on the rich managers boards, and could not take the bread out of his own mouth. But the poor scholar, and still poorer actor, could yet indulge himself, and take his covert fling at the rich charlatan :

"Though need make many poets, and some such
  As art and nature have not bettered much,
Yet ours for want hath not so loved the stage
  As he dare serve the ill customs of the age :
Or purchase your delight at such a rate
  As for it, he himself must justly hate.
To make a child now swaddled, to proceed
Man, and then shoot up in one beard and weed—
Past threescore years, or with three rusty swords
And help of some few foot and half foot words—
Fight over York and Lancaster's long jars,
And in the tiring-house bring wounds to scars !
He [*that is, Ben himself*] rather prays you will be pleased to see
One such to-day, as other plays should be;
          [*that is, one he wrote himself*]
Where neither chorus wafts you o'er the seas,
Nor creaking throne comes down the boys to please."

Ben says this himself—in the prologue to his " Every Man in his Humour."

Again, in the "Induction" to his " Bartholomew

Fair," he has this fling at "The Tempest:" "If there
be never a servant-monster in the fair, who can help
it," he says, "nor a nest of antiques? He is loth to
make Nature afraid in his plays, like those that beget
tales, tempests, and such like drolleries."[1]

But that Jonson never himself believed, or expressed
himself as believing, that William Shakespeare was a
poet (except in this rhymed panegyric which Heminges and Condell prefixed to the first folio), there is still
further and perhaps stronger proof. Three years after
William Shakespeare's death, Ben Jonson paid a visit to
William Drummond of Hawthornden, and spent with
him the greater part of the month of April, 1619 (or,
as some fix it, the month of January, in that year).
Drummond was a poet himself, and, it is said, his poetical reputation was what had attracted Jonson to
make the visit. At any rate, he did visit him, and
Drummond kept notes of Jonson's conversation.
These notes are in the form of entries or items,
grouped under Drummond's own headings or titles,
such as:

"HIS ACQUAINTANCE AND BEHAVIOR WITH POETS LIVING WITH HIM."

DANIEL was at jealousies with him.

DRAYTON feared him, and he esteemed not of him.

That Francis Beaumont loved too much himself and his own
verses.

---

[1] "The Tempest" of that day in William Shakespeare's hands,
then, was a "drollery." See some curious evidence going to
prove that, while the titles of the plays always remain the same,
the plays themselves may have been different at different times.
post VI, "THE NEW THEORY." Dr. Carl Elze (Essays on Shakespeare. London. Macmillans. 1874), thinks that Jonson meant
a hit at Shakespeare when he says, in Volpone, "all our English
authors will steal."

That Sir John Roe loved him; and when they, too, were ush-
ered by my Lord Suffolk from a mask, Roe wrott a moral Epistle
to him which began: *That next to Playes, the Court and the State were
the best.   God threateneth Kings, Kings Lords, (as) Lords do us.*

He beat Marston and took his pistol from him.

Sir W. Alexander was not half kinde unto him, and neglected
him, because a friend to Drayton.

That Sir R. Aiton loved him dearly.

Nid Field was his schollar, and he had read to him the satyres
of Horace, and some Epigrames of Martiall.

That Markam (who added his Arcadia) was not of the number
of the Faithfull, (*i. e*), Poets, and but a base fellow.

That such were Day and Middleton.

That Chapman and Fletcher were loved by him.

Overbury was first his friend, then turn'd his mortall enimie."

etc., etc.

There are, in all, between two and three hundred
entries of a similar character. Now, in one of these
entries, Jonson is represented as saying that he " es-
teemeth Done the first poet in the world in some
things;" but there is nothing put in Jonson's mouth,
in the whole category, about the " Star of Poets,"
save that, in another place, is the following item:

"That Shakspeer wanted arte,"

and, further on, the following:

"Shakespeare wrote a play, brought in a number of men saying they had suffered shipwreck in Bohemia, when there is no
see neer by some 100 miles."[1]

These notes were first printed by Mr. David Laing,
who discovered them among the manuscripts of Sir

---

[1] Works of Ben Jonson. By William Gifford. Edited by Lt.
Col. Francis Cunningham. Vol. III., p. 470. London. I. C. Hotten, 74 & 75 Picadilly.

Robert Sibbald, a well-known antiquary and physician of Edinburgh. They were preserved in the form
of a copy in Sibbald's handwriting. Sibbald was a
friend of the Bishop Sage, who edited Drummond's
works in 1711. These notes were believed by Sir
Walter Scott to be genuine, and, by his advice, were
printed first in the "Archæological Scotica," in or
about 1723. At any rate, they were never printed by
Sibbald himself, nor used by him in any way which
suggested a motive for forgery, and, internally, they
agree with Ben Jonson's own "Discoveries," especially as to his (Jonson's) estimate of William Shakespeare.

And yet Ben Johnson was the beneficiary and
friend of William Shakespeare — the "immortal
Shakespeare" — whom Ben "honours *this side* idolatry," but whom we are not fearful of passing the
bounds of idolatry in worshiping to-day. Ben Johnson was an overworked rhymester, and made his
rhymes do double and treble duty. The first couplet
of the prologue just cited

> "Though need make many poets, and some such
> As art and nature have not bettered much "—

needs only a little hammering over to become the

> "While I confess thy writings to be such
> As neither man nor muse can praise too much "—

of the mortuary verses which—as we say—made
Shakespeare SHAKESPEARE. When the rich manager's
alleged works were to be collected, the poor scholar,
who had borrowed money of him in his lifetime, was
called upon for a tribute. But the poor scholar for-

bore to draw on the storehouse of his wits, though willing to hammer over some of his old verses for the occasion. He once assured posterity, in rhyme, that they must not "give nature all," but remember his gentle Shakespeare's art, how he would "sweat and strike the second heat upon the muse's anvil" (in other words, bring by long toil the firstlings of his genius to artificial perfection). And yet he deliberately tells Drummond, long years after, and puts it down in black and white over his own signature, that this same Shakespeare "wanted art," and that the great trouble with him was that he talked too much. Is it possible that the ideal Shakespeare, the mighty miracle-working demigod, is only the accidental creation of a man who was poking fun at a shadow? Let us not proceed to such a violent surmise, but return to a serious consideration of Mr. Ben Jonson's unimpassioned prose.

If the paragraph from the "Discoveries" last above quoted—which estimates William Shakespeare precisely as history estimates him, namely, as a clever fellow, and a player in one of the earliest theaters in London—is not to be regarded as a confession that Ben Jonson's verses were written (or rewritten) more out of generosity to his late friend's memory—rather in the exuberance of a poetic license of apotheosis— than with a literal adherence to truth;[1] then it must be conceded that the result is such a facing both ways as

---

[1] A confession, say the Baconians, that Jonson, as long as Bacon lived, was eager to serve him by shouldering on his *incognito*—in poetry—while he was under no compunction to do so in his own posthumous remains. See *post* V, THE BACONIAN THEORY.

hangs any Jonsonian testimony in perfect equilibrium as to the Shakespearean controversy, and entitles Ben Jonson himself, as a witness for anybody or to any thing, to simply step down and out. For, admitting that his poetry is just as good as his prose—and probably the Shakespeareans would care to assert no more than that—it is a legal maxim that a witness who swears for both sides swears for neither; and a rule of common law no less than of common sense that his evidence must be ruled out, since no jury can be called upon to believe and disbelieve one and the same witness at the same time. And so we are relieved from accounting for the "Jonson testimony," as did Lord Palmerston, by saying: "O, those fellows always hang together; or, its just possible Jonson may have been deceived like the rest;"[1] or by asking ourselves if a score of rhymes by Ben Johnson, a fellow craftsman (not sworn to, of course, and not nearly as tropical or ecstatic as they might have been, and yet been quite justifiable under the rule nil nisi)—are to outweigh all historic certainty? If Jonson had written a life, or memoir, or "recollections," or "table-talk," of William Shakespeare, it might have been different. But he only gives us a few cheap lines of poetical eulogy; and FACT is one thing, and POETRY—unless there is an exception in this instance—is conceded to be altogether another.

But since numberless good people are suspicious of rules of law as applied to evidence, regarding them as over-nice, finical, and as framed rather to keep out truth than to let it in, let·us waive the legal maxim,

---

[1] Frazer's Magazine, November, 1865, p. 666.

and admit the Jonsonian testimony to be one single, consistent block of contemporary evidence. But, no sooner do we do this, than we find ourselves straight-way floundering in a slough of absurdities for greater, it seems to us, than any we have yet encountered. To illustrate: It is necessary to the Shakespearean theory that in the days of Elizabeth and James there should have been not only a *man*, but a genius, a wit, and a poet, of the name of William Shakespeare; and that all these—man, genius, wit, and poet—should have been one and the same individual. Taking all the Jonsonian testimony, prose and poetry, together, such an individual there was, and his name was William Shakespeare, as required. But—still following Jonson's authority—at the same period and in the same town of London there was a certain gentleman named Bacon, who was "learned and able," and who had, moreover, "filled up all numbers—and" in the same days "performed that which may be compared either to insolent Greece or haughty Rome." We have, then, not only a "wit and poet" named Shakespeare, but a "wit and poet" named Bacon; and, since Jonson is nowhere too modest to admit that he himself was a "wit and poet," we have, therefore, actually not one but three of a kind, at each other's elbows in London, in the golden age of English literature. We have already seen that, of this trio, TWO—Bacon and Shakespeare, if we are to believe the Shakespeareans —were personally unknown to each other. It is worth our while to pause right here, and see what this statement involves.

They are all three—Bacon, Jonson, and Shakespeare—dwelling in the same town at the same moment; are, all three, writers and wits, earning their living by their pens. Ben Jonson is the mutual friend. He is of service to both—he translates Bacon's English into Latin for him,[1] and writes plays for William Shakespeare's stage, and, as we have seen, he ultimately becomes the Boswell of both, and runs from one to the other in rapture. His admiration for Bacon, on the one hand (according to his prose), amounts to a passion; his admiration for Shakespeare, on the other hand (according to his poetry), amounts to a passion. He declares (in prose) that Bacon "hath filled up all numbers, and performed that in our tongue, which may be compared and preferred either to *insolent Greece or haughty Rome*." He declares (in poetry) of Shakespeare that he may be left alone—

> " . . . for comparison
> *Of all that insolent Greece or haughty Rome*
> Sent forth, or since did from their ashes come."

And yet he never, while going from one to the other, mentions Shakespeare to Bacon or Bacon to Shakespeare; never "introduces" them or brings them together; never gives his soul's idol Bacon any "order" to his soul's idol Shakespeare's theater, that this absolutely inimitable Bacon (who has surpassed insolent Greece and haughty Rome) may witness the masterpieces of this absolutely inimitable Shakespeare

---

[1] Jonson assisted Dr. Hackett, afterward Bishop of Litchfield and Coventry, in translating the essays of Lord Bacon into Latin. (Whalley, "Life of Ben Jonson," Vol. I. of works, cited *ante*.) Jonson was at this time "on terms of intimacy with Lord Bacon."—(W. H. Smith, "Bacon and Shakespeare," p. 29.)

(who has likewise surpassed insolent Greece and
haughty Rome); this Boswell of a Jonson, go-be-
tween of two men of repute and public character,
travels from one to the other, sings the praises of each
to the world outside (using the same figures of speech
for each), and, in the presence of each, preserves so
impenetrable a silence as to the other, that of the two
public characters themselves each is absolutely ignorant of the other's existence! And yet they ought to
have been close friends, for they borrowed each other's
verses, and loaned each other paragraphs to any extent. Persons there have been who asserted, as we
shall see, on merely the internal evidence of their
writings, that Bacon and "Shakespeare" were one
and the same man, and that what appeared to be "parallelisms" and coincidences in Bacon and "Shakespeare" were thus to be accounted for. But, admitting their separate identity, it is certain either that
the natural philosopher borrowed his exact facts from
the comedies of the playwright, or that the playwright
borrowed the speeches for his comedies from the natural philosopher; either of which looks very much
like, at least, a speaking acquaintance. For, as we
shall see further on,[1] some of these "parallelisms" are
not coincidences, but something very like *identities*.

It will not lighten this new difficulty to rule out the
prose and leave in the poetry, for we can not anni-
hilate Francis Bacon nor yet William Shakespeare
from their places in history. If, however, the Jonsonian poetry *were* wiped out, the Jonsonian prose would
receive, at least, a negative corroboration, as follows:

---

[1] *Post*, part V, The Baconian Theory.

At the same time that Bacon and Shakespeare are living, unknown to each other respectively, in London,
there also dwell there three other gentlemen—Sir
Walter Raleigh, Edmund Spenser, and Sir Tobie
Matthew. We, therefore, actually have four well-
known gentlemen of the day in London, gentlemen
of elegant tastes—poets, men about town, critics—who,
if the town were being convulsed by the production
at a theater of by far the most brilliant miracles of
genius that the world had ever seen, ought not, in the
nature of things, to have been utterly uninformed as
to the circumstance. We do not add to this list Southampton, Essex, Rutland, Montgomery, and the rest,
because these latter have left no memorandum or
chronicle of what they saw and heard on manuscript
behind them. But the first four have left just precisely such memoranda of their times as are of assistance to us here. Bacon, in his "Apothegms," Spenser
in his poems,[1] and Raleigh and Matthew in their re-

---

[1] Spenser's well-known lines in "Colin Clout's come Home
again," written in 1591, are:

> "And there, though last not least, is Ætion,
> A gentler shepherd may nowhere be found,
> Whose muse, full of high thought's invention,
> Doth—life himself—heroically sound."

"Æton" is generally assumed by commentators to stand in
the verse for "Shakespeare." But it is difficult to imagine how
this can possibly be more than mere speculation, since Spenser
certainly left no annotation explanatory of the passage, and it
does not identify itself as a reference to Shakespeare. In "The
Tears of the Muses," line 205, there is an allusion which on a
first glance appears so pat, that the Bard of Avon has long been
called "our pleasant Willy" on the strength of it. It runs:

> "And he, the man whom Nature's self had made,
> To mock herself and truth to imitate

mains—especially Matthew—who, like Bacon, kept a
diary, who wrote letters and postscripts, and was as
fond of playing at Boswell to his favorites as Jonson
himself—appear to have stumbled on no trace of such
a character as "Shakespeare" in all their saunterings
about London. Especially on one occasion does Sir
Tobie devote himself to a subject-matter wherein, if
there had been any "Shakespeare" within his ken,
he could very properly—and would, we think, very
naturally—have mentioned him. In the "Address to
the Reader," prefixed to one of his works,[1] he says,
speaking of his own date, "We have also rare compositions made among us which look so many fair
ways at once that I doubt it will go near to pose any
other nations of Europe to muster out in any age four
men who, in so many respects, should be able to excel

> With kindly counter under mimick shade,
> Our pleasant Willy, ah, is dead of late :
> With whom all joy and jolly merriment
> Is also deaded, and in dolour drent."

But, since Spenser died some seventeen years before Shakespeare, and if—as must be supposed from their flippancy—these
lines point to the enforced or voluntary retirement or silence of
some writer, rather than to his death—they appear more nearly
to refer to Sidney than to Shakespeare. And this now appears
to be conceded. (See Morley's "English Men of Letters: Spenser," by Dean Church. American edition, Harpers, New York,
1879, p. 106.) Besides, "The Tears of the Muses" was written
in 1580, when Shakespeare was a lad of sixteen, holding horses
at the theater door. "Will," or "Willy," appears to have been
the ordinary nickname of a poet in those days.—R. G. White's
"Shakespeare," vol. i., p. 57, *note*.)

[1] "A Collection of Letters made by Sir Tobie Matthew, with a
Character of the Most Excellent Lady Lucy, Countess of Car-
lisle. To which are added Many Letters of his Several Persons
of Honour, who were contemporary with him." London, 1660.

four such as we are able to show—Cardinal Wolsey, Sir Thomas More, Sir Philip Sidney, and Sir Francis Bacon. For they were all a kind of monsters in their various ways," etc.

Besides, these four—or, dismissing Spenser, who was a poet exclusively—then three, Bacon, Raleigh, and Tobie Matthew—however else dissimilar, were any thing but blockheads or anchorites. They were men of the court and of the world. They mingled among their fellow-men, and (by a coincidence which is very useful to us here) none of them were silent as to what they met and saw during their careers. They both live and move in the very town and in the very days when this rare poetry which Emerson says "the greatest minds value most" was appearing. But, if William Shakespeare was the author of it all, how is it possible to escape the conviction that not one of them all—not Bacon, a man of letters himself, a student of antique not only, but of living and contemporary literature, and overfond of writing down his impressions for the benefit of posterity (even if wanting in the dramatic or poetic perception, the scholarship of the plays could not have escaped him; and had these plays been the delight and town talk of all London, as Mr. Grant White says they were, some morsel of them must have reached his ear or eye)—not Raleigh, courtier, gallant, man-about-town, "curled darling," and every thing of that sort (who probably was not afraid to go to a theater for fear of injuring his morals)—not Tobie Matthew, who was all this latter with less of responsibility and mental balance—ever so much as heard his (Shakespeare's) name mentioned? That not one of these ever heard of a name that was in everybody's mouth—of a living man so famous that, as we shall presently consider, booksellers were using his name to make their wares sell, that his plays were filling the most fashionable theater in London from cockpit to the dome; whose popularity was so exalted that the great Queen Elizabeth herself stepped down from the throne and walked across his stage to do him honor, to whom in after days, her successor King was to write an autograph letter (for these must all be considered in the argument, though, as we have seen, the King James story is only one of the " yarns,"[1] cooked for occasion by commentators, or the growth of rumor —in orthodox procession from " might have been " to " was "—and so, doubtless, is the other) is a trifle incredible to a mind not already adjusted to swallow any and every fable in this connection rather than accept the truth of history! To be sure, it is not absolutely impossible that these three men should have been cognizant of William Shakespeare's existence without mentioning him in their favors to posterity. But, under all the circumstances, it is vastly improbable. At any rate, we fancy it would not be easy to conceive of

---

[1] The story of Elizabeth's order for "Falstaff in Love," resulting in the production of "The Merry Wives of Windsor" (which would prove that, whatever else she was, Elizabeth was no Anthony Comstock), is, to our mind, another sample of the same procession. Hazlitt (Lit. of Europe, Part iii., chap. 6, sec. iii., note,) is especially incredulous as to the King James letter. The truth is that Shakespeare, far from being flattered by James, was actually in disgrace, and not so much as to be mentioned in that monarch's hearing, from having permitted a representation of the sacred person of royalty on his stage, as is authenticated by the well-known lines of Davies:

Hadst thou not played some Kingly parts in sport, etc., etc.

three Englishmen in London to-day, in 1881—let us say Mr. Gladstone, Mr. Browning, and Mr. Swinburne —without collusion, writing down a list of their most illustrious contemporaries, and not one of them mentioning Mr. Tennyson! Or, assuming that Tennyson is the admitted first of poets of the Victorian age (as Mr. Ben Jonson and all the commentators at his heels, down to our own Mr. Grant White, tell us that " William Shakespeare" was the admitted first of poets of his contemporary Elizabethan age), it would not be the easiest thing in the world to conceive three chroniclers—Mr. Gladstone, Mr. Browning, and Mr. Swinburne—sitting themselves down to an enumeration, not of their illustrious contemporaries in general, but of their contemporaneous men of letters only, and, by a coincidence, omitting any mention of the great first of poets of their day! Either, then, it seems to us we are to infer that three such men as Raleigh, Bacon, (who, Emerson says, "took the inventory of the human understanding, for his time,") and his satellite Matthew, had never so much as heard that there was any Shakespeare, in an age which we moderns worship as the age of Shakespeare, or that there was no "Shakespeare" for them to hear about; that " William Shakespeare" was the name of an actor and manager in the Globe and Blackfriars play-houses, of a man not entitled, any more than any of his co-actors and co-managers in those establishments, to enumeration among the illustrious ornaments of an illustrious age, the stars of the golden age of English!

Of course, it can be well urged that all this is mere negative evidence; that not only three but three million of men might be found who had never mentioned or ever heard of Shakespeare, without affecting the controversy either way. But, under the circumstances, in view of what the Shakespearean plays *are*, and of what their author must have been, and of when and where these three men—Bacon, Raleigh, and Matthew[1] —lived and flourished, the chronicles left by these three men—Bacon, Raleigh, and Matthew—constitute, at the very least, a "negative pregnant" not to be omitted in any review of our controversy that can lay the faintest claim to exhaustiveness or sincerity; and, moreover, a negative pregnant which—if we admitted all the Ben Jonson testimony, in prose and poetry, as evidence on the one side—could not be excluded as evidence on the other. In which event it is fairest to the Shakespeareans to rule Ben out altogether.[2] Besides, Ben is what the Scotchmen call "a famous witness" (if the commentators, who enlarge on Shakespeare's bounty and loans to him, can be relied upon), as being under heavy pecuniary obligation to the stage manager, and so his testimony is to be scrutinized with the

---

[1] And we might add to these Sir John Davies, Selden, Sir John Beaumont, Henry Vaughn, Lord Clarendon and others.

[2] It is fair to note that another " negative pregnant" arises here, to which the Shakespeareans are as fairly entitled as the other side to theirs. Sir Tobie Matthew died in 1655. He survived Shakespeare thirty-nine years, Bacon twenty-nine years, and Raleigh thirty-seven years! Left in possession of the secret of the Baconian authorship, how could such a one as Matthew let the secret die with him? Although we do not meet with it among the arguments of the Shakespeareans, this strikes us as about the strongest they could present, except that the answer might be that at the date of Matthew's death, 1655, the Shakespearean plays were not held in much repute, or that Matthew might have reserved his unbosoming of the secret too long; but it is only one fact among a thousand.

greatest care, though he certainly did not allow his obligations to over-master him when writing the "Discoveries." But, in any event, it would be easier to believe that Ben Jonson once contradicted himself for the sake of a rhyme, and to "do the handsome thing" by the memory of an old friend and unpaid creditor, than to swallow the incredible results of a literal version of his prose and poetry, read by the light of the Bacon, Raleigh, and Matthew remains. And the conclusion of the matter, it seems to us, must be: either that the poetry was the result of his obligations to William Shakespeare and to William Shakespeare's memory, or that, having sworn on both sides, Mr. Ben Jonson stands simply dehors the case—a witness for neither.

It is not, then—it is very far from being—because we know *so* LITTLE of the man Shakespeare that we disbelieve in his authorship of the great works ascribed to him. It is because we know *so* MUCH. No sooner did men open their histories, turn up the records and explore the traditions and trace the gossip of the Elizabethan days, than the facts stared them in the face. Long before any "Baconian theory" arose to account for these anomalies: at the instant these plays began to be valued for any thing else than their theatrical properties, the difficulty of "marrying the man to his verse" began to be troublesome. "To be told that he played a trick on a brother actor in a licentious amour, or that he died of a drunken frolic, does not exactly inform us of the man who wrote 'Lear,'" cried Mr. Hallam.[1] "Every accession of in-

---

[1] "I laud," says Hallam, "the labors of Mr. Collier, Mr. Hunter, and other collectors of such crumbs, though I am not sure that

formation we obtain respecting the man Shakespeare renders it more and more difficult to detect in him the poet," cries Mr. William Henry Smith.[1] "I am one of the many," testifies Mr. Furness, "who have never been able to bring the life of William Shakespeare and the plays of Shakespeare within a planetary space of each other; are there any other two things in the world more incongruous?"[2] It was necessary, therefore, in order to preserve a belief in the Shakespearean authorship, either that William Shakespeare should be historically known as a man of great mental power, a close student of deep insight into nature and morals —a poet, philosopher, and all the rest—or else that, by a failure of the records, history should be silent altogether as to his individuality, and the lapse of time have made it impossible to recover any details whatever as to his tastes, manners, and habits of life. In such a case, of course, there would remain no evidence on the subject other than that of the plays themselves, which would, of course, prove him precisely the myriad-minded genius required. In other words, it was only necessary to so cloud over *the facts* as to make the "Shakespearean miracle" to be, *not* that William Shakespeare had written the works, but—that history should be so silent concerning a "Shakespeare!" So long as the Shakespeareans could cry, "Behold a mys-

---

we should not venerate Shakespeare as much if they had left him undisturbed in his obscurity. . . . If there was a Shakespeare of earth, as I suspect, there was also one of heaven, and it is of him we desire to know something."

[1] " Bacon and Shakespeare," p. 886.

[2] In a letter to Judge Holmes, printed at p. 628, third edition, of the latter's "Authorship of Shakespeare."

terious dispensation of Providence—that, of the two mightiest poets the world has ever held—Homer and William Shakespeare—we know absolutely nothing!" —so long as they could assign this silence to the havoc of a great deluge or a great fire, just so long the name " William Shakespeare" was as good and satisfactory a name as any other, and nobody could propose a better. But they can cry so no longer. It is not because we know *so little*, but because we know *so much* about the Stratford boy, that we decline to accept him as the master we not only admire and love, but in whose pages we find our wisdom vain and our discovery anticipated. As a matter of fact, through the accident of his having been a part-proprietor in one of the earliest English play-houses, we know pretty accurately what manner of man he was. We know almost every thing about him, in short, except—what we *do* know about Homer—that the words now attributed to him were *his*. Homer, at least, we can trace to his " Iliad" and his " Odyssey," as he sang them in fragments from town to town. But neither to his own pen nor his own lips, and only problematically (as we shall see further on) to his own stage, can we trace the plays so long assigned to William Shakespeare. Let the works be placed in our hands for the first time anonymously; given the chronicles of the age of Elizabeth and James in which to search for an author of these works, would any thing we found in either lead us to pronounce William Shakespeare their author? And has any thing happened *since* to induce us to set aside the record and substitute an act of pure faith, of faith blind and obedient, and make it almost a religion to blindly and obediently believe that William Shakes-

peare was not the man he was, lest we should be " dis-
respectful to our birthright?"

Nothing whatever has happened since, except the
labors of the commentators. By the most painfully
elaborate explorations on the wrong track, by ingenious postulation upon fictitious premises, and by divers
illicit processes of majors and minors, while steering
carefully clear of the records, they have evolved a
butcher, a lawyer, a physician, a divinity student, a
a schoolmaster, a candlestick-maker—but, after all, a
Shakespeare. That the error, in the commencement,
was the result of carelessness, there can be no doubt.
But that, little by little—each commentator, either in
rivalry for a new fact, and jealous to be one item ahead
of his competitor (even if obliged to invent it out of
hand), or being too indolent to examine for himself,
or too subservient to authority to rebel—it grew to
vast proportions, we have only to look at the huge
" biographies " of the last half century to be assured.
It will not detain us long, as an example of these, to
briefly glance at the labors of one of the most intrepid
of the ilk to identify the traditional poet with the
traditional man. In 1839, Thomas De Quincy contributed to the " Encyclopædia Britannica " its article " Shakespeare." That about the story of the
prankish Stratford lad, who loved, and wooed and
won a farmer's daughter, and between the low, smoky-
raftered cottage in Stratford town and the snug little
thatch at Shottery trudged every sunset to do his
courting, there lingers the glamour of youth, and love,
and poetry, no patron of the " Encyclopædia " would
probably have doubted. But that a staid and solemn
work, designed for exact reference, should have printed

so whimsical a fancy sketch as Mr. De Quincey supplied to it, and that it should have been allowed to remain there, must certainly command surprise. There
can surely be complaint as to the variety of the performance. Mr. De Quincey very ably and gravely spec-
ulates as to the size of the dowry old Hathaway gave
his daughter; as to whether old John Shakespeare
mortgaged his homestead to keep up appearances; and
whether that gentleman received the patronage of
Stratford corporation when (as there is no direct authority for saying they did not) they had occasion to
present a pair of gloves to some favored nobleman
(and this portion of the composition winds up with a
history of gloves and glove-making which can not fail
to interest and instruct the reader). And his speculations as to whether the messengers who sped to
Worcester for the " marriage-lines " did or did not ride
in such hot haste, in view of an expected but prema-
ture Susannah, that they gave vicious orthographies
of the names " Shakspeare " and " Hathaway " to the
aged clerk who drew the document, are, especially
pretty reading. But—with facilities in 1839 for writing a history of the Stratford lad, which the Stratford
lad's own contemporaries and near neighbors, two hundred years and more before Mr. De Quincey, seem never
to have possessed—Mr. De Quincey quite surpasses himself in setting us exactly right as to William Shakespeare. And, first, as to the birthday. There has always been a sort of feeling among Englishmen that
their greatest poet ought to have had no less a birthday than the day dedicated to their patron saint. The
Stratford parish records certifying to the christening
of William Shakespeare on the 26th day of April,

1564 (which Mr. De Quincy forgets was "old style,"
and so, in any event, twelve days before the corresponding date in the present or "new style"), and the
anniversary of St. George being fixed for celebration
on the 23d of April, it had come to be unanimously
resolved by the commentators that, in Warwickshire,
it was the custom to christen infants on the third
day after birth, and that, therefore, William Shakespeare was born on the anniversary of St. George,
April 23, 1564.   To baptise a three-days-old baby,
in an English April, a period five days earlier than,
in the mild latitude of Palestine, the Israelites
thought it necessary to circumcise their infants, seems
a very un-English proceeding.   So Mr. De Quincy,
who would rather perish than mislead, thinks, after
all, the birth might have been a day earlier.   "After
all," he says, "William *might* have been born on the
22d.   Only one argument," he gravely proceeds, "has
sometimes struck us for supposing that the 22d might
be the day, and not the 23d, which is, that Shakespeare's sole granddaughter, Lady Barnard, was married on the 22d of April, ten years exactly from the
poet's death, and the reason for choosing this day
might have had a reference to her illustrious grandfather's birthday, which, there is good reason for thinking, would be celebrated as a festival in the family
for generations!"   But even Mr. De Quincy appears
to concede that, in writing history, we must draw the
line somewhere; for he immediately adds, "Still this
choice may have been an accident" (so many things,
that is to say, are likely to be considered in fixing a
marriage-day, besides one's grandfather's birthday!),
"or governed merely by reason of convenience.   And,

on the whole, it is as well, perhaps, to acquiesce in the old belief that Shakespeare was born and died on the 23d of April. We can not do wrong if we drink to his memory both on the 22d and 23d."[1] Mr. De Quincy's proposition to drink twice instead of once ought to forever secure his popularity among Englishmen; but it remains, nevertheless, remarkable that a ponderous encyclopædia should admit this sort of work among its articles on sugar, snakes, Sardinia, soap, Savonarola, and its other references in S! Like his fellow Shakespeareans, Mr. De Quincy makes no use of Aubrey, or the old clerk, or the Rev. Richard Davies, or any one else who, having lived at dates inconveniently contiguous to the real William Shakespeare, were awkward customers about whom it was best to say nothing. He cannot claim never to have heard of Aubrey, because he quotes him as saying that William Shakespeare was "a handsome, well-shaped man." But this is the only allusion he makes to Aubrey or to any body else who lived within eye-sight or ear-shot of the William Shakespeare who (we admit), if a well-conducted person, *ought* reasonably to have been the man Mr. De Quincy and his ilk turn him out, and not the man his neighbors, or any body who happened to be born within a hundred years

---

[1] Mr. De Quincy's own estimate of this performance we take from a preface to the article itself, in the American edition of his collected works (Boston: Shepard & Gill, 1873), vol. xv., p. 11: "No paper ever cost me so much labor; parts of it have been recomposed three times over." And again, "William Shakespeare's article cost me more intense labor than any I ever wrote in my life and, I believe, if you will examine it, you will not complain of want of novelty." We should say not.

of him, knew him. As to the difficulties Coleridge, Goethe, Schlegel, Richter, Carlyle, Palmerston,
Emerson, Gervinius, Hallam, Holmes, William Henry
Smith, Furness, and Delia Bacon find so insurmountable—namely, as to where the material of the plays
came from—Mr. De Quincy skips over these with
his airy two terms at the little grammar-school on
Stratford High Street! (The identical desk which
William occupied during this period of attendance at
that institution of learning was promptly supplied by
the Stratford guides, upon hearing Mr. De Quincy's
discovery.) "Old Aubrey," two hundred years nearer
his subject, was careful to give his school-master's
story "for what it was worth," admitting that his
authority for the statement that William Shakespeare
was a school-master was only a rumor, founded on the
statement of one "Beeston;" but who was "Beeston?" Some of our modern commentators have conjectured that possibly William, being a sort of model
or head boy, was trusted to hear some of the little
boys' lessons, which gave rise to the "school-master"
story. But Mr. De Quincy allows no demurrer nor
doubt to his assertions in the Encyclopædia Britannica.
And for these "two terms" (of course), no further
authority than himself being necessary, he vouchsafes
none. Such dry things as references are gracefully
compensated for by favoring the reader in search for
Shakespearean data with two dissertations upon
the loveliness of female virtue, one of which covers
fourteen pages octavo.[1]   His cue has had prolific fol-

---

[1] Of Sheppard & Gill's reprint (pp. 41, 69–83). But if Mr. De
Quincy could have lived until November, 1879, even he might
have been taught something. The Rev. John Bayley, in an

lowing. Now-a-days our "biographies" of William Shakespeare are huge tomes of Elizabethan and other antiquarian lore, commentary, conjecture, argumentation ; that stupefy us, as it were, by mere bulk and show of research, into accepting the whole rather than plunge into so vast and shoreless a sea of apparent labor, and, therefore, alleged learning. For such is the indolence of man, that the bulkier the book the less likely is it to be read or refuted. And so, in view of the great eye-filling books labeled "biographies" of William Shakespeare—volumes commensurate with the idea of a life which might, in time at least, have compassed the mighty works—one need not doubt that "William Shakespeare" was the name of the marvelous man who wrote the plays.

But, when one left the fiction of Mr. De Quincy and his ilk, and was forced to confront the William Shakespeare who wrote the Lucy lampoon and the epitaph on Elias James, who stuck calves and stole

article on "The Religion of Shakespeare," in the "Sunday Magazine" (New York: Frank Leslie, November, 1879, p. 518), says of William Shakespeare," "During the last years of his life it is stated that he and his family attended the parish church where the Rev. Richard Byfield, an eminent Puritan minister, and father of the distinguished commentator on the Epistle to the Colossians, commenced his ministry, A. D. 1606." Of course, the reverend contributor to the "Sunday Magazine" does not inform us where this fact "is stated," but concludes from the fact (he is sure it *is* a fact) that Shakespeare was "during the last years of his life the constant hearer of this eminent and energetic preacher of the gospel," and that "we may reasonably hope for the best of consequences." So simple a process has Shakespeare-making become!

14

deer, the difficulty only recurred with redoubled emphasis.

It is not, of course, because William stuck the calves and stole the deer, because he wrote the lampoon or the epitaph, nor because he was son (or apprentice, as some say), to a butcher or a glover, a tallow-chandler or a seedsman, that he is conceived to have been unequal to the Shakespearean authorship. There never yet was cradle too lowly to be the cradle of genius, or line too ignoble for its genesis. George Stephenson was a colliery-stoker, Turner was the son of a barber, and Faraday the son of a horseshoer. Coleridge was a charity-lad, and the number of tanners' and tallow-chandlers' offspring, without whose names history could not be written, is something amazing. We may trace the genius of Turner from the first impulse of his pencil to its latest masterpiece, but we can not find that he discovered the solar spectrum or described the Edison phonograph. He knew and practiced what he was *taught* (albeit he taught himself), and died quite contented to leave his own works behind him. Robert Burns was fully as unlettered and as rustic a plowboy as could be desired to prove the mighty miracle of genius. His history, up to a certain point, is the very duplicate of the history of William Shakespeare, the butcher's boy and prodigy of Stratford village. Both were obscure, schoolless, and grammarless. But, in the case of Robert Burns, this heaven-born genius did not set him straightway on so lofty a pinnacle that he could circumspect the past, and forecast the future, or guide his untaught pen to write of Troy and Egypt, of Athens and Cyprus, or to reproduce the very counterfeit civiliza-

tions and manners of nations born and buried and
passed into history a thousand years before he had
been begotten, the very names of which were not
dreamed of anywhere in the neighborhood of his
philosophy; of the most unusual and hidden details
of forgotten politics and commercial customs, such as,
for instance, the exceptional usage of a certain trade
in Mitylene, the anomalous status of a Moorish mer-
cenary in command of a Venetian army, of a savage
queen of Britain led captive by Rome, or a thane of
Scotland under one of its primitive kings—matters of
curious and occult research for antiquaries or dilettanti
to dig out of old romances or treatises or statutes,
rather than for historians to treat of or schools to
teach! In the case of Robert Burns we are content
not to ask too much, even of genius. Let us be content if the genius of Robert Burns could glorify the
goodwives' fables of his wonted firesides and set in
aureole the homeliest cipher in his vicinage, until a
field-mouse became a poem or a milkmaid a Venus!
It were unreasonable to demand that this genius, this
fire from heaven, at once and on the instant invest a
letterless peasant-lad with all the lore and law which
the ages behind him had shut up in clasped books and
buried and forgotten—with all the learning that the
past had gathered into great tomes and piled away in
libraries. And yet, if Robert Burns had sung of the
Punic wars or the return of the Heraclides, some
Malone or DeQuincey or Charles Knight would doubtless—with history staring him in the face—have arisen
to put his index-finger upon the sources of his authority. Judging by the record in the case of William
Shakespeare, history is able to oppose no difficulty

over which a Malone or DeQuincey or Charles Knight
can not easily clamber.

If William Shakespeare was a born genius, a true
son of nature, his soul overflowing with a sense of
the beauty of life and of love, and of all around him,
we might expect to find his poems brimful of the
sweet, downcast eyes of his Anne, of sunny Stratford
fields, of Shottery and the lordly oaks of Charlecote
—to find him, " Fancy's child," warbling " his native
wood-notes wild," indeed! But of Troy, Tyre, and
Epidamnium, of Priam and Cressid and Cleopatra, of
the propulsion of blood from the vital heart, and of
the eternal mysteries of physics, who dreams that
" sweetest Shakespeare, Fancy's child " could sing in
the very speech and idiom of those forgotten towns
and times, or within the mathematical exactitude of
sciences that had not yet been treated of in books?
Or, again, John Bunyan is a case in point. John
Bunyan was as squalid and irredeemable a tinker as
ever flourished in the days when " a tinker was rogue
by statute."[1] And yet he, according to Macaulay, produced the second of the two books of which England
should be proudest.[2] What was the miracle in the case
of John Bunyan? He produced a book which, " while
it obtains admiration from the most fastidious critics,
is loved by those who are too simple to admire it. . . .
This is the highest miracle of art, that things which

---

[1] Cockayne vs. Hopkins, 2 Lev., 214.

[2] " Though there were many clever men in England during the
latter half of the seventeenth century, there were only two minds
which possessed the imaginative faculty in a very eminent degree. One of these minds produced the ' Paradise Lost,' and
the other the ' Pilgrim's Progress.' "

are not should be as though they were; that the imaginations of one mind should become the personal
recollections of another. And this miracle the tinker
has wrought." But this great praise was not abstracted
from Macaulay by wealth of antique learning, universal accuracy of information, or vivid portraiture of
forgotten civilizations. There was no trace of Bunyan's perfect familiarity with Plato and Euripides,
with Galen, Paracelsus, Plautus, Seneca, and the long
line of authors down to Boccaccio, Rabelais, Saxo-
Grammaticus, and the rest! The critic did not find
in Bunyan's pages the careful diction of a scholar, the
sonorous speech of the ancients, or the elegant and
punctilious Norman of the court. "The Bunyan vocabulary," says Macaulay, "is the vocabulary of the
common people. There is not an expression, if we
except a few technical theological terms, which would
puzzle the rudest peasant." In short, we need not
pause, marvelous as are the pages of the "Pilgrim's
Progress," to ask of John Bunyan, as indeed we must
ask of William Shakespeare, the question, "how
knoweth this man letters, having never learned?"
Peerless as the result all is, there is nothing in the
writings of John Bunyan which can not be accounted
for by natural (that is to say, by what we have been
obliged by the course of human experience to accept
as not impossible) causes. "The years of Bunyan's
boyhood were those during which the Puritan spirit
was in the highest vigor over all England. . . . It is
not wonderful, therefore, that a lad to whom nature
had given a powerful imagination and sensibility which
amounted to a disease, should have been early haunted
by religious terrors. Before he was ten, his sports

were interrupted by fits of remorse and despair, and his sleep disturbed by dreams of fiends trying to fly away with him. . . . He enters the Parliamentary army, and, to the last, he loves to draw his illustrations of sacred things from camps and fortresses, guns, trumpets, flags of truce, and regiments arrayed, each under its own banner. . . . His 'Greatheart,' his 'Captain Boanerges,' and his 'Captain Credence' are evidently portraits of which the originals were among those martial saints who fought and expounded in Fairfax's army. . . . He had been five years a preacher when the Restoration put it in the power of the Cavaliers . . . to oppress the Dissenters. . . . He was flung into Bedford jail, with pen and paper for company,"[1] etc., etc. Here are the school and the experience, and the result is writings "which show a keen mother wit, a great command of the homely mother tongue, an intimate knowledge of the English bible, and a vast and dearly bought spiritual experience."[2] Moreover, here is a scholar like Macaulay striving to account for the extraordinary phenomenon of a "Pilgrim's Progress" written by a village tinker. But in the case of the at least equally extraordinary phenomenon of the Shakespearean drama, the creation of a village butcher, the scholar has not yet been born to the Shakespeareans who deems it necessary or profitable to try his hand at any such investigation. "Where did he get his material?" "Oh, he picked it up around Stratford, somehow!" "But his learning?" "Oh, he found it lying around the theater somewhere!" Prob-

---

[1] "Bunyan," in "Encyclopædia Britannica," by Macaulay.
[2] Ibid.

ably there were encyclopædias to be fished out of the mud of the bank-side in those days, of which we can find no mention in the chroniclers! And so, although scarcely a commentator on the glowing text has not paused in wonder at the vastness and magnificence of this material, leading him on to vaster and more magnificent treasuries at every step, so far as we are able to discover, not one of them has attempted to trace the intellectual experience of the man who wrought it all out of the book and volume of his unaided brain. Not one of them has paused to ask the Scriptural question, "How knoweth this man letters, having never learned?" For, it can not be too incessantly reiterated, the question is not, "Was Shakespeare a poet?" but, "Had he access to the material from which the plays are composed?" Admit him to have been the greatest poet, the most frenzied genius in the world; where did he get—not the poetry, but—the classical, philosophical, chemical, historical, astronomical, geological, etc., etc., information—the FACTS that crowd these pages?

And let us not be credited, in these pages, with a malignant rejection of every tradition or anecdote that works to William Shakespeare's renown, and a corresponding retention of every tradition or anecdote to his disparagement. For example, if it is asked, Why reject the story of King James's autograph letter, and retain the story of the trespass on Sir Thomas Lucy's deer? the answer must be: first; because, while there is nothing improbable in the latter, there is much of improbability in the former. King James was a king, and kings rarely write autograph letters to subjects. The Lord Chamberlain may give a sort of permission

to a haberdasher to call himself haberdasher to Queen
Victoria; but it would be vastly improbable that Queen
Victoria should write an autograph letter to the haberdasher to that effect.   Second, because the poaching
story (to use a legal test) appears to be so old that the
memory of man runneth not to a time when it was
not believed; whereas the King James story first appeared in the year 1710, in a biographical notice affixed to an edition of the plays prepared by one Bernard Lintot.   Mr. Lintot gave no authority for the
statement whatever, except to say that it rested on the
word of "a credible person then living."   But everybody can appreciate the zeal and appetite with which
rival biographers, like rival newspaper reporters, struggle to get hold of a new fact for their columns, and
nobody will wonder that, after Mr. Lintot, no "biographer" omitted to mention it.   As a matter of fact,
the letter from King James and the letter from Queen
Elizabeth, produced by young Ireland, are equally
genuine correspondence.   But the stories of the latter
class, while not beyond question, are at least not improbable, considering the record of the youth Shakespeare at Stratford, while those of the first are certainly improbable on their face, and can be in almost
every case traced to their exact source.

   So the story of his holding horses, while by no means
authentic, (Mr White says it was not heard of until
the middle of the last century), is by no means improbable, seeing that the lad ran away to London—
—and Rowe and the old sexton both agree that he began—as self-made men do—at the bottom.   The story
of Queen Elizabeth's crossing the stage and dropping
. her glove, which Shakespeare picked up and pre-

sented with an impromptu, Mr. White himself smiles at, with the remark that "the anecdote is plainly one made to meet the craving for personal details of Shakespeare's life,"[1] and he treats it as he does the "Florio" in the British Museum, supposed to have belonged to William Shakespeare, because that name is written— —after his mode—on a fly-leaf; with a pleasant wish that he were able to believe in it.[1]

Far from being of the class that kings delight to honor, it is simply impossible to turn one's researches into any channel that leads into the vicinity of Stratford without noticing the fact that the Shakespeare family left, in the neighborhoods where it flourished, one unmistakable trace familiar in all cases of vulgar and illiterate families; namely, the fact that they never knew or cared, or made an effort to know, of what vowels or consonants their own name was composed, or even to preserve the skeleton of its pronunciation. They answered—or made their marks—indifferently to "Saxpir" or "Chaksper;" or to any other of the thirty forms given by Mr. Grant White,[2] or the fifty-five forms which another gentleman of elegant leisure has been able to collect.[3]

In the records of the town council of Stratford, of which John Shakespeare was no unimportant part, the name is written in fourteen different forms, which may be tabulated as follows :

---

[1] Shakespeare's Works. Boston, 1865. Vol. I., p. 80, in, and see a note to the same volume, pp. 96-7, as to Ratzei's ghost, surmised to be an allusion to Shakespeare.

[1] Ib., p. 128.

[2] Shakespeare's Scholar, pp. 478-480.

[3] George Russel French, Shakespeareana Geologicana. p. 348.

4 times written Shackesper.

3 times written Shackespere.

4 times written Shacksper.

2 times written Shackspere.

13 times written Shakespere.

1 time written Shaksper.

5 times written Shakspere.

17 times written Shakspeyr.

4 times written Shakysper.

9 times written Shakyspere.

69 times written Shaxpeare.

8 times written Shaxper.

18 times written Shaxpere.

9 times written Shaxspeare.

In the marriage bond of November 28, 1582, it is twice written, each time Shagspere. On the grave of Susanna, it is Shakespere; and on the other graves of the family, Shakespeare, except that under the bust it is Shakspeare. That is to say, just as many orthographies as there are tombstones and inscriptions. Any lawyer's clerk who has had occasion to search for evidence among the uneducated classes, knows how certainly a lower or higher grade of intelligence will manifest itself primarily in an ignorance of or indifference to one's own name or a corresponding zeal for one's own identity, and anxiety that it shall be accurately "taken down." Whether this infallible rule obtained in the days of the Shakespeares or not, or whether a family, that was so utterly stolid as not to know if their patronymic was spelled with a " c," a " k," or an " x," could have appreciated and bestowed upon their child a classical education (not to ring the changes upon politics, philosophy, etc., right here), is for the reader to judge for himself.

Mr. W. H. Smith maintains that Shakespeare, like the rest of his family, was unable to write; and had learned, by practice only, to make the signature which he was assured was his name. Mr. Smith founds his theory on the fact that, in the Will the word "seale" (in the formula, " witness my seale," etc.) is erased,

and the word "hand" substituted. In a letter to Mr.
Shedding,[1] Mr. Smith claims that this erasure and substitution prove that the draughtsman who prepared
the Shakespeare Will, knowing that the testator could
not write, did not suppose that he would sign his
name, and so prepared it for the superimposition of
his seal. "I know," says Mr. Smith, "that you will
ingeniously observe that that might have been his belief, but that the fact could better have been proved if
'hand' had been erased and 'seale' inserted. But
Shakespeare, being proud of his writing, and, as this
would probably be his last opportunity, insisted on
exhibiting his 'hand.'" According to Mr. Smith,
therefore, Ben Jonson's speech about "never blotting
out a line," was redundant. But, whether able to
write, or, like his ancestors and descendants, signing
with a mark, he clearly cared no more than they
how people spelled his name. A Mr. George Wise,
of Philadelphia, has been able to compile a chart exhibiting one thousand nine hundred and six ways of
spelling the Stratford boy's name;[2] A commentary
on the efforts of Mr. Halliwell and others, to establish the canonical orthography, which might well reduce them to despair. The fact is, that there can no
more be a canonical spelling of the name Shakespeare
than there can be a canonical face of the boy William.
The orthography of Shakespeare, as now accepted,
and the face now accepted as belonging to William
of that name, are both modern inventions. Even the

---

[1] See third edition Holmes' "Authorship of Shakespeare,"
p. 627.

[2] Philadelphia, 1858. See Essays on Shakespeare, Carl Elze;
translated by Schmitz (London, Macmillan's 1874), note to p. 371.

"best of that family" (according to the old clerk),
William, when called to sign his own last will and
testament (obliged by law to sign each of the three
sheets upon which it was engrossed) three times,
spelled his name a different way each time.   His
daughter Judith lived and died without being able to
spell or write it at all; Milton, Spenser, Sidney, even
Gower and Chaucer (whom even our own Artemus
Ward pronounced " no speller "), had but one way of
writing their own names—and never dreamed of
one thousand nine hundred and six.   The name is now
supposed to have been simply "Jacques-Pierre" (James
Peter), which had been mispronounced—as Englishmen mispronounce French—for unnumbered generations.[1]   This is the present mispronunciation of Jac-
ques prevalent in Warwickshire.   And, such being
the true origin of the name, it is, of course, natural to
find it as we do, written in two words " Shake-speare,"
in those days.   It is not William Shakespeare's fault
that he sprang from an illiterate family, but that—after
growing so rich as to be able to enjoy an income of
$25,000 a year, he should never send his children—es-
pecially his daughter Judith—to school, so that the poor
girl, on being married, on the 11th day of February,
1616, should be obliged to sign her marriage bond with
a mark, shows, we think, that he was not that immortal
he would have been had he written the topmost literature

---

[1] " 'Thomas Jakes, of Wonersh' was one of the list of gentry
of the shire 12 Henry IV., 1433.   At the surrender of the Abbey
of Kenilworth 26 Henry VIII., 1535, the abbot was Simon Jakes,
who had the pension of £100 granted him." (Wilkes' "Shakespeare from an American Point of View." New York : D. Appleton & Co., 1877, p. 464.)

of the world—the Shakespearean Drama! But, still, this most unsatisfactory person—this man who answers, like Mr. Carroll's skipper, to "hi, or to any loud cry"—

> "To what-you-may-call-um or what-is-his-name
> But especially thing-um-a-jig,"

or to whatever the nearest actor or scene-shifter may happen to hit on when he wants the poor little "supernumerary," and "Joannes Factotum"—actually lived to clamber astride of the most immortal birthright of his own or of any century, and has clung thereon like another old man of the sea on Sinbad's shoulders, and been carried down through these three hundred years, and is being carried yet, down or up, to an undeterminate immortality of fame that is the true estate of somebody else! For, not only has the world not yet gotten its eyes half open, but it contumaciously refuses to open them to the facts in the case, and prefers to hug as tightly as it ever did this stupendous hoax—(" *Shakespearean* " indeed, in that it has outlasted and outlived all the other hoaxes put together—the witchcraft hoax, the Chatterton hoax, the Ossian hoax, the moon hoax, and all the rest of them); that has carried all sorts of parasite hoaxes, like Ireland's, Collier's, and Cunningham's upon its back, until their little day has been accomplished, and they have dropped off, just as, one of these days, the present hoax must drop off, and breathe its last, without a single mourner to stand by the coffin, and confess himself its disciple.

PART IV.

EXTRA SHAKESPEAREAN THEORIES: THE DELIA BACON THEORY.

HERE is a legal maxim to the effect that he who destroys should be able to build up. The anti-Shakespeareans have not neglected to observe it. The days when William Shakespeare first appeared in London, happened to be the days when the Renaissance had reached England, and the drama which began then for the first time to be produced, was the English Renaissant Drama—just throwing off the crudities of the old miracle and mystery plays borrowed from the continent, and beginning to be English and original. Moreover, letters and learning, so long exclusively confined to the rich and gentle, began to find expressions in other ranks. "The mob of gentlemen who write with ease" were, one and all, beginning to use their pens. There were no village newspapers with their "Poet's Corners," and these writers sent their manuscripts through the only channel at hand—the green-room door.

As these scores of manuscripts came in, William Shakespeare, of Stratford, now Mr. Manager Shakespeare of the Blackfriars, read them over; took out a scene here and an act there; scissored them as he pleased; made this "heavy" for the low comedian, and that for the "first old man;" adjusted the "love business," made "practical" for his boards all the nature and humor, and cut out all that came flat, stale, and unprofitable from the amateur's hand; even took a little of each to make a new one, if necessary, (thus retaining the indicia that *this* was written by a lawyer, *that* by a physician, *this* by a soldier, *that* by a chemist, etc., etc.). He did what Dumas, Boucicault and Daly do to-day; he was, in other words, the stage editor, not the author, of the Shakespearean drama; though, that it should be called by his name, is, perhaps, the least unusual thing about it.

Besides the gentlemen who used their pens, the very recent dissolution of the monasteries had thrown multitudes of "learned clerks," (the "clerical" profession then including lawyers and physicians, and indeed all book-learned men) upon their own resources for daily bread, and there was only one depot for their work. Not three, but three thousand men there were, other things being equal, more competent by education at least, than William Shakespeare to write the Shakespearean drama. But other things, as we shall see, were not equal. It is suggested, on the one hand, that William Shakespeare wrote the plays; on the other hand, that Francis Bacon wrote them; and, again, that Sir Walter Raleigh wrote them. So far as mere dates go, any one of the three might have written them. They were all three in London, and on the ground when the plays appeared. The truth is perhaps somewhere among the three. Francis Bacon was the most learned man of his time. He could and did read Greek in the original, and he did have access to untranslated manuscripts, such as the "Menæchmi" of Plautus. He was a philosopher, and he *did* come nearer to a prescience of the philosophy of ages to be, than any man who

ever lived—as witness his own acknowledged works.
Sir Walter Raleigh was a wit and a poet, a gentleman,
a man of elegant nonchalance, a very Mercutio, to the
day of his execution. He was liberally educated, cultured, and would have been all this in a more cultivated day than his own; moreover, he was idle and a
scribbler of belles-lettres. Perhaps he killed time by
writing speeches for the obsequious manager to put
into plays for his stage. Anonymous or pseudonymic
authorship has ever been a penchant of the gentle and
idle. Shakespeare, let us say, was a shrewd man of
business, who kept up with his times, as do managers
of theaters to-day; he was quick to perceive where a
point might be made in his plays, and moreover he
employed—or perhaps was fortunate enough to secure
by way of friendship—a poet to turn his ideas into
speech for the mouths of his players. That he used
his pen to prepare the prompter's manuscript of the
pieces performed at his theater, we have already seen
there is reason to believe. That he ever composed, on
his own account, we have only a sort of innuendo of
certain of his brother actors and playwrights, and a
Stratford tradition, which we can trace to no other
source than the source of the belief outside—that is to
say, to the fact that the plays were produced under his
management in London. The innuendo dubs him a
poet; the Stratford tradition makes him to have written doggerel verses. But some have ventured to disbelieve both the innuendo and the tradition.

Still, writing his life, as we do, from imagination, it
is much easier to imagine the three men—Bacon, Raleigh, and Shakespeare—producing between them
"Hamlet," "Othello," or the "Comedy of Errors,"

than to imagine William Shakespeare alone doing it.
Especially since, apart from the internal evidence of
the plays, he "had his hands full" of work besides—
the work in which he earned his competency.   It can
not be too clearly borne in mind that Shakespeare, in a
space of ten or twelve years, actually made what is a
fair fortune to-day.   That Bacon and Raleigh, whose
ambitions did not lead them to seek renown as playwrights, should have contributed their share to the
plays—the first for gold which he needed, and the second for pastime which he craved—is not remarkable;
we can see hundreds of young lawyers scribbling for
gold while waiting for practice, or young "swells" trying their hand at comedies for the sport of the thing,
by opening our eyes to-day.   That the shrewd and
successful manager should carefully pick into present-
able and playable shape for his stage, these productions of his young friends, is, likewise, the easiest
thing in the world to conceive of, or to see managers
doing to-day.   Possibly, William Shakespeare, or some
other skilled playwright, took the dialogues—let us
say, for example—of Bacon and Raleigh, put them
into the form of plays, introduced a clown here or a
jade there, interpolated saws and localisms, gave the
characters their names, looked out for the "business,"
arranged the tableaux—in short, did what Mr. Wallack, or Mr. Daly, or Mr. Boucicault would have to
do to-day to fit a play for the stage.   It is thought that
Shakespeare himself did it, because the plays are said
to have been seen in his handwriting, and because,
from that fact or otherwise, they went by his name in
the days when they were first produced in London.

This sort of joint authorship would not only explain

away the antagonism which grew up between the evidence of the man Shakespeare and the evidence of the Shakespearean plays, but account for the difficulties of accepting any anti-Shakespearean theory. This would explain the parallel passages in Bacon's writings and in the plays, which Judge Holmes has so painstakingly sorted out; the little inaccuracies of law and of grammar, of geography and of history, in the plays themselves; Mr. Greene's " sea-coast of Bohemia," or the introduction of gunpowder at the seige of Troy—absurdities which it is morally impossible to suppose of the portrayer of antiquity who wrote "Julius Cæsar," or the knowledge that framed the historical plays. If, however, we consider them as the interpolations of a stagewright[1] aiming at stage effect, they are easily enough accounted for. The stagewright saw an opportunity for the introduction of a stage ship or shipwreck, hence

---

[1] It is nothing less than marvelous that this simple explanation should not have occurred to the wise men who have been knocking their heads against "the sea-coast of Bohemia" for the last hundred years. That this error is a part of the "business" and not of the play, is very evident from a casual reading of Act III., Scene III. The stage direction for that scene is simply, "SCENE— a *desert country near the sea*," to be sure there is no stage direction of any sort in the "first folio" but we may be sure that this was the proper stage setting of the piece. And to fit it, Antigonus, the first speaker, says to the mariner: "Art thou perfect, then? Our ship hath touched the deserts of Bohemia." Robert Green makes the same mistake in his " Dorastus and Faunia." It was, if any thing, a vulgar error of the time. There is no further allusion to the troublesome geography in the play. So, too, the gunpowder used at the seige of Troy is a part of the " business," and should be assigned where it belongs—to the playwright and not to the dramatist. Not only did the stage editor put it in, but he took it out of Green's "Dorastus and Faunia."

he puts in the borrowed "sea-coast." He needs an alarum of guns to impress his audience on the coming evening with the fact that a fight is in progress. And even if it should occur to him to doubt if there were any guns at the siege of Ilium, he is pretty certain that it will not occur to the groundlings or the penny seats, from whose pocket all is grist that comes to his mill, if he makes the guns and the cannon a part of the "business." So, again, we have only to understand this, and the characters of Nym and Bardolph—supposed to have puzzled the critics since critics first began to busy themselves with these dramas—is explained. Bardolph is the walking comedian, inserted by the experienced manager to tickle the frieti ciceris et nucis emptor, with his fiery nose, and corporal Nym to break in with his "There's the humor of it," just as Rip Van Winkle dwells upon his favorite toast, and Solon Shingle upon his ancestor who "fitted into the Revolution." And to many minds this accounts for the little dashes of obscene display, the lewd innuendo, which came never from the same pen as the master-strokes, but which they prefer to conceive of an actor or manager interpolating to the delight of Monsieur Taine's audience, and for the stolen delectation of the maids of honor and city dames who went, in men's clothes, to mingle with them.

This, too, might account for the poems dedicated to Southampton. In the lax court and reign of the Virgin Queen, there was at least one man bold and reckless enough to stand patron to the "Venus and Adonis" and "The Rape of Lucrece"—the noble young libertine of nineteen, Southampton. Similarly, there may have been but one man available upon

whom to father them, and so the joint or several productions of certain young men about town, "curled
darlings" who affected Shakespeare's green-room,
were sworn upon the complacent manager, who doubtless saw his profit in it. We have rumor, indeed, that
his profit was no less a sum than one thousand pounds.
But, as we have seen, and shall see further, this thous-
and pounds story is not only without authority, but
incredible: that Southampton's means did not justify him in giving away any such sum—that Shakespeare did not need it, and that none of Southampton's
coterie ever heard of it.

Whether Bacon wrote these works or not (and we
may say the same of Raleigh), and whether the audiences before whom these Shakespearean dramas
were first presented could have estimated them as
what we of this age recognize them to be or not;
we may be sure that, had he chanced to light upon
them, Lord Bacon could have appraised them, and
the genius that created them, at their true worth.
But while Lord Bacon's writings teem with mention of his own contemporaries (Mr. W. H. Smith
points out the fact that we owe about all we know of
Raleigh's skill in repartee to Bacon's "Apothegms"),
he nowhere alludes to such a man as William Shakespeare!—to William Shakespeare—who, if popular belief is true, was his lordship's most immortal contemporary, the one mind mightier than Bacon's, and yet
not a rival or a superior in his own particular sphere,
of whom he could have been jealous. The truth
which makes this strange riddle plain is, according to
the Baconian theory, that (to use Sir Tobie Matthew's
words in his famous letter to his patron) "the most

prodigious wit that ever I knew, of my nation, and
of this side of the sea, is of your lordship's name,
though he be known by another,"[1] in other words, that
Bacon was "Shakespeare." And, indeed, Sir Tobie
was fonder of nothing than of indulging in sly allusions to Lord Bacon's secret, of which he had become
possessed. In another letter than that just quoted, he
says again to his lordship: "I will not promise to return you weight for weight, but *measure for measure* .
. . . and there is a certain judge in the world, who, in
the midst of his popularity toward the meaner sort of
men, would fain deprive the better sort of that happiness which was generally done in that time."[2]

Such considerations as these, as they came one by
one to light, began to suggest to thinking minds that
perhaps William Shakespeare was enjoying, by default,
estates belonging to somebody else. But it is curious
to see how gradually. In 1733, Theobald, a competent and painstaking scholar of the text, declares that
there were "portions of the plays which proved beyond a doubt that more than one hand had produced
them." More than fifty years after came Dr. Richard
Farmer (who wrote his famous letter on "The Learning of Shakespeare," in or about 1789), and appears to
have been the first actual anti-Shakespearean and un-
believer. Dr. Farmer sought—by demonstrating that
much of the learning of the plays COULD have been,
by sufficient research, procured at second-hand—to account for (what he could not overlook) the utter inadequacy of the historical man to the immortal work

---

[1] Holmes's "Authorship of Shakespeare," second edition, p. 175.
[2] "Bacon and Shakespeare," by W. H. Smith, p. 96.

assigned him; just as if it were not, if any thing, an
increase (or say a substitution) of marvels to suppose
a busy actor and manager rummaging England for
forgotten manuscripts in the days when no public libraries existed, and when students lived in cloisters;
or (let us say) that he knew precisely where to lay his
hand on every obscure tract, letter, or memorandum
ever drawn from a classical source! And just as if the
encyclopædic learning required was lessened by the
fact that the plot of the perfected play was borrowed
or rewritten from an older drama of the same name!

For example of Farmer's argument, take the following. In the play of that name, Timon says:

"The sun's a thief, and with his great attention
Robs the vast sea. The moon's an arrant thief,
And her pale fire she snatches from the sun.
The sea's a thief whose liquid surge resolves
The moon into salt tears. The earth's a thief
That feeds and breeds by a composture stolen
From general excrement: each thing's a thief."

Now, exclaim the men who upho'd the stage manager's ability to read Greek, the idea of this is from
Anacreon, and they give the ode in which William
Shakespeare found it. Not so fast, says Dr. Farmer.
He might have taken it from the French of Ronsard,
a French poet: because one Puttenham, in his "Arte
of English Poesie," published in 1589, speaks of some
one—of a "reasonable good facilitie in translation, who,
finding certain of Anacreon's odes very well translated
by Ronsard, the French poet—comes a minion and
translates the same out of French into English," and
" on looking into Ronsard I find this very ode of Anacreon among the rest!"

Letting pass the far-fetched conjecture which aims to prove that William Shakespeare could not read Greek by showing that he COULD reach French—or the observation, that the sum of Dr. Farmer's arguments (for the above is a sample of each and all of them) amounts simply to this, that: though the manager knew no Greek—he knew where every thing contained in Greek was to be obtained in translation: the question for us is simply, Why should the stage-manager have recourse to either Anacreon or Ronsard for a meteorological episode? This, and a thousand like passages, are nothing but digressions, with nothing whatever to do with the action or by-play of the comedy or tragedy in which they occur, and not apposite to any thing else in the part of the speakers who pronounced them. A scholar might be unable to keep them out; but why should a stage-manager—fitting a spectacle to the acting necessities of his boards or to the humor of his audience—put them in? Whereas, if a scholar *did* write the manuscript play and sell it to a stage-manager, it is useless to ask why the stage-manager did not cut out the digression or why he left it in, for that was a mere matter of whim or circumstance, not worth our while to speculate over. Dr. Farmer went just far enough to see that, if the William Shakespeare of history wrote the Book, something must be done to account for his access to the material he wrought with. If the Doctor had kept on a little further, the truth would have dawned upon him. But, as it was, he (without looking for them) observed traces of what he believed to be two hands in the Plays, and so followed Theobald. He says of Hamlet, that he considered it "extremely probable that the French ribaldry in the

last scene of Hamlet was the work of another than
the author of the body of the work"—but the hint
was altogether lost on him. He looked no further, and
so lived and died unsuspicious of the truth—namely,
that it was only the fair-copied manuscript that was
William Shakespeare's. The "without blotting a line"
of Ben Jonson—not a mere form of speech, but a
fact, confirmed by Heminges and Condell, the editors
of the "first folio" of 1623, who say in their preface,
"we have scarce received from him a blot in his papers"—as we shall see further on, ought to have itself
awakened suspicion. Lope de Vega, the Spaniard,
who supplied his native stage with upward of two
thousand original dramas—who is computed to have
written upward of 21,300,000 verses, and who wrote
so hurriedly that he never had time to unravel his in-
trigues, but cut them all open "with a knife" in the
last act—probably did write "without blotting a line."
At least so Mr. Hallam thinks, adding that, "nature
would have overstepped her bounds, and have produced the miraculous, had Lope de Vega, along with
this rapidity and invention, attained perfection in any
department of literature."[1] But in the case of these
marvelous Shakespeare plays, it was preferred to believe that nature *had* "produced the marvelous,"
rather than accept the simple truth that what Heminges and Condell and Ben Jonson saw, were the engrossed parts written out for each actor, and not the
first drafts of the poet, improvising as he wrote.

Except that Mr. Spedding, in the "Gentleman's Magazine" for February, 1852, printed a paper "Who wrote

---

[1] Literature of Europe, part ii., ch. vi., § 8.

Shakespeare's Henry VIII?"—in which he claimed to
have found startling traces of two hands in that play,
(and possibly some other floating papers which have
escaped our search)—prior to the year 1852 it had
occurred to nobody (except Kitty, in "High Life Below Stairs") to ask the question, "Who Wrote Shakespeare?" But, in August of that year an anonymous
writer, in Chambers' "Edinburgh Journal," distinctly
and for the first time discussed the question, "Who
wrote Shakespeare?"—when, after going over much of
the ground we have already traversed, arrived, to his
own "extreme dissatisfaction," (as he says, at the conclusion), that William Shakespeare "kept a poet." It
is curious to find this anonymous writer dealing, as airily
as Lady Bab herself, with the question: and (while un-
conscious of the elaborate network of evidence he
might have summoned, and suggesting no probable
author by name) actually foreshadowing the laborious
conviction which, four years later, Delia Bacon was to
announce. He surmises, indeed, that William Shakespeare was a sort of showman, whose interest in the
immortal plays was a purchased interest—precisely
what the law at present understands by "proprietary
copyright." "The plays apparently arise . . .
as the series goes on; all at once Shakespeare, with a
fortune, leaves London, and the supply ceases. Is
this compatible with a genius thus culminating, on any
other supposition than the death of the poet and the
survival of the employer?" Of this supposititious
hack-author, who dies, and leaves to William Shakespeare the halo of his genius as well as the profit
of his toil, this anonymous writer draws a picture
16

that has something familiar in its coloring. "May
not William Shakespeare," he asks, "the cautious,
calculating man, careless of fame, and intent only
on money-making, have found, in some farthest garret
over-looking the 'silent highway of the Thames,'
some pale, wasted student . . . who, with eyes
of genius gleaming through despair, was about, like
Chatterton, to spend his last copper coin upon some
cheap and speedy means of death? What was to
hinder William Shakespeare from reading, appreciat-
ing, and purchasing these dramas, and thereafter
'keeping his poet,' like Mrs. Packwood? . . .
With this view the disputed passages—those in which
critics have agreed that the genius is found wanting—
the meretricious ornaments sometimes crowded in—
the occasional bad taste—in short, all the imperfections discernible and disputable in these mighty dramas,
are reconcilable with their being the interpolations of
Shakespeare himself on his poet's works."[1] Miss Delia
Bacon, a remarkable lady, followed in a paper printed
in "Putnam's Magazine," in its issue of January,
1856, (and therefore must have written it in 1855), and
was supposed therein to distinctly announce and maintain that Lord Bacon—her namesake by coincidence—
was the "Shakespeare" wanted—a supposition which,
as we shall see, was erroneous.

The audacity of the assertion, by a young woman, a
school-teacher, in no way distinguished or anywise eminent, that the idol of these centuries, and of the English-
speaking race, was a mere effigy of straw—a mere dummy
for an unknown immortal, was too tremendous! Men

---

[1] Chambers' "Edinburgh Journal," August 7, 1852, p. 88.

stood aghast. Was it a chimera of a mind diseased! Sneered at in her own country, she went to England, but found that—while at home she was treading only on adverse sentiment—*there* she was openly tampering with vested rights, almost with the unwritten constitution of England. She made a few personal friends, and found some sympathizers, but all England was arrayed against her. She came back, heart-broken, and died eight months later. Mr. William Henry Smith, of London, in September, 1856, appeared with his " Was Lord Bacon the Author of Shakespeare's Plays? A Letter to Lord Ellesmere," in which the Baconian theory was very plainly and circumspectly laid down and admirably maintained.[1] The presumption once disturbed, inquiry began to be diverted from the well-worn track of the commentators, and the result has been, we think, a candid, rational, and patient attempt to study the Shakespearean writings by the aid of contemporary history rather than by mere conjecture, and by the record rather than by fancy, guess-work, and gossip. It is too early in the day—the time has been too short—for the reaction to have proved equal to the action, and verified the physical rule ; but three well-

---

[1] This " Letter," which was reprinted in " Littell's Living Age," (No. 56), for November, 1856, was, the following year (1857) elaborated into the valuable work on which we have so unsparingly drawn in these pages, and to which we acknowledge our exceeding obligation (" Bacon and Shakespeare: An Inquiry touching Players, Playhouses, and Playwriters in the days of Elizabeth. By William Henry Smith. London: Smith, Elder & Co., 1857 "). In this work Mr. Smith (in his preface) asserts that at the date of his letter to Lord Ellesmere, he had never seen Miss Bacon's article in " Putnam's," but, it is to be observed, no where claims to have been the originator of the " Baconian Theory."

defined anti-Stratfordian theories have offered themselves already, as substitutes for the mossy and venerable fossil remains of the commentators. These theories are:

1. The Delia Bacon Theory;
2. The Baconian Theory; and
3. The New Theory (as we are compelled, for want
of a better name, to call it).

THE DELIA BACON THEORY.

It was across no dethroned and shattered intellect
that there first flashed the truth it has been the essay
of these papers to rehearse. That Delia Bacon—who,
earliest in point of time, announced to the world that
"Shakespeare" was the name of a *book*, and not the
name of its author; and who, contenting herself with
the bare announcement, soon passed on to the theory
we are now about to notice—was pelted with a storm
of derision, abuse, and merciless malice, until in poverty, sickness, and distress, but still in a grand silence,
she passed out of sight for ever, is true enough.
That in the midst of it all she still struggled on in
what she believed to be " the world's work "—bearing
more than it was ever intended a woman should bear
—is not to overweigh any merit her scheme of the
Shakespearean plays may have possessed, however it
may have eventuated in the "madness" so insepar-
ably connected with her name. Wherever Delia Bacon
died, she lived and moved in the conviction that she
was a worker in the world's workshop. What to us
is a mere cold, historical formulary, seems, however,
we may smile at the absurdity, to have seized upon
her whole life and being; and, as in a great crusade

against a universal error, she seems to have struggled
in loneliness and wretchedness, with a crusader's faith
and a martyr's reward.

In all her tragic life, Delia Bacon appears never to
have paused to formulate the theory, for ever to be
associated with her name, as to the actual authorship
of the plays. The paper "William Shakespeare and
his Plays," which appeared in "Putnam's Magazine"
(and inaugurated the controversy, never thereafter to
"down" at anybody's bidding), seems to treat the matter as already settled. It is rather sarcasm at the
expense of those who rejected the theory of a non-
Shakespearean authorship than a formulation of the
theory itself. That the sarcasm, as a sustained effort,
has rarely if ever been equaled, there certainly can be
no question. Her indignation at the idea that the
magnificent plays sprang from the brain of "the Stratford poacher—now that the deer-stealing fire has gone
out of him; now that this youthful impulse has been
taught its conventional mental limits, sobered into the
mild, sagacious, witty Mr. Shakespeare of the Globe,"
is intense. "What is to hinder Mr. Shakespeare, the
man who keeps the theater on the bank-side, from
working himself into a frenzy when he likes, and
scribbling out, unconsciously, Lears, and Macbeths,
and Hamlets, merely as the necessary dialogues to the
spectacle he professionally exhibits!" Her allusion to
Bacon is equally impassioned: "We should have
found, ere this, *one* with learning broad enough and
deep enough and subtle enough and comprehensive
enough; one with nobility of aim and philosophic
and poetic genius enough to be able to claim his
own, his own immortal progeny, unwarped, un-

blinded, undeprived of one ray or dimple of that all-
pervading reason that informs them—one who is able to
reclaim them, even now, 'cured and perfected in their
limbs, and absolute in full numbers as he conceived
them!'" Long before its appearance, as we shall proceed to narrate; and still longer before the world had
well opened its eyes to the fact that a formidable
anti-Shakespearean proposition had been asserted, its
author had left the proposition itself leagues behind,
and was well along on her route to the fountain-head
of its inspiration. The problem she proposed to herself was not, " Did Bacon and others write the plays?"
but " WHY did Bacon and others write the plays
under the name of William Shakespeare?"

As the fruit of laborious study of the system and
structure of the plays, she reached the answer—
as she believed, and lived and died believing—hidden
and embalmed in the masterpiece of them all, the
tragedy of " Hamlet." " Hamlet," she maintained,
was the master-key that unlocked the whole magnificent system. They were not plays, but chapters in a
great Treatise—links in a great chain of philosophy—
a new philosophy of politics and of life; and, just as
the Lord Hamlet caused certain strolling players, with
the set speech he put into their mouths, to " catch the
conscience of the king," so had the greatest mind of
all the golden age put into the mouths of the vagabond Shakespeare and his crew the truth which should,
in the fullness of time, catch the conscience of the
whole world. But why should these great minds have
chosen to put their philosophy into enigmas and
ciphers? Miss Bacon's answer was convincing: " It
was the time when the cipher, in which one could

write 'omnia per omnia,' was in request; when even 'wheel ciphers' and 'doubles' were thought not unworthy of philosophic notice. It was a time, too, when the phonographic art was cultivated and put to other uses than at present, and when a nomme de plume was required for other purposes than to serve as the refuge of an author's modesty, or vanity, or caprice. It was a time when puns, and charades, and enigmas, and anagrams, and monograms, and ciphers, and puzzles were not mere sport and child's play; when they had need to be close and solvable only to those who *should* solve them. It was a time when all the latent capacities of the English language were put in requisition, and it was flashing and crackling through all its length and breadth, with puns and quips and conceits and jokes and satires, and inlined with philosophic secrets that opened down into the bottom of a tomb, that opened into the Tower, that opened on the scaffold and the block."[1] THIS was the " Delia Bacon theory." This was the " madness " forever associated with her plaintive story, and *not* the proposition that the author of the plays (whoever he might be—or they, if more than one) and William Shakespeare were persons—as distinctly two as were the noble Hamlet and the poor player who played " Gonzago " in the " Mousetrap " that day before the majesty of Denmark. But, madness or not, Miss Bacon never wavered in her conviction that the appointed time to read the oracles had come, and that *she*, Delia Bacon, a namesake, possibly, of the real Hamlet of the plays, had been raised in her appointed place to be the reader. Alas for her !

---

[1] " Philosophy of Shakespeare's Plays unfolded," p. x.

Like Cassandra, she announced her message only to be scorned and flouted in return !

By what whim of fortune or fancy the great plays had grown to be known as " Shakespeare's works," any more than Burbage's works, or Jonson's works, she never troubled herself to inquire ; but with the details of her mission she was careful to possess herself. She held that " the material evidence of her dogma as to the authorship, together with the key of the new philosophy, would be found buried in Shakespeare's grave."[1] She claims to have discovered, by careful study of Lord Bacon's letters, not only the key and clew to the whole mystery, but to an entire Baconian cipher In these letters—there were over five hundred of them extant, and others have been discovered, we believe, since Miss Bacon's day—however, it still remains, for the secret of Miss Bacon's clew died with her. But she stoutly maintained that in these letters were " definite and minute directions how to find a will and other documents relating to the conclave of Elizabethan philosophers, which were concealed in a hollow space in the under surface of Shakespeare's gravestone. . . . The directions, she intimated, were completely and precisely to the point, obviating all difficulties in the way of coming to the treasure, and so contrived as to ward off any troublesome consequences likely to arise from the interference of the parish officers. . . . There was the precious secret protected by a curse, as pirates used to bury their gold in the guardianship of a fiend."[2] The original manu-

---

[1] Hawthorne.

[2] Id. Delia Bacon was born in New Haven, in 1811, and early devoted herself to literature, writing two works " The Tales of

scripts of the plays she did not expect to find there.
These she believed the ignorant Shakespeare to have
scattered, after the blotless copies for the players had
been taken; to have devoted to domestic purposes, or
to have never concerned himself about further. This
was the gravamen of the charge she brought against
"Lord Leicester's groom," the co-manager, late of
Stratford, and this the vandalism for which she never
could forgive him. " This fellow," she cried, " never
cared a farthing for them, but only for his gains at
their hands. . . . What is to hinder his boiling his
kettle with the manuscripts . . . after he had done
with them? He had those manuscripts—the original
Hamlet, with its last finish; . . . the original Lear,
with his own fine readings . . . he had them all—
pointed, emphasized, corrected, as they came from the
gods! And he has left us to wear out our youth and
squander our life in poring over and setting right the
old garbled copies of the play-house! . . . For is he
not a private, economical, practical man, this Shakespeare of ours, with no stuff and nonsense about him;
a plain, true-blooded Englishman, who minds his own

the Puritans" and "The Bride of Fort Edward." She soon, however, abandoned miscellaneous writing and adopted the profession of a student and teacher of history, and began her career
as a lecturer on history in the city of Boston. Her method was
original with herself. She had models, charts, maps, and pictures to illustrate her subject; and we are told by Mrs. Farrar
(" Recollections of Seventy Years," Boston, Ticknor & Fields,
1866) that, being of a commanding presence and elegant delivery,
she was successful and attracted large audiences. Mrs. Farrar
says, " She looked like one of Dante's sibyls, and spoke like an
angel."

17

business, and leaves others to take care of theirs? . . .
What did he do with them? He gave them to his
cook, or Dr. Hall put up potions in them, or Judith—
poor Judith, who signified her relation to the author
of Lear and the Tempest, and her right to the glory
of the name he left her, by the very extraordinary
kind of 'mark' which she affixed to legal instruments
—poor Judith may have curled her hair with them to
the day of her death. . . . What did you do with
them? You have skulked this question long enough;
you will have to account for them! The awakening
ages will put you on the stand, and you will not leave
it until you answer the question, what did you do with
them?"[1]   This chain of dramas, so blindly perpetu-
ated by William Shakespeare, became, through Miss
Bacon's unlocking process, a great system of political
philosophy, dictated by the thoughtful Bacon and his
compeers, and locked up for the nineteenth century,
against the blindness of the centuries between.

But, of so startling a proposition, Miss Bacon
confesses that the world would require something
more than her own conviction. So she deliberately
set out to *prove*, from the very crypt and silence of the
grave itself, its truth. To St. Albans, whence the
mysterious letters were dated, to the lonesome tomb
at old Verulam and the vault in Stratford chancel, she
proposed a pilgrimage—thence to probe the secret,
and lay it open to a doubting world. "Her friends
regarded her theory as a delusion, and Miss Bacon as
a monomaniac. . . . They put their Shakespeares
out of sight when she approached, declined to listen

---

[1] "Putnam's Magazine," January, 1856.

to her conversations on the subject, and peremptorily
refused contributions to assist in her expedition. But,
by her lectures, and the friend she enlisted in her pro-
ject in New York City, she gathered together enough
money to get to London."[1]

It was while in London, in abject poverty and
friendlessness, that Thomas Carlyle, " upon whom she
had called and whom she had impressed with respect
for herself if not for her theory," says Hawthorne,
advised Miss Bacon to put her thoughts upon paper
first, before proceeding to the overt act of proof she
contemplated — namely, the opening of Willlam
Shakespeare's grave. It was upon his advice that
this most remarkable woman—sitting in bed in a
garret to keep warm without a fire, without sufficient
or wholesome food, " looking back," to use her own
words, " on the joys and sorrows of a world in which
I have no longer any place, like a departed spirit,"
and yet, doing " the world's work," and knowing
" that I had a right to demand aid for it "—undertook
to unfold out of the Shakespearean plays their hidden
system of philosophy." Meanwhile, under a contract
obtained for her by Mr. R. W. Emerson (though, it is
presumed, more for temporary supply of funds than
as rider to her great work), she furnished to " Putnam's Magazine " eighty pages of manuscript, which
became the famous paper " William Shakespeare and
his Plays," first announcing to the world the first anti-
Shakespearean theory of which it had ever heard.[2]

---

[1] Mrs. Farrar.

[2] This was contracted to be the first of a series of papers, but
the arrangement for some reason, probably because Miss Bacon
found it necessary to devote herself to the work to which she

Under such circumstances, and with such surroundings, this heroic woman accomplished the first half of
the work she had marked out for herself—the reading
of the sealed book, the unfolding of the philosophy
of the Shakespearean plays. Her book was written,
printed, published, and—damned![2] It failed so utterly

was to give her life, fell through, and no successive papers appeared in the magazine.

[2] "The Philosophy of Shakespeare's Plays unfolded. By Delia
Bacon." London: Sampson, Low & Co.; and Boston: Ticknor
& Fields, 1857. The book lies before us, and certainly is the
most difficult reading we ever attempted. Even so competent
and partial a critic as Hawthorne says of it: "Without prejudice
to her literary ability, it must be allowed that Miss Bacon was
wholly unfit to prepare her own work for publication, because,
among other reasons, she was too thoroughly in earnest to know
what to leave out. Every leaf and line was sacred, for all had
been written under so deep a conviction of truth, as to assume,
in her eyes, the aspect of inspiration. A practiced book-maker,
with entire control of her material, would have shaped out a
duodecimo volume, full of eloquent and ingenious dissertation—
criticisms which quite take the color and pungency out of other
people's critical remarks on Shakespeare. . . . There was a
great amount of rubbish, which any competent editor would
have shoveled out of the way. But Miss Bacon thrust the whole
bulk of inspiration and nonsense into the press in a lump, and
there tumbled out a ponderous octavo volume, which fell with
a dead thump at the feet of the public, and has never been
picked up. A few persons turned over one or two of the leaves,
as it lay there, and essayed to kick the volume deeper into the
mud. . . . I believe that it has been the faith of this remarkable book never to have had more than a single reader. I
myself am acquainted with it only in isolated chapters and scattered pages and paragraphs. But since my return to America,
a young man of genius and enthusiasm has assured me that he
has positively read the book from beginning to end, and is completely a convert to its doctrines. It belongs to him, therefore,

and miserably that nobody opened it, though that
fact deterred nobody, of course, from laughing at it
and its author to the utmost of their endeavor in ridi-
cule and abuse. "Our American journalists," says
Hawthorne, "at once republished some of the most
brutal vituperations of the English press, thus pelting
their poor countrywoman with stolen mud, without
even waiting to know whether the ignominy was deserved, and they never have known it to this day, and
never will." But none the less did Delia Bacon per-
severe to the end. The philosophy was unfolded. If
the world declined to receive the truth—"the truth,"
as she claimed, "that is neither yours nor mine, but
yours *and* mine"—it was not on her head, at least, that
the consequences would fall. The second half of her
work remained. She proceeded to Stratford to crown
her labors, by opening the vault in the chancel of the
parish church, and exposing the secret she had already
guessed, to the doubting Thomasses who clamored for
the tactual evidence so long entombed there.

Although on a mission so likely to be regarded as
predatory—as even coming under police prohibition,
Miss Bacon seems to have lived in open avowal of her
purpose, under the very shadows of the church she
meant to despoil, and to have made nothing but
friends. The regard was mutual, and, says Hawthorne,

---

and not to me, whom, in almost the last letter that I received
from her, she declared unworthy to meddle with her work—it
belongs surely to this one individual, who has done her so much
justice as to know what she wrote, to place Miss Bacon in her due
position before the public." ("Our Old Home.") The volume
is obtained to-day, only by chance, in old bookshops and at such
prices as the bookseller may choose to demand.

"she loved the slumberous town, and awarded the only
praise that I ever knew her to bestow on Shakespeare,
the individual man, by acknowledging that his taste
in selecting a residence was good, and that he knew
how to choose a suitable retirement for a person of shy
but genial temperament." She laid her plans before
the vicar, who, so far as Miss Bacon ever was permitted to learn, never opposed them.[1] At least he did
not hand her over to the first Dogberry at hand—a
most un-English omission on his part. He did, however, ask Miss Bacon's leave to consult a friend, "who
proved to be legal counsel," and who, doubtless, advised inaction, for the matter was allowed, so far as
the lady was concerned, to retain the form of a pend-
ing negotiation with the parish, never, as a matter of
fact, broken off on its part. The rest is best told in
Mr. Hawthorne's dramatic narrative: "The affair
looked certainly very hopeful. However erroneously,
Miss Bacon had understood from the vicar that no
obstacle would be interposed to the investigation, and
that he himself would sanction it with his presence.
It was to take place after nightfall; and, all preliminary arrangements being made, the vicar and the
clerk professed to wait only her word, in order to set
about lifting the awful stone from its sepulchre. . .
She examined the surface of the gravestone, and en-

---

[1] I cannot help fancying, however, that her familiarity with
the events of Shakespeare's life, and of his death and burial
(of which she would speak as if she had been present at the
the edge of the grave), and all the history, literature, and per-
sonalties of the Elizabethan age, together with the prevailing
power of her own belief, had really gone some little way toward
making a convert of the good clergyman.—*Hawthorne.*

deavored, without stirring it, to estimate whether it were of such thickness as to be capable of containing the archives of the Elizabethan Club. She went over anew the proofs, the clews, the enigmas, the pregnant sentences, which she had discovered in Bacon's letters and elsewhere. . . . She continued to hover around the church, and seems to have had full freedom of entrance in the day-time, and special license, on one occasion at least, at a late hour at night. She went thither with a dark lantern, which could but twinkle like a glow-worm through the volume of obscurity that filled the great, dusky edifice. Groping her way up the aisle, and toward the chancel, she sat down on the elevated part of the pavement above Shakespeare's grave. She made no attempt to disturb the grave, though, I believe, she looked narrowly into the crevices between Shakespeare's and the two adjacent stones, and in some way satisfied herself that her single strength would suffice to lift the former, in case of need. She threw the feeble rays of her lantern up toward the bust, but could not make it visible beneath the darkness of the vaulted roof. . . . Several times she heard a low movement in the aisle; a stealthy, dubious footfall prowling about in the darkness, now here, now there, among the pillars and ancient tombs, as if some restless inhabitant of the latter had crept forth to peep at the intruder. By and by the clerk made his appearance, and confessed that he had been watching her ever since she entered the church." This was the nearest she came to the overt act, all thought of which was finally abandoned; for, meanwhile, worn out with the absorbing mental activity of these last years, and her physical privations (she had only ar-

rived in Stratford in a condition so feeble and pros-
trated as to have believed herself beyond any necessity
of providing any further earthly sustenance; the
failure of her book and the miscarriage of her plans
did the rest), she finally consented to be borne back
to her home to die peacefully at the last, among friends.
Her life and her "theory" are only to be discussed
together, and both with tenderness. "Was there ever
a more wonderful phenomenon?" exclaims Hawthorne—"a system of philosophy, growing up in this
woman's mind, without her volition, contrary, in fact, to
the determined resistance of her volition, and substi-
tuting itself in the place of everything that originally
grew there! To have based such a system on fancy,
and unconsciously elaborated it for herself, was almost
as wonderful as really to have found it in the plays
. . . it certainly came from no inconsiderable depth
somewhere."

This was, so far as she herself put it on paper, Miss
Delia Bacon's theory. It is to be carefully noticed,
however, that it is a theory, not of a UNITARY but of a
JOINT authorship. There is one passage in the "Putnam's Magazine" article (which at that time was announced by the publishers as the first of a series of
papers, and was so intended by Miss Bacon) which
points to Bacon as the supposed sole author of the
plays. But, in the book which followed it, these plays
are repeatedly assigned to a conclave or junta of Elizabethan courtiers and scholars, and such was the faith,
we believe, in which Miss Bacon labored and died.

The UNITARY theory, we believe not unfairly, may
be assigned to Messrs. Smith and Holmes; the latter
of whom, in the preface to his work, most distinctly

rejects Miss Bacon's "junta" authorship, and undertakes to maintain the proposition that Bacon, and Bacon alone, was the author of the whole canon of "Shakespeare." According to Judge Holmes, Bacon had reasons in plenty for concealing his authorship, and for "loving better to be a poet than to be accounted one." Not only his personal safety :— Dr. Heywood was already in the tower for having incensed the Queen by an unlucky pamphlet dedicated to Essex; and "not long after this," says Holmes, "and while Essex is under arrest, and Bacon in sundry interviews with the Queen, is still interceding in his behalf, her Majesty brings up against him this affair of Dr. Heywood's book, and also, as it would seem, distinctly flings at Bacon himself about 'a matter which grew from him, but went after about in other's names (in fact no other than the play Richard II. we have to-day)." But the development of his plans made concealment particularly desirable. Political rivals were watching jealously his every utterance. He is known to be a "concealed poet," so he prepares a masque or two for the queen's own eye and audience; but he alone, according to Judge Holmes, writes "Shakespeare." "Had the plays (says Mr. Furness) come down to us anonymously—had the labor of discovering the author been imposed upon future generations, we could have found no one of that day but Francis Bacon to whom to assign the crown. In this case it would have been resting now upon his head by almost common consent." It is well! that this essential difference between the "DELIA BACON" and the "BACONIAN" theories should be emphasized here.

PART V.

THE BACONIAN THEORY.

HE English Renaissance Drama seems naturally to group itself into two grand divisions: the Elizabethan drama and—SHAKESPEARE. There is nothing in the first which surprises: which impresses us as too abrupt a departure from the brutish coarseness and grossness of the middle age mummeries—"miracle plays" and "mysteries"—or as being too refined or elaborate for the groundlings who swaggered and swilled beer, or the lords and maids of honor who ogled and flirted in the contemporary barns called "play-houses" in the days of Elizabeth. But that the proprietor of one of these barns should have found it to his profit to have overshot the intelligence of his audience by creating a Hamlet, a Lear, Brutus, and Macbeth—the action of whose roles are intellectual rather than scenic—for his players, or an Ophelia, Isabella, or Catharine for the small boys employed to render his female parts, is an incongruity—to put it mildly—which arrests our credulity at once.

The utmost that the Shakespeareans propose to do—the utmost they attempt—is to make out William Shakespeare to have been an Elizabethan Dramatist. But the Elizabethan Dramatist was a man who catered to the Elizabethan play-goer. Greene, Peele, Lodge, Nash, and the rest, were Elizabethan Dramatists. But

their names are only a catalogue to-day. If we happen to buy a set of their works at a bargain, at some
old book sale, we may put them on our shelves; but
we are not equal to the laborious task of reading
them. The ˆShakespearean Drama is a thing apart.
Its Dramatic form seems only an Incident; perfect as
that Incident is, there is so much more in it that we
find appealing to our hearts and intellects to-day, that
we hesitate to ascribe it even to an Elizabethan Dramatist. The Baconian theory, as elaborated by Holmes,
we understand to be that this element apart from the
Dramatic, in these days is the key-note and explanation of the whole Shakespeare mystery, and leads to
the discovery that "Shakespeare" was only a convenient name under which the popular ear was sought
to be arrested by a Philosopher, who wrote in cipher,
as it were, for a great purpose of his own.

The philosophical system contemplated by Francis
Bacon—say the Baconians—was divided into two
grand Divisions, the Didactic and the Historical. The
first—its author (despairing of contemporary fame, or
possibly distrustful of the permanence of the vernacular) locked up in the universal language of scholars,
and left it by his testament to "the next ages." The
other he chose to put into Dramatic form. The spirit,
motive, theme, and purport of two great phenomena
of English letters, synchronizing in date (the philosop-
ical canon of Bacon and the dramatic canon of
"Shakespeare,") are IDENTICAL, and form together es-
sentially ONE great body of philosophy and inductive
science, and, therefore, must have had the one author.
"It is a thing, indeed, if practiced professionally, of
low repute; but if it be made a part of discipline, it

is of excellent use—I mean stage playing," he says himself. And again: "Dramatic poetry is as history made visible." This Historical or preliminary division of the Philosophy did not need a dead, but a living language—the language of his race. This he left in English: and when, at the end, a broken, weak, despised old man—knowing himself only too well to be the meanest and weakest of his kind; but yet conscious of having, in a large sense, worked for the good of his fellow-men—he made no excuse or palliation, but only bespoke for himself and his life " men's charitable speeches."

But, if there was but one author for these two contemporary works, why not William Shakespeare as well as Francis Bacon? Why not ask the question, "Did William Shakespeare write Lord Bacon's works?"[1] as well as, "Did Lord Bacon write William Shakespeare's work?" While not within our scope to demonstrate the identical philosophy of the Novum Organum and the Shakespearean Drama—(a work to which Miss Bacon devoted her life—and whose demonstration has been followed by Judge Holmes)—it is properly within that scope to examine, from the outside, the question whether, as matter of fact, William Shakespeare could have written either; or whether, from circumstantial evidence merely, Lord Bacon was thus, and in pursuance of a great purpose, actually the author of the Dramatic canon of " Shakespeare."

Now, aside from any *opinion* as to their value, beauty, or eloquence, there are two characteristics of

[1] See this question asked and answered affirmatively in " North American Review." February, 1881. New York. D. Appleton & Co.

the Shakespearean works which, under the calmest
and most sternly judicial treatment to which they
could possibly be subjected, are so prominent as to be
beyond gainsay or neglect. These two characteristics
are—1. The encyclopædic universality of their information as to matters of fact; and, 2. The scholarly
refinement of the style displayed in them. Their claim
to eloquence and beauty of expression, after all, is a
question of taste; and we may conceive of whole peo-
ples—as, for example, the Zulus or the Ashantees—
impervious to any admiration for the Shakesperean
plays on that account. But this familiarity with what,
at their date, was the Past of history, and—up to that
date—the closed book of past human discovery and
research which we call Learning; is an open and indisputable fact; and the New-Zealander who shall sit
on a broken arch of London Bridge and muse over the
ruins of British civilization, if he carry his researches
back to the Shakespearean literature, will be obliged
to find that its writer was in perfect possession·of the
scholarship antecedent to his own date, and of the ac-
cumulated learning of the world down to his own actual day. Moreover, this scholar would not be compelled to this decision only by a careful examination of
the entire Shakespearean opera. He will be forced to
so conclude on an examination of any one, or, at the
most, of any given group of single plays. Let him
open at random, and fall upon, let us say, the "Julius
Cæsar." [1] Even the artificial Alexander Pope (who,
so far from being an over-estimator of the Shakes-

---

[1] See in this connection "The English of Shakespeare illus-
trated in a Philological commentary on his 'Julius Cæsar.' By
G. L. Craik." London. Chapman & Hall. 1857.

pearean works, only, from the heights of his superior
plane, admits them very grudgingly to a rank beside
the works of Waller) was obliged to confess as much.
"This Shakespeare," says Mr. Pope, "must have been
very knowing in the customs, rites, and manners of
antiquity. In 'Coriolanus' and 'Julius Cæsar,' not
only the spirit, but the manner of the Romans is exactly drawn; and still a nicer distinction is shown between the manners of the Romans in the time of
the former and of the latter. No one is more a master of the poetical story, or has more frequent allusions
to the various parts of it. Mr. Waller (who has been
celebrated for this last particular) has not shown more
learning in this way than Shakespeare,"[1] But, if the
New-Zealander be a philologist, he will scarcely need
perusal of more than a Shakespearean page to arrive
at this judgment. Wherever else the verdict of scholarship may err, the microscope of the philologist cannot err. Like the skill of the chirographical expert,
it is infallible, because, just as the hand of a writer,
however cramped, affected, or disguised, will unconsciously make its native character of curve or inclina-
tion, so the speech of a man will be molded by his
familiarity, be it greater or less, with the studies, learning, tastes, and conceits of his own day, and by the
models before him. He cannot unconsciously follow
models that are unknown to him, or speak in a language he has never learned. Young Chatterton deceived the most profound scholars of his day, and his
manuscripts stood every test but this; but under it
they revealed the fact, so soon to receive the mournful

---

[1] Smith, p. 86.

corroboration of history, that they were only the forgeries of a precocious boy. To just as moral a certainty
are the handiwork of the Elohist and the Jehovist discernible in the Hebrew Scriptures, and just as absolutely incapable of an alternative explanation are the
ear-marks of the Shakespearean text. Hallam, whose
eyes were never opened to the truth, and who lived
and died innocent of any anti-Shakespearean theory
(though he sighed for a "Shakespeare of heaven,"
turning in disgust from the "Shakespeare of earth,"
of whom only he could read in history), noticing the
phrases, unintelligible and improper except in the
sense of their primitive roots, which occur so copiously
in the plays, proceeds to say: "In the 'Midsummer-
Night's Dream' these are much less frequent than in
his later dramas; but here we find several instances.
Thus, 'Things base and vile, holding no *quantity*' (for
value); rivers that 'have overborne their *continents*'
(the *continenti riva* of Horace); '*compact* of imagination;' 'something of great *constancy*' (for *consistency*);
'sweet Pyramus *translated* there;' 'the law of Athens,
which by no means we may *extenuate*,' etc. I have considerable doubts," continues Mr. Hallam, "whether any
of these expressions would be found in the contemporary prose of Elizabeth's reign, which was less over-
run with pedantry than that of her successor. Could
authority be produced for Latinisms so forced, it is still
not very likely that one who did not understand their
proper meaning would have introduced them into
poetry."[1] When we remember the coarseness of

---

[1] "Literature of Europe," Part II, ch. vi, sec. 81. "To be told
that he played a trick to a brother player in a licentious amour, or
that he died in a drunken frolic . . does not exactly inform

social speech in those days, even in the highest walks
of life—we happen to have very graphic accounts of
Queen Elizabeth's sayings and retorts courteous (as,
e. g., when she boxed Essex's ears and told him to go
and be hanged)—it requires considerable credulity to
assign this classic diction to a rustic apprentice from
Stratford, who, at "about eighteen," begins his dramatic labors, fresh from the shambles, and with no
hiatus for a college course between.

Add to this the patent fact that the antique allusions in the plays " have not regard to what we may
call ' school classics,' but to authors seldom perused but
by profound scholars " [1] even to-day : and technical exploration, however far it proceeds beyond this in the
Shakespearean text, can bring evidence only cumulative as to the result already obtained.   But, if we pass
from the technical structure to the material of the
plays, we are confronted with the still more amazing
discovery that, not only the lore of the past was at the
service of their author, but that he had no less an access to secrets supposed to be locked in the very womb
of Time, the discoveries of which, in the as yet distant future, were to immortalize their first sponsors.
For example, Dr. Harvey does not announce—what is
credited to him [2]—his discovery of the circulation of

---

us of the man who wrote " Lear."   If there was a Shakespeare
of earth, as I suspect, there was also one of heaven, and it is of
him that we desire to know something."   Id. Part II, ch. vi, sec.
35, note.

[1] Smith, p. 85.

[2] Though not, perhaps, universally now-a-days.   The late John
Elliotson declared that the circulation through the lungs had
certainly been taught seventy years previously by Servetus, who
was burned at the stake in 1553.   Dr. Robert Willis asserts, in

the blood in the human system—until 1619 (his book was not published until 1628), three years after William Shakespeare's death. But why need Dr. Harvey have resorted to vivisection to make his "discovery"? He need only have taken down his "Shakespeare." Is there any thing in Dr. Harvey any more exactly definite than the following?

> "I send it through the rivers of your blood,
> Even to the court, the heart, to the seat o' the brain,
> And through the cranks and offices of man:
> The strongest nerves, and small inferior veins,
> From me receive that natural competency
> Whereby they live."
> —*Coriolanus, Act I, Scene 1.*

> ". . . had baked thy blood, and made it heavy-thick
> (Which, else, runs tickling up and down the veins").
> —*King John, Act III, Scene 3.*

---

his "Life of Harvey," that the facts he used were familiarly known to most of his predecessors for a century previous. Izaak Walton states that Harvey got the idea of circulation from Walter Warner, the mathematician; and that eminent physician, John Hunter, remarks that Servetus first, and Realdus Columbus afterward, clearly announced the circulation of the blood through the lungs; and Cisalpinus, many years before Harvey, published, in three different works, all that was wanting in Servetus to make the circulation complete. Wotton says that Servetus was the first, as far as he could learn, who had a distinct idea of this matter. Even the Chinese were impressed with this truth some four thousand years before Europeans dreamed of it. Plato affirmed —"the heart being the knot of the veins, and the fountain from whence the blood arises and briskly circulates through all the members." This, however, rather adds to than lessens the strength of the argument drawn from finding the "discovery" in the plays.

18

". . . As dear to me as are the ruddy drops
That visit my sad heart."
—*Julius Cæsar, Act II, Scene* 1.

Harvey's discovery, however, is said to have been
the theory of Galen, Paracelsus, and Hippocrates
(who substituted the *liver* for the *heart*), and to have
been held also by Rabelais. Neither Galen, Paracelsus, Hippocrates, nor Rabelais was a text-book at
Stratford grammar-school during the two terms Mr.
De Quincey placed William Shakespeare as a pupil
there—but William has them at his fingers' ends.
There are said to be no less than seventy-eight passages in the plays wherein this fact of the circulation
of the blood is distinctly alluded to; and, as to Galen
and Paracelsus, they intrude themselves unrestrictedly
all through the plays, without the slightest pretext or
excuse:

"*Parolles.* So I say; both of Galen and Paracelsus.
Lafeu Of all the learned and authentic fellows."
—*All's Well that Ends Well, Act II, Scene* 3.

"*Host of the Garter Inn.* What says my Æsculapius? my Galen?"
—*Merry Wives of Windsor, Act II., Scene* 3.

In King HenryIVf. Part II., Act ii, Scene 2, the eru-
dite Bardolph and Falstaff's classical page make a
learned blunder about Althea, whom the page con-
founds with Hecuba. And so on. Are we to believe
that this sometime butcher's boy and later stage manager has his head so brimming full of his old Greeks
and philosophers that he can not for a moment miss
their company, and makes his very panders and public-
cans prate of them? Even if it were the commonest

thing in the world, nowadays, in 1881, for our Mr. Boucicault or Mr. Daly to write a play expressly to catch the taste of the canaille of the Old Bowery (or, for that matter, of the urbane and critical audiences of Wallack's or the Union Square), and stuff all the low-comedy parts with recondite and classical allusion (for this is precisely what William Shakespeare is said to have done for the unroofed play-house in the mud of the Bankside in London, some three hundred years ago or less, and to have coined a fortune at)—even, we say, if it were the simplest thing in the world to imagine this sort of playwriting to-day, would it be a wilder flight of fancy to suggest a pale student in London in the days of Queen Elizabeth, somewhere among the garrets of Gray's Inn, writing dialogues into which Galen and Paracelsus would intrude unbidden—and a stage manager letting them stay there as doing no harm (or, may be, taking them for names of dogs or wenches—at any rate, as good, mouth-filling words, to be paid for at the lowest market price):[1] than to conceive a twelfth manager and proprietor of this home of the Muses, and whilom sticker of calves, after the day's labor, shunning his cups and the ribald mirth-making of those sad dogs, his fellow-

---

[1] Shakespeare married a woman older than himself. Why should he call attention to the fact, publish it to the rabble, or record it on his stage whenever he found opportunity?

See Midsummer-Night's Dream," Act I, Scene 1—"O, spite, too old to be engaged to young!" etc. Again—"Too old, by Heaven! Let still the woman take an elder than herself." Again—"Then let thy love be younger than thyself," etc., etc. ("Twelfth Night," Act II., Scene 4.)

It is very difficult to suppose that Shakespeare should have wantonly in public insulted his own wife (however he might

managers, to seek, in the solitude of his library and
Greek manuscripts, the choice companionship of this
same Galen and Paracelsus?

Newton, who was only born in 1642—twenty years
after Shakespeare was laid away in his tomb—surely
need not have lain under his appletree in the orchard
at Woolsthorpe, waiting for the falling fruit to reveal
the immutable truth of gravitation. He had but to
take down his copy of "Troilus and Cressida"
(printed in 1606) to open to the law itself, as literally
stated as he himself could have formulated it:

" *Cressida.* . . But the strong base and building of my love
Is as the very center of the earth,
Drawing all things to it."
         —*Troilus and Cressida, Act IV., Scene 2.*

Are we called upon to tax our common sense to
fancy our manager, on one of his evenings at home,
after the play at the Globe was over, snugly in his
library, out of hearing of the ribaldry of his fellows
over their cups, stumbling upon the laws of the circulation of the blood and of gravitation, engrossing
them "without blotting out a line," and sending
the " copy " to the actors so that they could commit
it to memory for the stage on the following evening?

What a library it was—that library up among the
flies (if they had such things) of the old Globe Theater! What an Elihu Burritt its owner must have
been, to have snatched from his overworked life—from
the interval between the night's performance and the

snub her in private); though it is very easy to imagine his passing it over in another man's manuscript in hurried perusal in
the green-room."—*Chambers's Journal, August* 7, 1852, *p.* 89.

morning's routine—the hours to labor over Galen and Paracelsus and Plato in the original Greek! It was miracle enough that the learned blacksmith at his forge, in the nineteenth century—surrounded with libraries, and when books could be had for the purchasing—could have mastered all the known languages. But that William Shakespeare, with only two terms at Stratford school, (or, let us say, twenty years at Stratford School, or at the University of Oxford—for there is as much evidence that he was at Oxford as that he was at Stratford school) *without* books, since there were no books purchasable, should have known every thing that was written in books! Surely there never was such a miracle as this!

"He was the prophet of geology," says Fullom,[1] before it found an exponent in Werner;"

> "O Heaven! that one might read the book of fate;
> And see the revolution of the times
> Make mountains level, and the continent
> (Weary of solid firmness) melt itself
> Into the sea! and, other times, to see
> The beechy girdle of the ocean
> Too wide for Neptune's hips."[2]

And yet William Shakespeare had but two terms of Hunt, Jenkins and Stratford school! And, Mr. Malone believed, had never even gone so far into the classics as to have read Tacitus![3]

What was, or was not, taught at this marvelous

---

[1] "History of William Shakespeare, Player and Poet, with New Facts and Traditions." By W. S. Fullom, London: Saunders, Otley & Co., 66 Brook street, 1864.

[2] "King Henry IV.," Part II., Act 3, Scene i.

[3] See ante, p. 88.

Stratford school, "two terms" of which—between his poaching and his beer-bouting—were all the schooling William Shakespeare ever had, according to all his biographies. (We say, all he ever had, because his father was so illiterate that he signed every thing with a mark, and so did his mother, and so did the rest of William's family; and the boy William was too busy at skylarking—according to those who knew him—to have had much opportunity of private instruction at the parental knee, even had the parental acquirements been adequate.)   Were the theory and practice of the common law taught there?   "Legal phrases flow from his pen," says Mr. Grant White, "as a part of his vocabulary and parcel of his thought. . . . This conveyancer's jargon ('fine and recovery,' 'tenure,' 'fee simple,' 'fee farm,' etc., etc.) could not have been picked up by hanging around the courts in London, two hundred and fifty years ago, when suits as to the title of real property were comparatively rare.   And, besides, Shakespeare uses his law just as freely in his early plays, written in his first London years, as in those produced at a later period."[1]   And not only in the technique, but in the groundwork of "that mighty and abstruse science, the law of England," is he perfect.   A chief justice of England has declared that "while novelists and dramatists are constantly making mistakes as to the law of marriage, of wills, and of inheritance, to Shakespeare's law, lavishly as he expounded it, there can neither be demurrer, nor bill of exceptions, nor writ of error."[2]   Were medicine and

---

[1] "Memoir," p. 47.   And see "Was Shakespeare a Lawyer?" By H. T——.   London: Longmans, Green, Reader & Dyer, 1871.

[2] "Shakespeare's Legal Acquirements," Lord Campbell, p. 108.

surgery taught there? Dr. Bucknill[1] asserted in 1860 that it has been possible to compare Shakespeare's knowledge with the most advanced knowledge of the present day. And not only in the general knowledge of a lawyer and a physician, but in what we call in these days "medical jurisprudence," the man that wrote the historical play of Henry IV. seems to have been an expert. Mr. David Paul Brown[2] says that in "Frost's case" (a cause celebre of his day), on a trial for murder, the defense set up that the deceased had committed suicide. A celebrated physician being on the stand as an expert on this question, was examined as follows:

Q. What are the general indications of death from violence?

A. My knowledge will not enable me to answer so broad a question.

And yet Mr. Brown points out that "William Shakespeare's knowledge had enabled him" to answer so "broad a question:"

> "WARWICK. See how the blood is settled in his face!
> Oft have I seen a timely parted ghost
> Of ashy semblance, meagre, pale and bloodless.
> * * * * * * *
> But see, his face is black and full of blood;
> His eyeballs further out than when he lived,
> Staring full ghastly, like a strangled man;
> His hair upreared, his nostrils stretched with struggling;

And see "Shakespeare a Lawyer," by W. L. Rushton. London, 1858.

[1] "Medical Knowledge of Shakespeare." J. C. Bucknill, M. D. London, 1860. And see Appendix I.

[2] The Forum. By David Paul Brown. Philadelphia, 1856.

His hands abroad displayed, as one that grasped
And tugged for life, and was by strength subdued.
   *   *   *   *   *   *   *
It can not be but he was murdered here;
The least of all these signs were probable."[1]

All the arts, sciences, and literatures must have been
mastered by our sleepless Shakespeare, either at Stratford school, or in the midst of his London career,
when operating two theaters, reading plays for his
stage, editing them, engrossing the parts for his actors,
and acting himself. (And Mr. Cohn will have it
that in these unaccounted-for times, he had visited
Germany with his troupe and performed in all its principal cities, coining money as he went.)[2] Mr. Brown,
Dr. Bell, and others, announce that they believe that
these travels of his extended to Italy, and Mr. Thoms
and Mr. Cohn, to some extent, account for Shakespeare
on the continent, by believing that, instead of going at
once to London, when fleeing from Stratford before
Sir Thomas Lucy, he enlisted under Leicester for the
Netherlands in 1585, but left the ranks for the more
lucrative career of an actor. But these theories only
crowd still more thickly the brief years in which the
great works (which are, after all, what the world regards in these investigations), appeared. Either at
Stratford school, or in the Blackfriars, or else by pure

---

[1] 2 Henry VI., Act 3, scene ii.
[2] " Shakespeare in Germany. By Albert Cohn. London and
Berlin: Asher & Co., 1865. And see Shakespeare's Autographical
Poems, by Charles Armitage Brown. Essays on Shakespeare, by
Karl Elze. London, Macmillan & Co., 1874. The Suppose
Travels of Shakespeare. Three Notelets on Shakespeare.
Thoms: London, 1865.

intuition, all this exact learning must have been absorbed.

The classical course conducted by Hunt and Jenkins must have been far more advanced than is common in our modern colleges, in Columbia or Harvard, for example. For not only did Rowe and Knight find traces in "Shakespeare" of the Electra of Sophocles, Colman of Ovid, Farmer of Horace and Virgil, Steevens of Plautus, and White of Euripides, which are read to-day in those universities; but Pope found traces of Dares and Phrygius, and Malone of Lucretius, Statns and Catullus, which are not ordinarily used as text-books to-day in our colleges.

The name and character of "Imogen" is derived from an Italian novel not then—and perhaps not how—translated into English. Tschischwitz finds in "Hamlet" the philosophy of Giordano Bruno, professor at Wittemberg in 1583–86. All these are no stumbling-blocks to those who adhere to the Baconian authorship.

But, Spanish, Italian, Greek and Latin aside, was English taught at Stratford school? If it were, it would have been the most wonderful of all, for, as a matter of fact in those days, and for many long years thereafter, English was a much snubbed acquirement. The idea of education was to read, talk, and quote Latin, Greek, and the dead languages, the child was put to his "accidence," instead of his horn-book, and scholars scorned to spend much time on their own vernacular. But even should we concede that it was genius that made the village boy master of a diction the grandest of which his mother tongue was capable, there is a greater difficulty beyond, over which

19

the concession will not lift us. This difficulty has
been so succinctly stated by Mr. Grant White, in his
" Essay Toward the Expression of Shakespeare's Genius," that we can not do better than quote his words.
" It was only in London that those plays could have
been written. London had but just before Shakespeare's day made its metropolitan supremacy felt as
well as acknowledged throughout England. As long
as two hundred years after that time the county of each
member of Parliament was betrayed by his tongue.
. . . . Northumberland, or Cornwall, or Lancashire
might have produced Shakespeare's mind; but had
he lived in any one of those counties, or in another,
like them remote in speech as in locality from London,
and written for his rural neighbors instead of for the
audiences of the Blackfriars and the Globe, the music
of his poetry would have been lost in sounds uncouth
and barbarous to the general ear, the edge of his fine
utterance would have been turned upon the stony
roughness of his rustic phraseology. His language
would have been a dialect which must needs have
been translated to be understood by modern English
ears." [1]   As Mr. White wrote these words, did it not
occur to him that, by his own chronology,[2] this Warwickshire rustic came to London with " Venus and
Adonis " in his pocket, and began, almost immediately,
the production of plays, not in the Warwickshire dialect, which he had grown up in from his birth, but
in a diction that needs no translating " to be understood by modern English ears? " Robert Burns became

[1] Shakespeare's Works, Vol. I., p. cxcvi.
[2] Id., p. cxxi.

great in the dialect of his home, which he made into
music through the alembic of his genius. When, later
in life, he essayed to write in metropolitan English,
says Principal Shairp, "he was seldom more than a
third-rate—a common clever versifier."[1] But this uncouth Warwickshire rustic writes, as his first essay in
English composition, the most elegant verses the age
produced, and which for polish and care surpass his
very latest works! Every step in the received Shakespeare's life appears to have been a miracle: for, according to them, the boy Shakespeare needed to be taught
nothing, but was born versed in every art, tongue,
knowledge, and talent, and did every thing without
tuition or preparation.

And in the long vacation of this precious school
how much our worthy pupil—whose paternal parent
was in hiding from his creditors so that he dare not be
seen at church—supplemented its curriculum by
feasts of foreign travel! For it is only the careful
student of these plays who knows or conceives either
their wealth of exact reference to the minutest
features of the lands or the localities in which their
actions lie, or the conclusions to be drawn there-
from. There were no guide-books or itineraries of
Venice published until after William Shakespeare
had ceased writing for the stage: and yet, while school-
boy facts—such as that Venice is built in the sea, or
that gondolas take the place of wheeled vehicles, or
that there is a leaning tower at Pisa, or a coliseum at
Verona or Rome—are not referred to (the out-door
action in "Othello" or the "Merchant of Venice" is

---

[1] "English Men of Letters. Robert Burns.

always in a street or open place in that city, canals
and gondolas being never mentioned), the most casual,
inadvertant, and trivial details of Italian matters
(such as a mere tourist, however he might have observed, would scarcely have found of enough interest
to mention to his neighbors on returning home), are
familiarly and incidentally alluded to, making the phenomena of all this familiarity with Italy quite too
prominent to be overlooked.   A poet like Samuel
Rogers writes a poem on Italy.   All that is massive,
venerable, and sublime; all that touches his heart as
pitiful, or appeals to his nature as sensuous and romantic, goes down in his poem.   The scenes Mr. Rogers depicts are those which crowd most upon the cultivated tourist to-day—the past of history that must stir
the soul to enthusiasm.   But here are plays, written
before the days of guide-books (and if there had been
any such things, they would have enlarged upon the
same features that Mr. Rogers did), which are at home
in the unobserved details which the fullest Murray or
Baedeker find it unnecessary to mention.   Portia
sends her servant Balthazar to fetch "notes and gar-
ments" of her learned cousin, Bellario, and to meet
her at the "common ferry which trades to Venice."
There are two characters named "Gobbo" in the play
—a frequent Venetian name in a certain obscure walk,
and one which a mere tourist would be most unlikely
to meet with.   Othello brings Desdemona from her
father's house to his residence in the "Sagittary."
In "Two Gentlemen of Verona," Valentine is made to
embark at Verona for Milan, and in "Hamlet," Baptista
is used as the name of a woman.   Both of these latter
were sneered at as mistakes for some hundred years,

until one learned German discovers that Baptista is not uncommonly used as a woman's name in Italy,[1] and another learned German that, in the sixteenth century, Milan and Verona were actually connected by canals,[2] with which the surface of Italy was intersected![2] etc., etc. Dr. Elze was made a careful collation of these instances (which need not detain us here except by way of reference), in an essay on the supposed travels of Shakespeare,[2] wherein he, from the same internal evidence, regards it certain that the writer (William Shakespeare he calls him), not only visited Italy, but Scotland, absorbing all he saw with the same microscopical exactness.

And were the modern languages also taught by this myriad-minded Jenkins? Mr. Grant White says emphatically, No! "Italian and French, we may be sure, were *not* taught at Stratford school."[3] And yet William Shakespeare borrowed copiously from Boccaccio, Cinthio, and Belleforest.

Ulrici[4] says (quoting Klein) that the author of "Romeo and Juliet" must have read "Hadriana," a tragedy by an Italian named Groto, and Mr. Grant White points out that Iago's speech, "Who steals my purse, steals trash," etc., is a perfect paraphrase of a stanza in Berni's "Orlando Innamorato," of which poem, says Mr. White, to this day (1864) there is no English version. Mr. White furnishes a translation of

---

[1] A Von Beumont. Allgemeine Zeitung, Oct. 21, 1870.

[2] Karl Elze on Shakespeare, p. 296. London. Macmillan & Co. 1874.

[3] Memoir. Works, p. xxi.

[4] Vol. I, p. 253.

the stanza of Berni, which is certainly startingly like.[1]
And yet Mr. White clings to his Stratford school,
where " Beeston " told Aubrey that William Shakespeare was once a school-master.   Perhaps Mr. White
refuses to be converted because he has discovered that
Dr. Farmer discovered that, when, in the " Taming of
the Shrew," Tranio quotes Terence, " he is inaccurate,
and gives the passage, not as it appears in the text of
the Latin dramatist, but as it is misquoted in the Latin
grammar of William Lily; a school-book in common use among our forefathers when William Shakespeare was a boy."[2]   But (though somebody has suggested that William might have risen to be " head boy"
at Stratford grammar school; and been, in that capacity,
intrusted with hearing the lessons of the smaller boys,
whence the school-master story may have arisen), the
Beeston story has been rejected by all the commentators with a unanimity of which, we believe, it is the
only instance, in case of a Shakespearean detail.   So
far as we know, there has been but one effort to prove
that William Shakespeare was a university man.[3]
But if, instead of going to school, or operating a
theater, William had passed his days as a journeyman
printer, he could hardly have been more at home to
the mysteries of that craft.   Mr. Blades, a practical
printer, has found in the Works so many terms, technical to and employed in the exact sense of the composing and press-rooms, that they seriously add to

[1] Ante, p. 64, note.
[2] Id. p. xx.
[3] "Some Shakespearean and Spenserian MSS.," "American
Whig Review," December, 1851.

the enumeration of possible Shakesperean vocations. For example:

> " Behold, my Lords,
> Although the PRINT be little, the whole MATTER
> And COPY of the father,
> The very MOULD and FRAME of hand, nail, finger."

Witness, also, the following:

> " You are but as a FORM in wax, by him IMPRINTED.
> —*Midsummer-Night's Dream, I*, 1.

> " His heart, with your PRINT impressed.
> —*Love's Labours Lost, II*, 1.

A small type, called nonpareil, was introduced into English printing houses from Holland about the year 1650, and became admired and preferred beyond the others in common use. It seems to have become a favorite type with Shakespeare, who calls many of his lady characters " Nonpareils." Prospero calls his daughter "a Nonpareil." (Tempest, Act III, Scene 2d) Olivia, in " Twelfth Night," is the " Nonpareil of Beauty" (Act I, Scene 5), and in Cymbeline, Posthumous is made to call Imogen the " Nonpareil of her time" (Act II, Scene 5).

When a certain number of pages of type have been composed they are placed in an iron frame called a " chase," laid upon an " imposing" stone, a piece of beveled wood, called a " sidestick," is placed beside the pages, and small wedges of beveled hard wood, called " coigns," or " quoins," are tightly driven in, holding the pages firmly in their places, and making a compact " form." Surely there is an allusion to this in PERICLES III, 1.

> " By the four opposing COIGNS
> Which the world together joins."

Before the "form" is taken from the stone to be put on the press, the QUOINS are made very tight with a "mallet" to insure its "lifting" safely.

"There is no more conceit in him than there is in a MALLET."
—2 *Henry IV*, 2.

which process is called "locking-up," and when completed, the form is said, technically, to be "locked-up," or fast.

"FAST LOCKED-UP in sleep."
—*Measure for Measure, IV*, 2.

And to what but the care taken by a printer to make his forms "register" can we attribute the use of that word in Anthony and Cleopatra, Act IV, Scene 9.

"But let the world rank me IN REGISTER—
A master leaver and a fugitive."

Punctuation is a fruitful source of misunderstanding between an author and his printer. Very few authors punctuate their manuscript as they would wish to see it in the print, and fewer yet are apt to be good natured and satisfied when the printer punctuates for them. William Shakespeare may have remembered this when he wrote :

"Wherefore stand you on nice POINTS?"
—3 *Henry VI*, iv, 7.

"Stand a COMMA 'tween their amities."
—*Hamlet, V*, 2.

"My POINT and PERIOD, . . . ill or well."
—*Lear, IV.* 7.

"POINTS that seem impossible."
—*Pericles, V*, 1.

" Puts the PERIOD often from his place."
—*Lucrece*, line 565.

" You find not the APOSTROPHES, and so miss the ACCENT."

" No levelled malice infests one COMMA."
—*Timon*, I, 1.

"Come we to FULL POINTS here? And are ET CETERAS nothing?"

Possibly a book-worm, or even a bookseller might draw as many similes as Shakespeare did, from books—as for example:

" Show me your image in some antique book."
—*Sonnet*, l. ix.

" Has a book in his pocket with red letters in it."
—*2 Henry VI*, ix, 2.

" My red dominical—my golden letter!"
—*Love's Labours Lost*, V, 2.

referring to the rubricated editions of books so common in the seventh century, or the golden letters used in the calendar; or again,

" To place upon the volume of your deeds
As in a title-page, your worth of arms."
—*Pericles*, II, 3.

"'This man's brow, like to a title-leaf,
Foretells the nature of a tragic volume."
—*2 Henry IV*, i, 1.

But in the following:

" The VACANT LEAVES thy mind's IMPRINT will bear."
—*Sonnet*, l. xxvii.

it is hard to be persuaded that direct allusion is not

made to the English custom (which still obtains, as any
body may see for himself by opening a book PRINTED—
wherever PUBLISHED—in England) of placing the typo-
grapher's imprint upon the vacant or extra leaf or
leaves—where the text runs short, at the end of
the volume; just as, if an American publisher, who
buys a hundred copies of an English work, may
stipulate to have his imprint put upon the title-
page (or, perhaps, print his own title-page in this
country), the last page of the book itself will invariably reveal whether the actual manufacture was in
England or not; an analogy which implies technical
information. An image employed by Othello, who
takes his wife's hand in his, and says,

> " Here's a young and sweating devil."
> —*Othello, III, 4.*

is, Mr. Blades thinks, misunderstood. If his wife's
palm was the messenger, as Othello suspected, of her
desires to Cassio, there would be some propriety—
from a printer's standpoint—in calling it "a devil,"
for a printer's "devil" is his messenger or errand boy:
though another meaning is not so far fetched in sound
to a non-professional.

We have mentioned that the Stationer's Company
was a fraternity composed only of monopolists, each
of whom had a monopoly, from the crown, of the
printing of certain books. It was a part of their duty
to give notice of this monopoly upon every impression
of the book, precisely as the notice of copyright entry
is obliged by law to be printed to-day upon copy-
righted books. The entry was to be expressed, after
the printer's name, or at least, conspicuously on the

title-page, in the formula, "*cum privilegio ad impri-mendum solum;*" and as the formula was to be incessantly used it was undoubtedly "kept standing" in the composing room.

It is curious to notice, in the "Taming of the Shrew," Act iv., Scene 4, the recurrence of this formula in a speech of Biondello:

> *Bion.* I can not tell; except they are busied about a COUNTERFEIT assurance; take you assurance of her CUM PRIVILEGIO AD IM-PRIMENDUM SOLUM to the church.

It is to be noticed that the word "counterfeit" in the above speech, was a printer's term in those days; and, used in the printer's technical sense, would be applicable; for Biondello is counseling Lucertio to marry Bianca out of hand, and without waiting for her father and his counselor who are discussing the marriage treaty. A "counterfeit" was a reprint (as we would say now, a "reprint in fac-simile").[1]

Again: it might be supposed that a country lad should know the ways of dogs and birds and beasts and creeping things. But it happens to be human experience that the country lad is the least likely person to turn out a naturalist. It is much more probable that some over-worked shoemaker, in some rare escape from his city garret, should find his thoughts awakened by watching an ant-hill, and succeed in years in making himself an entomologist; than that the farmer's boy, who catches bugs every day to bait his fish-hook, should turn out an entomolo-

---

[1] Marahren's Parallel List of technical Typographical Terms—art., "Counterfeit." We take the above from Mr. Blades' "Shakespeare and Typography." London, 1872.

gist; just as it is not the farmer's daughter, but the fashionable young lady from town who tramps the fields and tears her hands for wild-flowers or wets her feet for the pond lilies. But whoever wrote the plays had found time to learn all the ways of these. Says Bottom, to Cobweb, the fairy, in "Midsummer Night's Dream," "Monsieur, get your weapons in your hand and kill me a red-hipped bumblebee on the top of a thistle." In the United States as well as England, there is no more likely place to find a bumblebee in midsummer than on a thistle. In "Much Ado about Nothing," Benedict says to Margaret "Thy wit is as quick as a greyhound's mouth. It catches." The peculiarity of a greyhound is that, unlike other dogs, it is able to catch game in its mouth as it runs; other hounds must stop to do this. In "As You Like It," Celia tells Rosalind that Monsieur Le Beau, who comes with his mouth full of news, will feed it to them "as pigeons feed their young," and Rosalind replies, "Then we shall be news crammed." Pigeons bring food to their young in their crops, and cram it down their young ones' throats, as no other birds do. In "Twelfth Night" the clown tells Viola that "fools are as like husbands as pilchards are to herrings—the husband's the bigger." The pilchard closely resembles the herring, but is thicker and heavier, with larger scales. In the same play Maria says of Malvolio, "Here comes the trout which must be caught with tickling." Expert anglers know that by gently tickling a trout's sides and belly, it can be so mesmerized as to be taken out of the water with the hand. In "As you Like It," we have the lines "For look where Beatrice, like the lapwing, runs close by the ground to hear our conference." The lapwing is a kind of plover which is very swift of foot and which, when trying to avoid being seen, keeps its head close to the ground as it runs. Says Lear's fool, "The hedge-sparrow fed the cuckoo so long that it had its head bit off by its young." The hedge-sparrow in England is a favorite bird for the cuckoo to impose its young upon. In "All's Well that Ends Well," Lafeu says of Parolles "I took this lark for a bunting." The English bunting is a field bird of the same form and color as the lark, but inferior as a singer. And so the figures are always accurate, "the ousel-cock so black of hue," "the throstle with his note so true," "the wren with little quill," "the russet-pated chough, rising and cawing at the guns report." And so of flowers, as when Perdita speaks of

> —daffodils,
> That come before the swallow dares, and take
> The winds of March with beauty—

the writer knew that in England the daffodil blooms in February and March, while the swallow never appears until April. In none of the allusions to nature or natural phenomena in the plays, is there any such thing as guess work.[1] Now, what was the necessity for all this technical, geographical, botanical, and occult learning, in a simple drama thrown off by an Elizabethan dramatist, earning his living by catering to an Elizabethan audience? It was not only unnecessary, but almost fatal to his success. The Elizabethan audience did not want scientific treatises. But

---

[1] And see further "The natural History of the Insects mentioned in Shakespeare," by R. Paterson. London: A. K. Newman & Co., Leadenhall street, 1841.

nothing—from governmental polity to the stuffing of
a fowl—from processes of the human mind to the
management of kitchen gardens—was too small or
rude for a philosopher's (let us say for Francis Bacon's)
vast purposes.   How otherwise are they to be accounted for ?

That Shakespeare borrowed Greene's famous " sea-
coast " is a point either way.   If he took it supposing that Bohemia had a sea-coast, the omnipotent knowledge assigned him by his worshipers failed
him at least once.   And if he knew (as is now claimed,
though on what authority we know not), that Bohemia once possessed provinces on the Adriatic, he knew,
as usual, what the acute research of three hundred
years has only just developed.   And was agriculture
taught at this Stratford school, and politics and the art
of war ?[1]   And was there any thing that William
Shakespeare did not know ?   We are entitled to
ask these questions, for it must be remembered that,
before the appearance of the Shakespearean dramas,
there was practically no literature written in the
English tongue.   To use the words of Macauley,
"A person who did not read Latin and Greek could
read nothing, or next to nothing. . . .   The Italian
was the only modern language which possessed any
thing that could be called a literature."[2]   One possessing, then, merely " small Latin and less Greek," could
not have written " Shakespeare."   Still less could he
have written it out of Gower and Chaucer, and the

---

[1] See " Was Shakespeare ever a Soldier?"   Three Notelets on
Shakespeare, by Wm. J. Thoms, London.   John Russell Smith,
1865.

[2] Essays.   Lord Bacon.

shelf-full of English books that made up all there was in English letters.

But if the Stratford grammar-school confined its teachings to the pages of the English bible alone, it worked wonders, for Bishop Wadsworth goes so far as to declare, that "take the entire range of English literature—put together our best authors, who have written on subjects not professedly religious, and we shall not find, I believe, in them all, printed so much evidence of the Bible being read and used, as in Shakespeare alone.[1] Yet William Shakespeare had little opportunity for self-education, except these two terms at Stratford school; he was a lad-of-all-work at the Bankside Theater, when a mere child. He was only fifty-two years old when he died. He was one of several partners in certain theatrical establishments in London, in the years when he must have put all this multitudinous learning, he had carried in his head so long, on paper. He was so active, industrious, and shrewd in those years, that he alone of the partners was able to retire with a fortune—to purchase lands and a grant of arms for his father (whence he himself might become an esquire by descent); and, in the years of leisure after his retirement, he wrote only three or four epitaphs, which no other graduate of Stratford school would probably have cared to claim.

It has only been within the last few years that hardy spirits—like Nathaniel Holmes—whose education has led them to look judicially backward from effects to causes—and whose experience had impressed

---

[1] Shakespeare's use of the Bible. By Charles Wadsworth, p. 345. London. Smith Elder & Co., 1880.

them with the idea that most effects come in natural procession from causes somewhere—were courageous enough to seek the solution of this mystery—not in what is called the "internal evidence" of the plays themselves, but in the circumstances and surroundings, that is to say, in the external evidence of their date and production.

The Baconian theory is simply that, so far as the records of the Elizabethan period are accessible, there was but one man in England, at the date at which this Shakespearean literature appeared, who could have produced it.[1] The history of Bacon's life, his massive acquirements, his profound scholarship even as a child : his advantages of foreign travel, his ambitious acquaintance with the court : and, joined to all, his dire necessities and his successive retirements (the dates of which, when collated, coincide with the dates at which the plays—tallying in matter with the circumstantial surroundings of Bacon's life (as, for example, Shylock appeared at about the time when Bacon was most helplessly in the toils of what he calls "the Lombardo") :—all this need not be recapitulated here. He was born and bred in the atmosphere of libraries. While William Shakespeare was poaching on Avon banks, the little Francis was impressed with the utter inadequacy of Aristotle's method to grapple with

---

[1] "Had the plays come down to us anonymously, had the labor of discovering the author been imposed upon after-generations, I think we could have found no one of that day but Bacon to whom to assign this crown. In this case it would have been resting now on his head by almost common consent."—(W. H. Furness to Judge Holmes, third edition of "Authorship of Shakespeare," p. 628).

modern needs, and meditating its supersedure with labors of his own. The gray-haired Queen, who in youth had called him her little Lord Keeper, will not lift a hand to aid him in his poverty, or to advance him in the State, regarding him as a man of study rather than of practice and experience; and so Bacon is known to have remained, bemoaning (as he himself says in a letter to Burleigh, written in 1592) "the meanness of my [his] estate; for though I can not accuse myself that I am either prodigal or slothful, yet my health is not to spend, nor my course to get.¹ This is the very year, 1592, in which Robert Greene "discovers that a new poet has arisen who is becoming the only shake-scene in a county;" and so far forgets himself as to become "jealous" of William Shakespeare, who, up to this time, has only been a "Johannes Factotum," of not much account until he borrows "our feathers."² And so, until 1611, Bacon is driven to the Jews. Why should he not, in his pressing necessity for "lease of quick revenue," bethink him of the resources within himself, and seek a cover whereunder—without embarrassing his hope of future preferment—he may turn into gold his years of study and travel, by means of a quick pen?

In 1611, when he is suddenly created attorney-general, the Shakespearean plays cease abruptly, to appear no more for ever. William Shakespeare closes out his theatrical interest in London, and retires, to money-lending (as some say), in Stratford. He dies in 1616. Lord Bacon reaches his highest pinnacle of greatness,

---

¹ Spedding, "Letters and Life of Bacon," vol. i, p. 108.
² Ante, p. 125

and falls, in 1621. In 1623, while Bacon is again spending his time in the strictest privacy and retirement, there suddenly appears a folio, "The Complete Works of William Shakespeare," amended, revised, enlarged, and improved, including at least seventeen (Mr. Smith says twenty-three) p'ays which had never appeared or been heard of in Shakespeare's lifetime.

Few of us—outside the ranks of commentators, like Mr. Grant White, and others, who give their valuable lives to this study—dream how vast were the emendations and revisions, enlargements and corrections of the old Shakespearean plays given to the world in this folio of 1623. Mr. White says that in the one play of "Love's Labours Lost" there are inserted new lines in almost every speech.[1] Another, "The Merry Wives of Windsor," according to Knight,[2] has double the number of lines it originally possessed in 1600. The "Henry V." has nineteen hundred new lines. The "Titus Andronicus" has an entire scene added, and the "Much Ado about Nothing" and "The Lear" are so altered and elaborated, with curtailment here and enlargement there, as to lead Mr. Knight to declare that "none but the hand of the master could have superadded them."[3] But, if William Shakespeare was the "master," how did his hand reach up out of the grave under Stratford chancel, where it had rested seven years, to make these improvements? And if William Shakespeare in his lifetime made those revisions for Heminges and Condell (who appear on the title-page of this folio of 1623 as editors, and an-

---

[1] Cited by Holmes, "Authorship of Shakespeare," third edition, p. 71.

[2] "Studies of Shakespeare," p. 337.   [3] Id.

nounce in the preface that this edition is printed from
the "true original copies") at Stratford (where, according to his own inventory, he had neither library
nor books—nor bookcase, nor writing-table, for that
matter), why did he not print them himself, for his
own benefit, instead of performing all this labor of
emendation for somebody else? He could not have
been fearful lest he would lose money by them, for
they had been the foundation and source of all his
fortune. Nor had he grown, in his old age, indifferent to gain (let the ghost of the poor "delinquent for
malt delivered" assure us of that!). He could not
have revised them for pure glory : for, in his previous
career, while in London, he had shown no interest in
them, permitting them to be surreptitiously printed
by whoever, in the same town with himself, listed so
to do. He had even allowed them to be mixed up
with other people's trash, his name signed to all indifferently, and the whole made footballs of by the
London printers, under his very nose, without so much
as lifting a voice in protest, or to declare which were
his and which were not.[1] Besides, if he had revised
them for the glory of his own name, why did he not
cause them to be printed? Nor can we suppose that
he was employed to revise them, for pay, by Heminges
and Condell, because, if they did so employ him, why
did they carry the expense of the revision for seven
long years, until he and his wife were both in their
graves, before reimbursing themselves by printing the
first folio for the market! Last, and most wonderful

---

[1] See *post*, "The New Theory," where it appears that, at the
time Shakespeare was producing certain plays on his stage, certain others were being printed and circulated, as his, outside.

of all, in this first folio are included all these entirely new plays which had never been heard of before! Who wrote those, and why? The answer to
these riddles, the Baconians say, is that, when again
at leisure, Bacon bethought himself of his scattered
progeny, and—whether proposing to publicly own
them or not—whether to secure them for posterity or
merely for his own pastime—he devoted that leisure to
a revision of the works by means of which he had
bridged the first long interval in his career. At any
rate, when the revision appeared, it is matter of fact
that William Shakespeare was dead and in his grave,
and speculation has nothing to do with that.

Besides the coincidence of the plays appearing during Bacon's first retirement: ceasing altogether at his
first elevation, and appearing in revised and improved
form again after his final downfall, and during his
second privacy, the Baconians cite: I. Contemporary
statements, which include (A), Sir Tobie Matthew's
famous postscript :[1] " The most prodigious wit of these
times is of your name, though he be known by another" (which Mr. Weiss[2] explains, very lamely in our
opinion, by arguing that the *other* name by which
Bacon was known, and to which Matthew alludes, was
" *Viscount St. Albans*); (B), a letter from Bacon him-

---

[1] Bacon was in the habit of sending certain of his lighter manuscripts to Sir Tobie, and this postscript was appended to a letter
acknowledging the receipt of Bacon's " great and esteemed favor
of the 9th of April."

[2] "Wit, Humor and—Shakespeare." By John Weiss. Boston.
Roberts Brothers, 1876. Matthew writes this in a letter acknowledging receipt of a volume sent him by Bacon. If that
volume was a copy of the " First Folio," the postscript would be
intelligible.

self, to Sir John Davies, who is going to meet the new king James (with whom Bacon is striving for favor, looking to his own preferment), in which he commits to Sir John's "faithful care and discretion" his interests at court, and adds, "So, asking you to be good to concealed poets, I continue," etc., etc.;[1] II. Evidence by way of Innuendo, including another of Matthew's postscripts (the one in which he writes to Bacon, "I will not return you weight for weight, but measure for measure," etc.); also, perhaps, the injunctions of secrecy in Bacon's own letters to Matthew, to "be careful of the writings submitted to you, that no one see them." There is, besides, in many of Bacon's preserved letters something suggestive of a "curious under-meaning, impressing the reader with an idea of more than appears on the surface." The idea of the stage, as a figure of speech, occurs in a letter to the Queen: "Far be it from me to stage myself," etc.; and in one to lady Buckingham, "I do not desire to stage myself but for the comfort of a private life," etc. "Dramatic poesy," he declares, "is as history made visible." Writing to Matthew, he refers to a "little work of my recreation;" and Matthew, in return, banters him on writing many things "under another name." This is in 1609, and no more "Shakespeare" plays appear until Othello, in 1621. The Jonson obituary verse—in which occur the encomiums so rung in our ears by the Shakespeareans (and which we have—earlier in these pages—seen was all they really had behind them), which we have thought could be most easily explained on the "nil mortuis nisi bonum" theory—are also re-

---

[1] Holmes, " Authorship of Shakespeare,"

garded, we believe, by the Baconians, as Innuendo.[1]
III. The Parallelisms. That is to say, an almost
identity of phraseology, found in both the Baconian
and Shakespearean writings. The best list of these is
to be found in Judge Holmes' book, covering some
twenty-five closely-printed pages.[2] Of the value of
this latter class of evidence, it is for every reader to
judge for himself; but that a writer of exact science
and moral philosophy should plagiarize from the
theater, or the theater from the writer of exact science
and moral philosophy; or (still more improbable) that
two contemporary authors, in the full glare of the
public eye, should select each other's works to habitu-
ally and regularly plagiarize upon, are altogether, it
seems to the Baconians, out of the question. But
even the conceiving of so unusual a state of affairs as
a political philosopher and playwright contracting
together to mutually plagiarize from each other's writ-

---

[1] It is curious to find the Baconians appealing to this "best evidence" for the other side. But they read it as an Innuendo.
For example, the verses—

> "Shine forth, thou star of poets, and with rage
> Or influence, cheer the drooping stage!
> Which—since thy flight from hence, hath mourned like night
> And despaired day—but for thy volume's light—"

they say, do not and can not, refer to William Shakespeare at
all. For this was published in 1623, and William Shakespeare
had been dead seven years. He could not "shine forth" again,
except figuratively, in his volume, and this he already does by
the publication of his works, and is admitted to do in the next
line, where it is said that but for "thy volume's light" the stage
would "mourn in night." The Baconians, who believe that Ben
Jonson himself was the "Heminges and Condell" who edited the
first folio, regarded this whole poem as a sop to Bacon, on Ben
Jonson's part.
[2] Pp. 306–326.

ings would hardly account for the coincidence between the cottage scene (Act IV, Scene 3) in "A Winter's Tale," and Bacon's "Essay on Gardens," in which he maintained that "there ought to be gardens for all the months of the year; in which severally things of beauty may be in their season," which he proceeds to suggest:

BACON.

For December and January, and the latter part of November, you must take such things as are green all winter . . . rosemary . . . lavender . . . marjoram.

BACON.

Primroses for March, there come violets, especially the single blue—the yellow daffodil: in April follow the double white violet, the cowslip, flower-de-luce, and lilies of all natures, the pale daffodil.

In May and June come pinks of all sorts: the French marigold, lavender in flowers; in July come gilliflowers of all varieties.

PERDITA.

. . . , Reverend sirs,
For you there's rosemary, and rue; these keep
Seeming and savor all the winter long.

PERDITA.

. . . daffodils,
That come before the swallow dares, and take
The winds of March with beauty; violets dim
. . . pale primroses . . .
bold oxlips, and
The crown-imperial; lilies of all kinds,
The flower-de luce being one!

Sir, the year growing ancient—
Not yet on summer's death, nor on the birth
Of trembling winter,—the fairest flowers o' the season
Are our carnations, and streaked gillyvors, . . .
Hot lavender, mints, savory, marjoram;
The marigold, that goes to bed with the sun;
And with him rises, weeping;
These are flowers of middle summer.

Were we assured that the prose in the left-hand column was the poet's first rough notes for the exquisite poetry in the second, would there be any internal evidence for doubting it? And when it appears that "The Essay on Gardens" was not printed until 1625, nine years after William Shakespeare's death and burial, and two years after an edition of his alleged plays, rewritten and revised, had appeared (when so deliberate a "steal" would hardly be profitable), the exoteric evidence seems at least to command attention.

A coincidence between a passage in "The Advancement of Learning" and in the play of "Troilus and Cressida," Act II., Scene 2 (which, we shall see later on, first appeared in print, advertised as the work of a novice, in 1609, thereafter, within a few months, to be reissued as by William Shakespeare [1]—who was not, at the date of that edition, either a novice or a first appearance), is worth pausing to tabulate:

BACON.	HECTOR.
Is not the opinion of Aristotle worthy to be regarded, where he saith that young men are not fit auditors of moral philosophy, because they are not settled from the boiling heat of their affections nor attuned by time and experience?	. . . Not much Unlike young men, whom Aristotle thought Unfit to hear moral philosophy.

That the manager of a theater, in dressing up a play for the evening's audience (and *such* an audience) should tuck in an allusion to Aristotle, to " catch the

---

[1] *Post,* " The New Theory."

[2] It is to be noticed that no similarity of *style* in these opposed extracts is alleged or relied upon.

ear of the groundlings"—or, finding it already in, should not have a sufficient acquaintance with Aristotle to scent an impropriety and take it out—is no less or no more absurd than that a philosopher, in composing so profound and weighty an essay as the "Advancement of Learning," should go to a cheap play-house for his reference to the Greek sage. If Bacon *did* attend the theater that night to learn the opinion of Aristotle (whom he had criticised at college at the age of fifteen) on young blood and philosophy, he was misled, for Aristotle said not that young men ought not to *hear moral*, but ought not to *study political* philosophy. And the error itself is proof positive—it seems to the Baconians—of an identical source for the two passages. It must not be forgotten, however, that the evidence from these coincidences is cited not to an ANTI-SHAKESPEAREAN case—which is purely historical —but as cumulative to the BACONIAN case alone. And yet, though the evidence from the "parallelisms" is the least forcible of any presented by the Baconians, so systematically do they occur that the ablest Baconian writer (Judge Holmes) claims that he has been able to reduce them to an ordo, and to know precisely where to expect them, by reference merely to a history of the life of Lord Bacon, and the date of the production. "When I got your 'Letters and Life of Bacon,'" he writes to Mr. Spedding, "and read that fragment of a masque; having the dates of all the plays in my mind, I felt quite sure at once in which I should find that same matter, if it appeared anywhere (as I expected it would) and went first straight to the 'Midsummer-Night's Dream,' and there came upon it, in the second

21

act, so palpably and unmistakably that I think nothing else than a miracle could shake my belief in it."[1]

The facts that Lord Bacon expressed himself to the
effect that the best way of teaching history was by
means of the drama; that there is a connected and
continuous series of historical plays (covering by
reigns the entire period of the War of the Roses), in
the Shakespearean drama "from 'King John,' by way
of prelude—in which the legitimate heir to the throne
is set aside, and the nation plunged into civil war—to
'Richard III.,' where the two roses are finally united
in one line in Henry VII., and winding up with the
reign of Henry VIII.—wherein, as a grand finale to
the whole, the splendor of the new line is shown
in its reunited vigor"—which (with but one hiatus, the missing reign of Henry VII.) is one
complete cycle of English history: and that, on
searching among the remains of Francis Bacon, a
manuscript "History of Henry VII." is found, which
might well be the minutes for a future drama (the
opening paragraph of which seems to be a recapitula-
tion of the last scene of the Richard III. of the dramas),
is certainly startling. Not necessarily connected with
this discovery is the further fact that Mr. Spedding
has found, in the library of Northumberland house,
among certain of Bacon's manuscripts, a slip of paper,
upon which is scrawled eight times, in a clerky hand
(not Bacon's), the name "William Shakespeare," together with the names of certain of the known
Shakespearian Historical plays, and of certain (as
Judge Holmes conjectures) other plays not now

---

known.[1] But there is nothing in this discovery more startling than the numberless other coincidences—if they be nothing more—which Judge Holmes has massed in his scholarly work.

Henry Chettle, in 1603, in his "England's Mourning Garment (a rhyme)," wonders that "Melicert does not drop a single sable tear" over the death of " Our Elizabeth." It might, indeed, seem strange had William Shakespeare (supposing these lines to apply to him) been the favorite he is said to have been with Elizabeth. But, while neither Shakespeare nor Bacon sing mortuary strains, of the two (if these stories about Elizabeth's love for Shakespeare are true) it is certainly not strange that Bacon did not; for Bacon, at least, had no cause to idolize his queen.

Ben Jonson's eulogies of Shakespeare, in verse, nowhere surpass, as we have seen, his eulogies of Bacon, in prose. He calls Lord Bacon "the ἀκμή of our language," and, as Mr. Thompson suggests, "no pinnacle has two acmes." "On every variety of court enfolding," continues that writer, "was Bacon daily employed, writing in others' names; and, if we do not think worse of Plato for personating Socrates, or of Cicero for personating Cato," neither should ill be thought of Bacon for borrowing a name "to cover his aim," etc.[2] Meanwhile, "this ἀκμή of our language was poor and a borrower." In 1605, is published an anonymous pamphlet, called " Ratsei's Ghost." In it, one Ratsei, a highwayman, is about to be hung, and gives some parting advice to a strolling player; tells

---

[1] Holmes' "Authorship of Shakespeare," 3d edition, pp. 657–682.

[2] The Renascence Drama, p. 59.

him to go to London, where he would learn to be
frugal and thrifty; to feed upon all men, but let none
feed on him; make his hand stranger to his pocket,
his heart slow to perform his tongue's promise; and
when he felt his purse well lined, to buy some place
of lordship in the country; that, growing weary of
playing, his money may then bring him to dignity and
reputation; that he need care for no man—no, not for
them that before made him proud with speaking their
words on the stage." "If this satirical passage," says
Mr. Thompson, "plainly alludes to him who went to
London very meanly, and came, in time, to be exceedingly wealthy, it confirms Greene's saying, that
Shakespeare made his money by *acting*, not by writing, plays, and by usury." [1]

As to Miss Bacon's question, "What did William
Shakespeare do with Bacon's manuscripts?" Mr.
Thompson [2] seems to think that they may yet be
brought to light. They "appear to have been so many
times hypothetically burned, at Stratford, in the Globe
theater, the London fire, by their owners (by purchase)
at the play-house, to hinder rivals from using them,"
that Mr. Thompson argues that "it is probable they
are still to the fore." Bacon's Will directs certain papers laid away in boxes, cabinets, and presses, to be
collected, sealed up, and put away, "so as not to have
them ready for present publication." He was "not
ignorant that those kind of writings would, with less
pains and embracement (perhaps), yield more luster
and reputation to my name, than those other which I

---

[1] Id., p. 209.

[2] Renascence Drama, or History made Visible. By William
Thompson. Melbourne, 1880.

have in hand." They could bide their time, an , since William Shakespeare and his fellows do not dispose of them, the inference is that they were not allowed to retain them.

The Baconian theory, it is to be noticed, is quite indifferent as to whether William Shakespeare, on first turning up at London, found employment (as Mr. Grant White asserts) in his "cousin's law-office" or not: or whether, at any stage in his career, either in Stratford or London, he was an attorney's clerk, hard 'prentice at the trade of "noverint." (By which slur Mr. Fullom believes that Nash meant, not that Shakespeare was a "noverint," but that the young "noverints" of the time were "Shakespeare's;" that is to say, that they scribbled, out of hand, for the stage.) The Shakespearean problem is neither increased nor diminished by the proposition; even an attorney's clerk could not have written all the Shakespearean pages. Should it be necessary, however, to find a law-student in London who could have managed some of them, why not allow Francis Bacon his claim among the rest? He has, at least, this advantage of his rival; that, while it is the general impression now-a-days that William Shakespeare was not a law-student, as a matter of fact Francis Bacon *was*.[1]

---

[1] And too good a law student, we think, to have written the law in the "Merchant of Venice." For, although Lord Bacon was apt to discover the public feeling, and quick to array himself on the right side (and spitting at Jews has always been accounted of Gentiles for righteousness), he must have seen that Shylock had a standing in court on the merits of his case.

But Portia begins her extraordinary (according to common law at least) judgment by deciding for the Jew in that, not having paid the principal sum, Antonio must suffer in the foreclosure

As to the bibliography of the Baconian theory, there are two volumes which will probably always remain its text-books, viz., Judge Holmes's book, of which the first edition appeared in 1862; and Mr. Smith's, printed in 1857, which made a convert of

---

of the mortgage, as it were, upon his person. This is against the letter of any known law, which gives an equity of redemption to the debtor in all such cases. Her next decision is, that the Jew has his election between the principal sum and the penalty, and that, with his election, not the law itself can interfere. This, again, is not *law*; for the law abhors a penalty, and even in a foreclosure will not allow the debtor to be mulcted in more than the face of his debt, interest, and costs. But now, having decided, against all law, for the Jew, Portia begins deciding for the Christian, and the first point she makes is that, when Shylock takes his pound, he must not take a hair's weight more or less, nor yet one ounce of blood. This, again, is clearly not law, since it is an eternal principle of jurisprudence that, when the law grants any thing it also grants everything that is necessary to the conversion of that thing to possession (as, when it grants a farm, it likewise tacitly grants a right of way to that farm). So, if Shylock had had any title to his pound of flesh, he would certainly have had a title to draw as much blood as it was absolutely necessary to draw in cutting out that pound, and such portions of flesh over and above a pound as it would be absolutely necessary to cut out, providing the cutting out was done by a skillful operator and not a bungler. Astounded at this turn of the tide, Shylock deliberates, and finally cries, "Well, give me my principal and let me go!" Portia thereupon renders her fourth decision, which is the most astounding of all—namely, that, having once refused a tender of the money in open court, the Jew is not entitled to change his mind and take it! Since the days of Moses—certainly since the days of Littleton—a tender has never quite destroyed a debt, but only the interest and costs accruing upon it, after the tender! Such a glaring and high-handed sacrifice of common law and common sense to stage effect might have been conceived of by a manager anxious for the plaudits and pence of a crowded house, scarcely by a future lord chancellor of England.

Lord Palmerston. Mr. Wilkes's exceedingly fresh and readable work, "Shakespeare from an American Point of View," and Mr. King's "Bacon versus Shakespeare; a Plea for the Defendant," as text-books on the other side, could hardly be expected to produce much disorder in Messrs. Holmes and Smith's stern and compact columns of facts and argument.

Mr. Wilkes[1] decides off-hand against this Baconian theory at the start, and then goes on, like his predecessors, to construct a Shakespeare to suit himself. It is to his praise that he has endeavored to construct this Shakespeare out of the Shakespearean pages, rather than to have unreined his fancy. But he makes his own particular Shakespeare, nevertheless. The Wilkes Shakespeare is a Romanist. We consider this to William Shakespeare's praise, for to be a good Romanist is to be a good Christian, and to be one in a Protestant reign is to be a consistent Christian as well. But this is all the good Mr. Wilkes's Shakespeare is. Beyond that he is base-born, a man despised of his equals, and a flunkey and tidewaiter at the knees of an aristocracy to which he can not attain—an obscene jester, etc., etc.—and this author he calls Shakespeare. Such a one, whoever he is, is neither Bacon nor Raleigh, at all events. In 1880, Mr. Thompson, of Melbourne, Australia, published a volume, "Renascence Drama; or, History made Visible,"[2] devoted to an accumulation of fact and argument—rather than to a presentation of the case already made—in favor of the Baconian theory. Mr.

---

[1] Shakespeare from an American Point of View. New York: D. Appleton & Co., 1877.

[2] Melbourne: Sands & McDougall, Collins street, west, 1880.

Thompson aims to answer the more refined objections to that theory, by showing that Bacon's mind and art rather overgrasped than undergrasped the matter and form of these Shakespearean drama, and his work is an extremely valuable and charming contribution to the pro-Baconian view.

In his abounding zeal for "our Shakespeare," Mr. King[1] gives us much eulogy, very little argument, and remakes but one or two points, namely, that a large proportion of the Shakespearean characters are made to bear Warwickshire names, such as Ford, Page, Evans, Hugh, Oliver, Sly, Marion Hacket, the fat ale-wife of Wincot, Curtis, Burton Heath, Fluellen, Bardolph, and so on; and that certain expressions which have puzzled commentators, such as "make straight" (meaning "make haste"), "quoth" (meaning "went"), the use of the word "me" in place of "for me," "old" for "frequent," etc., are Warwickshire expressions, and current in no other parts of England. But, as anybody can see, the majority of these are far from being uncommon names, and are quite as prevalent in New York, for example, as they are or were in Warwickshire. And if, as has been suggested, Mr. Manager Shakespeare dressed up his friends' dialogues for his own stage, and tucked in the clowns and jades, this usage of Warwick names might well be accounted for. Four of these names are taken out of "The Merry Wives of Windsor," and three of them from the induction to the "Taming of the Shrew"— matter in the composition of which Shakespeare or

[1] Bacon and Shakespeare: A Plea for the Defendant. By Thomas King. Montreal: Lovell Printing and Publishing Company, 1875.

any other playwright might have had the largest hand, without entitling himself to any Olympus. And if, in the dressing up, Shakespeare inserted a clown or a sot here and there, to make sport, what would be more natural than that he should put into their mouths the *argot* he had grown up amid in his boyhood, and make the drunken turnkey in " Macbeth " to say, with hiccoughs, " If a man were porter of hell-gate, he should have *old* turning the key?" For, as Mr. King can see for himself, the cardinals and kings do not use these phrases; nor, we may add, are the surnames he particularizes ever bestowed on them, but only on the low-comedy characters of the plays.

Surely, if William Shakespeare ever were forced "upon the country," as the lawyers say, as against my Lord Bacon, he would wish his case to the jury rather without Mr. King's " plea " than with it. As a " plea " on any side of an historical question, it is, to be sure, nothing, if not candid ; but, as a personal appeal to posterity to, willy-nilly, believe that certain players and others in the age of Elizabeth knew not guile, it is touching and beautiful in the extreme. " Who shall say Heminges and Condell lied?"[1] " Could rare Ben Jonson, who is worthy of our love and respect, have lied?"[2] Did Shakespeare practice a deceit upon his

---

[1] "Bacon versus Shakespeare: A Plea for the Defendant." By Thomas King. Montreal, and Rouse's Point, New York : Lovell Printing, etc., Company, 1875, p. 9.

[2] Ibid., p. 10. Heminges and Condell " profess that ' they have done this office to the dead only to keep the memory of so worthy a friend and fellow alive as was our Shakespeare.' Yet their utter negligence, shown in their fellow's volume, is no evidence of their pious friendship, nor perhaps of their care or their intelligence. The publication was not, I fear, so much an

noble and generous patron ?   Could *he* be guilty of a
lie ?"[1]   And so on. To much the same effect (the
reverence due the name "Shakespeare," the improbability of Jonson and others telling an untruth, etc.) is
an anonymous volume, "Shakespeare not an Impostor,
by an English Critic,"[2] published in 1857 ; and finally,
in 1877, was published a paper, read before the Royal
Society of Literature, by C. M. Ingleby, M. A., LL.D.,
a vice-president[3] of the same. Dr. Ingleby is severe
upon all anti-Shakespeareans, whose minds he likens
to "Macadam's sieves," which "retain only those in-
gredients which are unsuited to the end in view"
(whatever that may mean), and thinks that "the profession of the law has the inevitable effect of fostering
the native tendency of such minds." Unlike the others, however, Dr. Ingleby does not confine himself to
expressions of his interest in the anti-Shakespeareans
"as examples of wrong-headedness," but attempts an
examination of the historical testimony. In favor of
the Shakespearean authorship, he names seven witnesses, viz., John Harrison, Francis Meres, Robert
Greene, Henry Chettle, Heminges, Condell, and Ben
Jonson. John Harrison was the printer (publisher)
who published the "Venus and Adonis" in 1593, and
the "Lucrece" in 1594. Each of these was without

offering of friendship as a pretext to obtain the copyright.'
(Disraeli, "Amenities of Authors—Shakespeare.")

[1] Ibid., p. 13.

[2] George Townsend (according to Allibone), London : G. Routledge & Co., Farringdon street, 1857.

[3] "Shakespeare: The Man and the Book." London : Josiah
Adams, Trübner & Co., 1877, Part I., p. 38. "The Authorship of
the Works attributed to Shakespeare."

an author's name on the title-page, though each was dedicated to Southampton, in an address dedicatory, signed "William Shakespeare." This is all that the Harrison evidence amounts to, except that Dr. Ingleby says, " It is to me quite incredible that Harrison would have done this unless Shakespeare had written the dedications, or at least had been a party to them." [1] As to Meres, anybody can see by reading him that he wrote as a *critic*, and not as an historian.[2] To subpœna Greene as a witness to Shakespeare's genius, is at least a bold stroke; for, as has been seen, Greene is very emphatic to the effect that William Shakespeare was a mere "Johannes Factotum," or Jack-of-all-trades, who trained in stolen plumage, and the Shakespeareans (Dr. Ingleby alone excepted) have universally exerted themselves to break the force of this testimony by proving Greene a drunkard, jealous, etc.[3] Greene

---

[1] Ibid., p. 42.

[2] " Palladis Tamia, Wit's Commonwealth," 1598.

[3] That Robert Greene was much more than a drunkard and a pretender, but that, to the contrary, he had many admirers who were not unaware of the effrontery of his debtor, Shakespeare, a search among the old literature of the day would reveal. In a quarto tract, dated 1594, " Greene's Funeralls, by R. B., Gent.," is a copy of verses, the last stanza of which runs :

> " Greene is the pleasing object of an eye
> Greene pleased the eye of all that looked upon him;
> Greene is the ground of every painter's dye,
> Greene gave the ground to all that wrote upon him:
> Nay, more; the men that so eclipsed his fame,
> Purloined his plumes, can they deny that same?"

Hallam believes that the last two lines are directed principally at William Shakespeare. (" Literature of Europe," Part II., ch. vi., p. 32, note.)

A selection of his poems, edited by Lamb, is printed in Bohn's Standard Library. But by far the most careful ac-

was a graduate of Cambridge—a learned man—" one of the fathers," says Lamb, " of the English stage." He does not seem to have approved of William Shakespeare's borrowing his plumes; but the impression that he was a monster of debauchery and drunkenness is derived wholly from his own posthumous work, " The Confessions of Robert Greene," etc., London, 1592, which lays the black paint on so thickly that it should have put the critics on their guard. Greene was probably no worse than his kind. Henry Chettle edited Greene, and personally deprecated some of its hard sayings as to Shakespeare, on account of his (Shakespeare's) being a clever, civil sort of fellow, and of " his facetious grace in writing;" but more particularly, no doubt, because " divers of worship" had taken him up, and he (Chettle) did not wish to appear as approving slander of a reigning favorite. Heminges and Condell were men of straw, whose names are signed to the preface to the " first folio," who otherwise bear no testimony one way or the other, but whose book, as will be demonstrated further on, is an unwilling witness against its purported author. And Ben Jonson, who brings up the rear of this precious seven, has been already disposed of. That theory must be pretty soundly grounded in truth, against which there is nothing but rhetoric to hurl, and, in our opinion, it would be entirely safe—if not for the Baconians, for the anti-Shakespeareans, at least—to rest their case on the arguments for the other side. And we believe the more

count of Greene's career, as connected with William Shakespeare, is to be found in " The School of Shakespeare," by Richard Simpson, London: Chatto & Windus, 1878, Vol. II., p. 339.

thoughtful among Shakespeareans are beginning to recognize it, and coming to comprehend that, if they are to keep their Shakespeare they must re-write their "Biographies;" spend less time in proving him to have been an epitome of the moral virtues—beyond the temptation of deer stealing, beer drinking, and skylarking, etc.—and devote more attention to his opportunities for acquiring the lore and technical knowledge his alleged pages so accurately handle. Especially has Mr. Halliwell Phillips, in his little book (in which he binds himself to cite no dates or authorities subsequent to 1616),[1] impressed us as endeavoring to meet this emergency. But we find that he has not met it. He has, indeed, developed many details of curious interest—as that John Shakespeare was, in April, 1552, fined twelve pence for throwing muck into the street in front of his house; and that he was several times a candidate for high bailiff of Stratford (or mayor, as the office was afterward called) before finally arriving at that dignity in 1568; that July 15, 1613, there was heard at Worcester Assizes a curious lawsuit, brought by Dr. John Hall, Shakespeare's son-in-law, against a neighbor for slandering his wife (Susannah Shakespeare), which suit appears to have been "fixed" in some way before coming to trial. Mr. Phillips brings much learning to prove that William may have been "pre-contracted" to Anne Hathaway— that his death may have been from malarial fever

---

[1] Outlines of the Life of Shakespeare. Brighton. Printed for the Author's friends, 1881. We should add to our list of books Mr. O. Follet's two able pamphlets on the Baconian theory. Sandusky, Ohio, 1880.

rather than inebriation—which have nothing at all to
do with the question or the practical difficulties cited
by the anti-Shakespeareans, one way or the other.
But as to those practical difficulties, he brings no light
and has no word to say.

PART VI.

THE NEW THEORY—THE SONNETS—CONCLUSION.

F a matter so indifferent as the number of pebbles in Demosthenes' mouth when he practiced oratory on the beach, no effort of credulity can be predicated. But when a proposition is historical and capable of proving itself, it is, indeed, the skeptic who believes the most. It would be interesting, for example, to compile a catalogue of the reasons why A, B, and C, and their friends, doubt the real Shakespeare story, and cling to the manufactured tradition. A will tell us he believes it because somebody else (Bacon will do as well as anybody) wrote enough as it was, and was not the sort of man who would surrender any of the glory to which he was himself entitled, to another. B, because, when somebody else wrote poetry (for example, Bacon's "Paraphrase of the Psalms"), his style was quite another than the style of the dramas. C, because he is satisfied that William Shakespeare spent some terms at Stratford school, and was any thing but unkind to his wife. D, because the presumption is too old to be disturbed; as if we should always go on believing in William Tell and the man in the moon, because our ancestors believed in them! And so on, through the alphabet. It is so much easier, for instance, to believe that miracles should appear by the page, or that universal wisdom should spring fully

armed from the brain of a Warwickshire clown, than that Francis Bacon, or somebody else, should write anonymously, or in two hands, or use as a nomme de plume the name of a living man, instead of inventing one de novo.

Now, say the New Theorists, if at about that time, a living nomme de plume should happened to be wanted, whose name was more cheaply purchasable than that of a young "Johannes Factotum," of the Blackfriars, who, by doing any thing and every thing that was wanted, and saving every honest penny he turned, actually became able to buy himself a coat-of-arms (the first luxury he ever appears to have allowed himself out of his increasing prosperity) [1] and a county seat ?

Four or five years before our historical William Shakespeare had bethought himself of wandering to London, one James Burbage, father of Richard, the actor, had built the Blackfriars Theater, a plain, rough-building on the site of the present publishing office of the "Times." Before its door (for the Blackfriars will answer as well as the Globe) we may, perhaps,

---

[1] We happen on traces of the fact that William Shakespeare's particular weakness was his "noble descent" very often, in exploring the annals of these times, and that his fellow actors by no means spared his weakness. "It was then a current joke to identify Shakespeare with 'the Conqueror,' or ' Rufus,' as if his pretensions to descent from the Norman dukes were known" ("Ben Jonson's Quarrel with Shakspeare," "North British Review," July, 1870). And certain lines in the "Poetaster" are supposed to be a fling at this weakness of Shakespeare, as the whole play is believed to be a hit at Marlow (id.). We shall see how this weakness was fostered by the new set into which circumstances forced Shakespeare, later on.

imagine a rustic lad—fresh from Stratford, and foot-
sore from his long tramp, attracted by the crowd and
the lights, standing idle and agape. Possibly, then,
riding up, some gallant threw young William his
horse's bridle, and William Shakespeare had found
employment in London. By attention to business,
William, in time, may have, as Rowe thinks, come
to control the horse-holding business, and take his
predecessors into his pay; until they became known
as "Shakespeare's boys," and the young specula-
tor's name penetrated to the inside of the theater.
In course of time he becomes a "*servitour*" (what
we now call a "super," i. e., supernumerary) inside,
and ultimately (according to Rowe, an actor himself, and the nearest in point of time to William
Shakespeare to write his biography) "the reader"[1] of
the establishment; and naturally, therefore, stage editor of whatever is offered. He has no royal road to
learning at his command, nor does he want one. The
"knack at speech-making," which had delighted the
rustic youth of Stratford, mellowed by the new expe-
riences which surround him, is all he needs. Not
only the plays of Greene and others, which he now
remodeled (and improved, no doubt), but essays of his
own, became popular. The audience (we shall see
more of them further on) called for "Shakespeare's
plays," and his name came to possess a market value.

The dramas we now call "Shakespearean" surely
did appear in his lifetime, and under his name. Were

---

[1] In this capacity he read and accepted Ben Jonson's "Every
Man in his Humour," which was the beginning of the intimacy
which ended with their lives.

22

they ever performed at his theater? Let us glance at the probabilities.

The "theaters" of this day are barely more than inclosures, with a raised platform for the performers, and straw for the audience to stand or go to sleep in, as they prefer. Wotton, in a letter to Bacon,[1] says that the fire that destroyed the Globe theater burned up nothing but "a little wood and straw and a few forsaken cloaks." Sir Philip Sidney, writing in 1583, ridicules the poverty of the scenic effects and properties of the day in an often-quoted passage: "You shall have Asia of the one side and Africke of the other, and so many other under king-domes that the plaier, when hee comes in, must ever begin with telling where hee is, or else the tale will not be conceived. Now, you shall have three ladies walk to gather flowers, and then you must believe the stage to be a garden: by-and-by we have news of a shipwreck in the same place; and we are to blame if we accept it not for a rock. Upon the back of that comes a hideous monster, with fire and smoke, and the miserable beholders are bound to take it for a cave, while, in the mean time, two armies fly in, represented with four swords and bucklers, and then what hard heart will not receive it for a pitched field!"[2]

And M. Taine has drawn a life-like picture of the audience which applauded this performance: "The poor could enter as well as the rich; there were six-penny, twopenny, even penny seats. . . . If it rained, and it often rained in London, the people in

---

[1] Smith's "Bacon and Shakespeare," p. 74.
[2] "The Defence of Poesie," edition 1626, p. 592.

the pit, butchers, mercers, bakers, sailors, apprentices,
receive the streaming rain on their heads . . .
they did not trouble themselves about it. While waiting for the pieces they . . . drink beer, crack
nuts, eat fruit, howl, and now and then resort to their
fists: they have been known to fall upon the actors,
and turn the theater upside down. At other times
they were dissatisfied and went to the tavern to give
the poet a hiding or toss him in a blanket. . . .
When the beer took effect there was a great upturned
barrel in the pit, a receptacle for general use. The
smell arises, and then comes the cry, 'Burn the juniper!' They burn some in a plate in the stage, and the
heavy smoke fills the air. Certainly the folk there
assembled could scarcely get disgusted at any thing,
and can not have had sensitive noses. In the time of
Rabelais there was not much cleanliness to speak of.
Remember that they were hardly out of the middle
age, and that, in the middle age, man lived on a dung-
hill." Mr. White assures us further, that pickpockets
were apt to be plentiful among this audience, and when
discovered, were borne upon the stage, pilloried in full
view,[1] and there left, the play going on meanwhile
around them; and, moreover, that the best seats sold
were on the stage itself; where any of the audience, who
could pay the price, could sit, recline, walk, or con-
verse with the actors engaged in the performance,"
while pages brought them rushes to stretch upon, and

---

[1] " Kempe, the actor, in his 'Nine Days' Wonder,' A. D. 1600,
compares a man to 'such an one as we tye to a poast on our stage
for all the people to wonder at when they are taken pilfering.' "
(" Shakespeare," by Richard Grant White, Vol. I., p. 183.)

pipes of tobacco with which to regale themselves.[1]
"Practicable" scenery of any sort, even the rudest,
was utterly unknown,[2] and it is thought that the actors relied on barely more than the written action of
the piece for their guidance. In the plays of this period we come continually on such stage directions as
"Here they two talke and rayle what they list;" "All
speak;" "Here they all talke," etc.,[3] which proves that
much of the dialogue was trusted to the inspiration of
the moment—to which inspiration the gallants and
pickpockets may not unnaturally have contributed.
The principal burden of entertaining the audience
rested with the clown, who, unembarrassed by any

---

[1] Ibid.

[2] Whenever we come on a stage direction, therefore, which supposes "practicable" scenery in a play, we may assert with confidence, that the same was written in or after 1662, up to which
date there was no such thing as practicable machinery. In the
original edition of "The Tempest," for instance, there is no intimation, by way of stage direction, that the first scene occurs on
shipboard. In the first edition of "As You Like It" there is
no mention of a forest in the stage direction. Nor in the early
quartos of "Romeo and Juliet" is there any intimation that Juliet makes love in a balcony. "What child is there, that, coming to a play, and seeing Thebes written in great letters upon an
old door, doth believe that it is Thebes?" says Sidney, in his
"Defence of Poesie."—(R. G. White's "Shakespeare's Scholar,"
p. 489, note.) Trap-doors, however, were probably in very
early use; at least, we find in a comedy by Middleton and Dekkar
a character called "Trap-door." There seems, also, to have been
pillars that turned about, and a writer in the times of James I.
mentions that "the stage varied three times in one tragedy."

[3] These stage directions are taken from Greene's "Tu Quoque,"
A. D. 1614, two years before Shakespeare died, and long after, according to the commentators, he had ceased writing for the
stage.

reference to the subject-matter of the play, popped in
and out at will, cracked his jokes, danced and sung
and made himself familiar with the outsiders upon
the stage. Before an audience satisfied with this
rudimentary setting, upon a stage crowded with
smirking gallants and flirting maids of honor, we
are assured that Hamlet and Wolsey delivered their
soliloquies, Anthony his impassioned oratory, and
Isabella her pious strains; while the clowns and pot-
wrestlers discoursed among themselves of Athens and
Troy, and Hecuba and Althea, of Galen and Paracelus,
of "writs of detainer," and "fine and recovery," and
"præmunire," and of the secrets of the pharmacopœia!
"At this public theater," says Mr. Smith, "to which
every one could obtain access, and the lowest of the
people ordinarily resorted . . . . we are called upon
to believe that the wonderful works which we so
greatly admire and feel we can only appreciate by
careful private study—that not only Englishmen like
Coleridge confess, in forty years of admiring study of
Greek, Latin, English, Italian, Spanish, and German
philosophers, literature, and manners, to have found
bursting upon him with increased power, wisdom, and
beauty in every step," [1] but foreigners like Schlegel,
Jean Paul, and Gervinus, "have fallen down before
in all but heathen adoration"—were performed. In
1880, when we force a common-school education at
state expense upon the people, the Shakespearean
plays are disastrous to managers. They "lose money
on Shakespeare," and unless "carpentry and French"—
unless ballet and spectacle are liberally resorted to, are

---

[1] Bacon and Shakespeare, p. 91.

dragged down to desolate houses and financial ruin. "Shakespeare" is "over the heads" of ὅι πόλλοι in these days of compulsory education. And yet we are calmly asked to credit the astounding statement that in and about the year 1600, in London, these grave, intellectual, and stately dialogues are taking by storm the rabble of the Bankside, and entrancing the trades-men and burghers of the days when to read was quite as rare an accomplishment as serpent-charming is to-day—when, if sovereigns wrote their own names, it was all they could do—and when the government could not afford to hang a man who could actually write his name.[1] "And yet," to quote Mr. Smith again, "it was from the profit arising from this wretched place of amusement that Shakespeare rea-lized the far from inconsiderable fortune with which in a few years he retired to Stratford upon-Avon." If not actual intellectual giants, the rabble of that day must have been the superiors in literary perception of some very eminent gentlemen who were to come after them, like, for example, Fuller, Evelyn, Pepys, Dryden, Dennis, Rymer, Hume. Pope, Addison, Steele, and Johnson, whose comments on our immortal drama we have set forth in the First Part of this work.[2] Only we happen to know they were not.

As an alternative to believing that these pearls, over which this nineteenth century gloats, were cast before the swine of the sixteenth; the theory we are now con-

---

[1] Benefit of clergy was only abolished in England by acts 7 and 8, George IV., c. 28, sec. 3, in 1827, fifty-three years ago; in the United States it had been disposed of (though it had never been availed of) by act of Congress, April 30, 1790.

[2] Ante, pp. 20-29.

sidering offers, as less violent an attack upon common sense, the supposition that what we now possess under the name of "Shakespeare's plays" were *not* produced upon the stage of any play-house in those days, but were *printed* instead, the name of William Shakespeare having been attached to them as surety for a certain circulation. The well-attested fact that William Shakespeare was a play-writer is not ignored by this supposition; for the new theorists believe that, although no fragment of the Shakespeare work now survives, its character can be readily determined. From what knowledge we possess of the tone and quality of the audiences of those days, it is not difficult to imagine the rudeness and crudity of the plays.

These were the formative days of audiences, and, therefore, the formative days of plays. Sir Henry Wotton, in a letter from which we have just quoted, written to Lord Bacon in 1631, refers to one of these plays called "The Hog hath lost its Pearl." Says this letter: "Now it is strange to hear how sharp-witted the city is; for they will needs have Sir Thomas Swinnerton, the Lord Mayor, be meant by the hog, and the late Lord Treasurer by the pearl." There is no disputing the fact, at least, that the plays we call " Shakespeare's " are cast in a mold by themselves, and have no contemporary exemplar. The student of these days knows the fact that Dekker, Webster, Massinger, Jonson, or any other who wrote in periods that are counted " literature," made no fortunes at their work. That such as this one alluded to by Wotton—and one example will suffice—were what the town ran to see in those days, mere local sketches -

lampoons on yesterday's events; coarse parables, the allusions in which could be met and enjoyed by the actors themselves (were to the popular taste, that is to say), is much easier to conceive than that the "Hamlet" and the "Lear" were to the popular taste. One Dr. Heywood (who, it is to be noted, is sometimes called the "prose Shakespeare") is understood to have produced some two hundred and twenty of this sort of sketches alone; and, possibly, this was the sort of "early essays at dramatic poetry" which Aubrey speaks of: this "the facetious grace in writing that approves his wit" which Chettle assigns to William Shakespeare—mere sketches in silhouette of the town's doings, such as would appeal, as this sort still do in cities, to a popular and local audience. There is some curious testimony on the subject, which looks to that effect.

Cartwright,[1] in his lines on Fletcher, says :

> " Shakespeare to thee was dull, whose best jest lies
> I' th' ladies' questions, and the fools' replies,
> Old-fashioned wit, which walked from town to town
> In turned hose, which our fathers called the clown ;
> Whose wit our nice times would obsceneness call,
> And which made bawdry pass for comical.
> NATURE WAS ALL HIS ART: thy vein was free
> As his, but without his scurrility."

One Leonard Digges—who, Farmer says (in his essay on " The Learning of Shakespeare "), was " a wit of the town " in the days of Shakespeare—wrote some verses laudatory of William Shakespeare, which (Farmer says again) " were printed along with a spurious edi-

---

[1] Poems, 1651, p. 273.

tion of Shakespeare" in 1640. In this copy of verses occur such lines as—

> "Nature only led him, for look thorough
> This whole book, thou shalt find he doth not borrow
> One phrase from Greeks, nor Latins imitate,
> Nor once from vulgar languages translate."

A startling declaration to find made, even in poetry, concerning compositions which Judge Holmes has demonstrated are crowded with classical borrowings, imitations drawn from works untranslated from their originals at the date when quoted; so that it would be impossible to say that the quoter found them in English works and took them with no knowledge of their original source![1] "Nature itself was all his art," says Fuller, and Denham, again, asserts that "all he [Shakespeare] has was from old mother witt."[2] And Dominie Ward says, to the same effect, in his diary, "I have heard that Mr. Shakespeare was a natural witt, without any art at all;"[3] though, of course, this was, and could have been, nothing more than matter of report.

It is probable that, in the production of these plays, William Shakespeare was not always scrupulous to compose "without blotting out a line" himself. That he was a reckless borrower, and scissored unconscionably from Robert Greene and others (so much so that

[1] See Holmes's "Authorship of Shakespeare," third edition, p. 5.

[2] Farmer, p. 13.

[3] "Diary of Rev. John Ward, Vicar of Stratford, extending from 1648 to 1679," p. 183; London, 1839, p. 30.

Shakespeare took his "Taming of the Shrew" from Greene's "Taming of A Shrew," there being no copyright to prevent.

23

Greene wrote a whole book in protest), we have Greene's book itself to testify. From its almost unintelligible pages we can glean some idea of the turgid English of the day. It was, of course, in the composition of this popular English that Shakespeare, by surpassing Greene, awakened the latter's jealousy. Otherwise, there would have been no superiority in Shakespeare over Greene which Greene could have perceived: or, at least, no cutting into Greene's profits wherein Greene could have found cause for jealousy. For, if Greene had continued to earn money indifferently to whether Shakespeare carried on his trade or not, he would not have been "jealous." But so fluent and clever a fellow as this William Shakespeare of Stratford, who could hold, when a mere boy, his rustic audience with a speech over a calf-sticking, was a dangerous rival among the hackney stock-playwrights of London, and would easily have made himself invaluable to his management by dashing off scores of such local sketches as " The Hog hath lost his Pearl," suggested by the current events of the day.

But, even if " Hamlet," " Othello," " King Lear," " Macbeth," and " Julius Cæsar" could have been produced by machinery, and engrossed currente calamo, (so that the author's first draft should be the acting copy for the players), they could have hardly been composed, nowadays, without a library. And even had William Shakespeare possessed an encyclopædia (such as were first invented two hundred years or so after his funeral) he would not have found it inclusive of all the reference he needed for those five plays alone. They can not be studied as they are capable of being

studied—as they were found capable of being studied
by Coleridge and Gervinus—without a library. And
yet are we to be asked to believe they were composed
without one?—in the days when such a thing as a dic-
tionary even was unknown! Who ever heard of
William Shakespeare in his library, pulling down volumes, dipping into folios, peering into manuscripts, his
brain in throe and his pen in labor, weaving the warp
and woof of his poetry and his philosophy, at the expense of Greece and Rome and Egypt; pillaging alike
from tomes of Norseman lore and Southern romance—
for the pastime of the rabble that sang bawdy songs
and swallowed beer amid the straw of his pit,
and burned juniper and tossed his journey-actors in
blankets?

It is always interesting to read of the habitudes
of authors—of paper-saving Pope scribbling his
"Iliad" on the backs of old correspondence, of Spenser by his fireside in his library at Kilcolman Castle,
of Scott among his dogs, of Gibbon biting at the
peaches that hung on the trees in his garden at Lau-
sanne, of Schiller declaiming by mountain brook-
sides and in forest paths, of Goldsmith in his garrets
and his jails. Even of Chaucer, dead and buried before Shakespeare saw the light, we read of his studies
at Cambridge, his call to the bar, and his chambers in
the Middle Temple. But of William Shakespeare—
after ransacking tradition, gossip, and the record—
save and except the statement of Ben Jonson how he
had heard the actor's anecdote about his never blotting
his lines—not a word, not a breath, can be found to
connect him with, or surprise him in any agency or
employment as to the composition of the plays we

insist upon calling his—much less to the possession of
a single book! Did William Shakespeare own a library? Had we found this massive draught upon antiquity in the remains of an immortal Milton or a
mortal Tupper, or in all the range of letters between,
we should not have failed to presume a library. Why
should we believe that William Shakespeare needed
none?—that, as his pen ran, he never paused to lift
volume from the shelf to refresh or verify his marvelously retentive recollection? There was no Astor or
Mercantile Library around the corner from the Globe
or the Blackfriars, in those days. And, as for his own
possessions, he leaves in his Will no hint of book or
library, much less of the literature the booksellers had
taken the liberty of christening with his name! Where
is the scholar who glories not in his scholarship? By
universal testimony, the highest pleasure which an author draws from his own completed work, the pride
of the poet in his own poem, is their chiefest payment.
The simple fact—which stands out so prominently in
the life of this man that nobody can gainsay it—that
William Shakespeare took neither pride nor pleasure
in any of the works which passed current with the
rest of the world as his, might well make the most
casual student of those days suspicious of a claim that,
among his other accomplishments, William Shakespeare was an author at all.

Just here we are referred to a passage in Fuller's
" Worthies:" " Many were the wit combats," says
Fuller, " between Shakespeare and Ben Jonson; . . .
I beheld them," etc. But Fuller was only eight years
old when Shakespeare died, and possibly spoke from
hearsay, as it is hardly probable that an infant of such

tender years was permitted to spend his nights in
" The Mermaid." Besides, these " wit combats" at
" The Mermaid" are now said to be " *wet* combats,"
i. e. drinking-bouts, by a long-adopted misprint.
As a matter of fact, unless we are misled by a typo-
graphical error in the edition before us,[1] what Fuller

---

[1] The History of the Worthies of England. Endeavored by
Thomas Fuller, D.D. Two volumes. (First printed in 1622.) A
new edition, with a few Explanatory Notes by John Nichols,
F. A. S. London, Edinburgh, and Perth. Printed for F. C. & J.
Rivington and others. The reference to William Shakespeare
is at page 414 of volume II., and is as follows:

"WARWICKSHIRE

" WRITERS SINCE THE REFORMATION.

" William Shakespeare was born at Stratford-on-Avon, in this
county, in whom three eminent Poets may seem in some sort to
be compounded. 1. *Martial* in the *warlike* sound of his surname
(whence some may conjecture him of a *military extraction*), *Hasti-
vibrans* or Shake-speare. 2. *Ovid*, the most *naturall* and *witty* of
Poets; and hence it was that Queen Elizabeth, coming into a
grammar school, made this extemporary verse—
" *Persius* a Crab-Staffe, Bawdy *Martial*, *Ovid* a fine Wag.
"3. *Plautus* who was an exact Commedian, yet never any
Scholar, as one *Shake-speare* (if alive) would confess himself.
Adde to all these that, though his genius generally was *jocular*,
and inclining him to *festivity*, yet he could (when so disposed) be
solemn and *serious*, as appears by his Tragedies ; so that *Heraclitus*
himself (I mean if secret and unseen) might afford to smile at
his Comedies, they were so merry ; and *Democritus* scarce forbear
to sigh at his tragedies, they were so mournfull.
" He was an eminent instance of the truth of that Rule, Poeta
non fit sed nascitur, ' One is not made but born a poet.' Indeed, his learning was very little, so that as Cornish diamonds
are not polished by any lapidary, but are pointed and smoothed
even as they are taken out of the earth, so *nature* itself was all
the *Art* which was used upon him. Many were the *wet-combates*

did actually say was, not "wit combats," but "WET COMBATS." But even if they were "wit combats," and not friendly contests at ale-guzzling, like the early tournament at "Piping Pebworth" and "Drunken Bidford," the "wit" could not have been colossal, if we may judge from one example preserved in the Ashmolean manuscripts at Oxford, as stated by Capell. "Ben" (Jonson) and "Bill" (Shakespeare) propose a joint epitaph.

Ben begins:

> "Here lies Ben Jonson,
> Who was once one—"

Shakespeare concludes:

> "That while he lived, was a *slow* thing,
> And now, being dead, is *no*-thing."

This being the sort of literature which William Shakespeare's pen turned out during his residence in London, he could manage very well without a library. And it was the most natural thing in the world that, after retiring to the shade of Stratford, it should have produced, on occasion, the famous epitaphs on his friends Elias James and "Thinbeard." At all events, this is a simpler explanation than the "deterioration of power, for which no one has assigned a sufficient reason," which Halliwell[1] was driven to assume in order

---

betwixt him and Ben Jonson; which two I beheld like a *Spanish great gallion* and an *English man of war*, lesser in *bulk* but lighter in *sailing*, could turn with all tides, tack about and take advantage of all winds, by the quickness of his *wit* and *invention*. He died Anno Domini . . . and was buried at Stratford-upon-Avon, the town of his nativity."

[1] "Life of Shakespeare," p. 270. London, 1848.

to account for this drivel from the pen which had written " Hamlet.' And, moreover, it is a satisfactory explanation of what can not be explained in any other way (and which no Shakespearean has ever yet attempted to explain at all), of the fact that William Shakespeare, making his last Will and Testament at Stratford, in 1515, utterly ignored the existence of any literary property among his assets, or of his having used his pen, at any period, in accumulating the competency of which he died possessed. Had William Shakespeare been the courtly favorite of two sovereigns (which Mr. Hallam doubts[1]), it is curious that he never was selected to write a Masque. Masques were the standard holiday diversions of the nobles of the day, to which royalty was so devoted that it is said the famous Inigo Jones was maintained for some years in the employment of devising the trappings for them alone (though, of course, it is no evidence, either way, as to the matter we have in hand). But if William Shakespeare was the shrewd and prosperous tradesman that we have record of (and, that he came to London poor and left it rich, everybody knows), was he not shrewd enough, as well, to see that his audiences did not require philosophical essays and historical treatises; that he need not waste his midnight oil to verify the customs of the early Cyprians, or pause to explore for them the secrets of nature? We may assert him to be a " great moral teacher " to-day ; but, had he been a " great moral teacher " then, he would have set his stage to empty houses. He could have earned the same money with much less trouble to

---

[1] Literature of Europe," vol. iii., p. 77 (note).

himself. The gallants would have resorted to his stage
daily (as they would have gone to the baths if they
had been in old Rome); and the ha'penny seats have
enjoyed themselves quite as much had he given them
the school of "The Hog hath lost his Pearl," or
"The Devil is an Ass," or the tumbles of a clown.
Why should this thrifty manager have ransacked
Greek and Latin and Italian letters, the romance of
Italy and the Sagas of the North (or, according to Dr.
Farmer, rummaged the cloisters of all England, to get
these at second hand)? Had these all been collected
in a public library, would he have had leisure to sit
down and pull them over for this precious audience of
his, these gallants and groundlings—when his money
was quite as safe if he merely reached out and took
the nearest spectacle at hand (as he took his "Taming
of the Shrew," "Winter's Tale," "sea-coast of Bohemia," and all—from Robert Greene)? But, if we may
be allowed to conceive that it was the *action* (that is to
say, the "business") of the Shakespearean plays that
delighted this Shakespearean audience (that filled the
cockpit, galleries, and boxes, while poor Ben Jonson's,
according to Digges, would hardly bring money enough
to pay for a sea-coal fire), and that certain greater than
the manager used this action thereafter as a dress for
the mighty transcripts caused to be printed under
voucher of the popular manager's name—if we may
be allowed to conceive this—however exceptional, it is
at least an accounting for the Shakespearean plays as
we possess them to-day, without doing violence to
human experience and the laws of nature.

Southampton, Raleigh, Essex, Rutland, and Montgomery are young noblemen of wealth and leisure,

who "pass away the time merely in going to plays every day."[1] We have seen that the best seats were on the stage, and these, of course, the young noblemen occupied. There were no actresses in those days— the female parts were taken by boys—but titled ladies and maids of honor were admitted to seats on the stage as well as the gallants, and a thrifty stage manager might easily make himself useful to both. If my Lord Southampton was bosom friend to William Shakespeare (as rumor has it), their intimacy arose probably through some such service. A noble youth of nineteen, of proverbial gallantry and sufficient wealth (though, it must be remembered, as among the fortunes of his day, a comparatively poor man; not able to give away $25,000 at a time, for instance), was not at so great a loss for a friend and alter ego in London in 1593 (the date at which the "Venus and Adonis" is dedicated to him) as to be forced to forget the social gulf that separated him from an economical commoner (lately a butcher in the provinces), however popular a stage manager, except for cause; and it takes considerable credulity to believe that he did forget it (if he did), through being dazzled by the transcendent literary abilities of the economical commoner aforesaid. For Southampton lived and died without ever being suspected of a devotion to literature or literary pur-

---

[1] "My Lord Southampton and Lord Rutland come not to the court, the one but very seldom; they pass away the time merely in going to plays every day."—(Letter from Rowland White to Sir Robert Sidney, dated October 11, 1599, quoted by Kenny, "Life and Genius of Shakespeare." London: Longmans, 1864, p. 34, note.) But it may be noted that Southampton and Raleigh were opposed to each other in politics.

suits; and, besides, the economical commoner had not
then written (if he ever did write) the "Hamlet" and
"Lear," and those other evidences of the transcendent
literary ability which could seduce a peer outside his
caste.   That the gallants and stage managers of the
day understood each other, just as they perhaps do to-
day, there is reason to believe.   Dekker, in his "Gull's
Horn-Book," says that, "after the play was over, poets adjourned to supper with knights, where they in
private unfolded the secret parts of their dramas to
them."   By "poets" in this extract is meant, as appears from the context, the writers of dramas for the
stage; such as, perhaps, William Shakespeare was.
But whether these suppers after the play were devoted
to intellectual and philosophical criticism is a question
for each one's experience to aid him in answering.
Whether William Shakespeare was admitted to this
noble companionship, or was only emulous of the
honor, we have no means of conjecture, as either might
account for the fact that with his first savings he purchased a grant of arms for his father, thus obtaining
not only an escutcheon, but one whole generation of
ancestry; a transaction which involved, says Dr.
Farmer, the falsehood and venality of the father, the
son and two kings at arms, and did not escape protest;[1] for if ever a coat was "cut from whole cloth,"
we may be sure that this coat-of-arms was the one.

---

[1] A complaint must have been made from some quarter that
this application had no sufficient foundation, for we have, in the
Herald's college, a manuscript which purports to be "the answer
of Garter and Clarencieux, kings of arms, to a libellous scrowl
against certain arms supposed to be wrongfully given;" in which
the writers state, under the head "Shakespeare," that "the per-

Whoever wrote Hamlet's soliloquy and Antony's oration might well have written the "Venus and Adonis," and the "Lucrece," and was quite equal to the bold stroke of describing the former (the most splendidly sensuous poem in any language—a poem that

---

son to whom it was granted had borne magistracy, and was justice of peace, at Stratford-upon-Avon; he married the daughter and heir of Arden, and was able to maintain that estate." The whole of this transaction is involved in considerable, and, perhaps, to a great extent, intentional obscurity; and it still seems doubtful whether any grant was actually made in the year 1596. In the year 1599, the application must have been renewed in a somewhat altered form. Under that date, there exists a draft of another grant, by which John Shakespeare was further to be allowed to impale the ancient arms of Arden. In this document a statement was originally inserted to the effect that "John Shakespeare showed and produced his ancient coat-of-arms, heretofore assigned to him whilst he was her Majesty's officer and bailiff of that town." But the words "showed and produced" were afterward erased, and in this unsatisfactory manner the matter appears to have terminated.

It is manifest that the entries we have quoted contain a number of exaggerations, one even of positive misstatements. The "parents and antecessors" of John Shakespeare were not advanced and rewarded by Henry VII.; but the maternal ancestors, or, more probably, some more distant relatives of William Shakespeare, appear to have received some favors and distinctions from that sovereign. The pattern of arms given, as it is stated, under the hand of Clarencieux (Cooke, who was then dead), is not found in his records, and we can place no faith in his allegation. John Shakespeare had been a justice of the peace, merely *ex officio*, and not by commission, as is here insinuated; in all probability he did not possess "lands and tenements of the value of five hundred pounds;" and Robert Arden, of Wilmecote, was not a "gentleman of worship."—(Kenny, "Life and Genius of Shakespeare," p. 38. London: Longmans, 1854.)

breathes in every line the blasé and salacious exquisite),
as the first heir of the invention of a busy London
manager and whilom rustic Lothario among Warwickshire milkmaids. The question as to the authorship of the one hundred and fifty-four "Sonnets,"
which appeared (with the exception of two, printed
in 1598, in a collection of verses called for some un-
suggested reason "The Passionate Pilgrim") in 1609,
need not enter into any anti-Shakespearean theory at
all. Except that one Francis Meres, writing in 1598
—eleven years before—had reported William Shakespeare to have circulated certain "sugared sonnets
among his private friends;"[1] and that the one hundred
and thirty-sixth of the series says the author's name is
"Will" (the common nickname of a poet of those days),[2]
there is nothing to connect them with William Shakespeare except his name on the title-page—in the days
when we have seen that printers put whatever name they
pleased or thought most vendable, upon a title-page.
(When the aforesaid "Passionate Pilgrim" was printed
in 1598—also as by William Shakespeare—Dr. Heywood recognized two of his own compositions incor-
porated in it, and promptly claimed them. "No evidence," says Mr. Grant White,[3] in commenting on this
performance, "of any public denial on Shakespeare's
part is known to exist. It was not until the publication of the third edition of the poem, in 1612, that
William Shakespeare's name was removed.") But
what involves the authorship of the sonnets in still

---

[1] Hallam does not think these are the sonnets mentioned by
Meres.—("Literature of Europe," vol. iii., p. 40, note.

[2] See ante, p. 000, note.

[3] "Shakespeare's Works," vol. iii., p. 77.

deeper obscurity is the fact that their publisher, Thomas Thorpe, himself dedicates them to a friend of his own. He addresses his friend as " Mr. W. H.," and signs the dedication with his own inititials " T. T." Perhaps it was just as the name " Shakespeare " was fastened to the title-page of " The Passionate Pilgrim," and the plays to which, as we shall notice the Shakespeareans declare it never belonged, that Mr. Thomas Thorpe calls his book " Shakespeare's Sonnets, never before imprinted," and makes in the pages of the Stationers' Company the entry: " 20 May, 1609. Tho. Thorpe. A book called Shake-speare's Sonnets." They appear conjointly with a long poem entitled "A Lover's Complaint," and two of them (as we have said) had already been printed in " The Passionate Pilgrim," published by Jaggard in 1598. This unhappy dedication has been so twisted by the commentators to serve their turns, that the only safety is to print it as it stood in this first edition :

" TO . THE . ONLIE . BEGETTER . OF .

THESE . INSUING . SONNETS .

MR . W . H . ALL . HAPPINESSE .

AND . THAT . ETERNETIE .

PROMISED .

BY .

OUR . EVER . LIVING . POET .

WISHETH .

THE . WELL-WISHING .

ADVENTURER . IN .

SETTING

FORTH .   T . T ."

For a dedication composed in the turgid fashion of nearly three hundred years ago, the above would seem to be peculiarly intelligible. All publications were ventures in those days. The printer might get his money back and he might not. But, until he did, he was an adventurer. So Mr. Thorpe, in setting forth on his adventure, wishes well to his publication and to some unknown patron whom he desires—as was the custom—to compliment with wishes of long life and happiness. At least this would seem to be the reading on the face of it. To be sure, there is a slight uncertainty as to whether " Mr. W. H." is dedicator or dedicatee. But the moment the name of Shakespeare appears this little trouble becomes insignificant —and, as usual, difficulties begin to crowd and multiply.

The title reads : " Shake-speares Sonnets never before imprinted : at London, by G. Eld, for T. T.   And are to be sold by William Apsley.   1609."

At that name the commentators appear, and swarm like eagles around a carcass.

Mr. Armitage Brown, who flourished in or about the year 1838, and appears to have been the first gentleman who ever took the trouble to read them, has demonstrated[1] that these sonnets are actually six poems of different lengths[2]— each poem having a consistent theme and argument (and he made this discovery by the simple process of reading them).   Can any body believe that, if these six poems had been the work of the mighty Shakespeare of the Shakespear-

---

[1] "Shakespeare's Autographical Poems, being his Sonnets clearly developed," etc.   By Charles Armitage Brown.   London: James Bohn, 1838.

[2] We find, however, that Coleridge had earlier advanced the same theory.—*Table Talk* (Routledge's edition), p. 2071.

cans, they would have waited until 1838 without a
reader? And, most wonderful of all, that this mighty
poet in his own lifetime would allow six of his poems
to be torn up into isolated stanzas by a printer, stirred
together and run into type hap-hazard, and sold as his
" Sonnets?" The Shakespeareans tell us sometimes of
their William's utter indifference to fame, but they
have never claimed for him an imperturbability quite
so stolid as this. And while we could not well imagine Mr. Tennyson regarding with complaisance a
publisher who would print his " Maud," " Locksley
Hall," " Lady Clara," etc., each verse standing by itself,
and calling the whole " Mr. Tennyson's Sonnets," so
we fancy even Mr. Shakespeare of the Globe, had he
been their author, would have thought the printers
were going a little too far.

But, all the same, the Shakespeareans, Mr. Armitage
Brown among the rest, are determined that these sonnets shall be Shakespeare's and nobody else's, and
proceed to tell us who " Mr. W. H." (to whom Mr.
Thorpe, at William Shakespeare's request—as if the
the man who wrote the sonnets could not write a
dedication of them—dedicated them) is. Certain of
them believe the letters " W. H." to be a transposition
of " H. W.," in which case they might stand for
" Henry Wriothesley," Earl of Southampton. Mr.
Boaden and two Mr. Browns[1] read them, as they stand,
to mean William Herbert, Earl of Pembroke (in either
case accounting for William Shakespeare addressing
in earl as " Mr."—which may mean " Mister ' or " Mas-

---

[1] Shakespeare's Autographical Poems." By Charles Armitage
Brown. London, 1838. " The Sonnets of Shakespeare solved,"
etc. By Henry Brown. London, 1870.

ter "—on the score of earl and commoner having
been the closest of "chums "). A learned Frenchman, M. Chasles, has conjectured that Thomas Thorpe
wrote the first half of the dedication, including the
"Mr. W. H.," and William Shakespeare the second
half (including, perhaps, though M. Chasles does not
say so, the " T. T.") One equally learned German
(Herr Bernsdorff) suggests that " W. H." means
" William Himself," and that the great Shakespeare
meant to dedicate these poems to his own personality
(as George Wither, in 1611, dedicated his satirical
poems, " G. W. wisheth himself all happiness;") and
another supposes Shakespeare to have been in love
with a negress, "black but comely," like the lady of
the Canticles. Yet another, that this dark lady typi-
fied " Dramatic art," the Roman Catholic church, etc.,
etc. Mr. Dowden will have it that Shakespeare and
Spenser, and Mento that Shakespeare and Chapman
were rivals for the lady's favor. And there have been
other and even more puerile speculations put gravely
forth by these same learned and venerable commentators : such as, since the word " Hewes " (in the line, "A
man in Hewes all Hewes in his controlling"), is spelled
with a capital letter, that, therefore, " W. H." is William Hewes (whoever he might have been). Wadsworth believes that these sonnets were the repository
of the REAL emotions of William Shakespeare, as a
relief to long simulation of other people's emotions
in his dramas ; while Mr. William Thompson[1] believes
them to be THE SONNETT, which Bacon mentions writ-

---

[1] The Renascence Drama, or History made Visible. By William Thompson, F. R. C. S., F. L. S. Melbourne: Sands & Mc-
Dougal, Collins street, West, 1880, p. 113, et seq.

ing in or about 1598, saying: "It happened a little
before that time that her Majesty had a purpose to
dine at Twickenham Park, at which time I had
(though I profess not to be a poet) prepared a *sonnet*,
directly tending and alluding to draw on her Majesty's
reconcilement to my lord, which I remember I also
showed to a great person," etc. Now, Mr. Thompson
believes that this " great person" was William Herbert, who read them among the friends of the putative
author—was, in short, the " W. H." Mr. Thompson
points out that, if these sonnets are not Bacon's *Sonnet*, the latter has never been found, among Bacon's
papers or elsewhere.

If these are the sonnets distributed by William
Shakespeare among his private friends—of which
Meres seems to have known in 1598—there would be
this historical difficulty in connecting them with Lord
Herbert, afterwards Earl of Pembroke, viz: In the
Sydney Papers[1] is preserved a letter from Rowland
White to Sir Robert Sydney, in which the writer
says: " My Lord Herbert hath, with much ado, brought
his father to consent that he may live at London, but
not before the next spring." This letter is dated April
19, 1597. " The next spring" would be 1598, the very
year in which Meres speaks of these sonnets as in existence among William Shakespeare's friends. Of
course, they might have been afterwards collected and
dedicated by their author. But at the time they were
so collected, Lord Herbert was Earl Pembroke, and
was surely not *then*, if he had ever been (which he had

---

[1] Vol. II., p. 43.

24

not), plain "Mr. W. H." In other words, if the sonnets were William Shakespeare's, he must either have
dedicated them to a stranger—a boy at Oxford—or
have waited until that boy had become of age and an
earl, and then dedicated them to him in either case
by a title not his own. In the absence of explanation,
nowadays, we would be obliged to regard such a dedication an insult rather than a compliment. And men
were at least no less punctilious about titles in the age
of Elizabeth than they are to-day.

It is interesting, in this connection, to note that in
1595, and while young Lord Herbert was at Oxford, a
play, "Edward III.," was entered in the register of
the Stationers' Company. In both this play and in
Sonnett XCIV. occur the line,

> " Lilies that fester smell far worse than weeds."

Were there any means of ascertaining in which the
line is original and in which quotation, it might be of
aid in solving this question of authorship. But, unhappily, none are at hand.

Mr. Niel believes that " W. H." means " William
Hathaway," Shakespeare's brother-in-law, and that
"onlie begetter" of these sonnets means " only collec-
tor;" (going into considerable philology to make good
his assertion), and that Hathaway collected his brother-in-law's manuscripts and carried them to Thorpe.
Mr. Massey has, for his part, constructed a tremendous
romance out of the sonnets,[1] in which " W. H." means

---

[1] Shakespeare's Sonnets, never before interpreted. London,
1866. Vide, a volume " Remarks on the Sonnets of Shakespeare,
showing that they belong to the Hermetic class of writings, and
explaining their general meaning and purpose." New York:

William Herbert, Earl of Pembroke. But all these commentators alike agree to ignore the fact that William Shakespeare did not dedicate the sonnets to any body, or, so far as we know, procure Thomas Thorpe to do so for him. A poem, "The Phœnix and the Turtle," is sometimes bound up with these, described as "Verses among the Additional Poems to Love's Martyr; or, Rosalin's Complaint," printed in 1601, but nobody knows by what authority, except that publishers have got into the habit of doing so.

Then, again, anonymous authorship was a fashionable pastime among the gallants and the gentle of this Elizabethan day, and joint authorship a familiar feature in Elizabethan letters. It is said that the great dramas we call Shakespeare's so persistently nowadays, and which began to appear unheralded at about this time, bear internal traces of courtly and aristocratic authorship. The diction is stately and sedate. No peasant-born author could have assumed and sustained so haughty a contempt for every thing below a baronet (for only at least that grade of humanity— it is said by those who have carefully examined the drama in this view [1]—does any virtuous or praiseworthy attribute appear in a Shakespearean character: while every thing below is exceedingly comic and irresistible, but still "base, common, and popular"). If certain noblemen of the court proposed amusing themselves at joint anonymous authorship, they were certainly right in concluding that the name of a living

James Miller, 1866. Printed Anonymous, but written by Judge E. A. Hitchcock.

[1] Mr. Wilkes' Shakespeare from an American Point of View. New York: Appletons, 1876.

man, in their own pay, was a safer disguise than a
pseudonym which would challenge curiosity and speculation. At least—so say the New Theorists—such
has turned out to be the actual fact. It is the New
Theory that, while in employment in the theater,
William Shakespeare was approached by certain gentlemen of the court. Perhaps their names were Southampton, Raleigh, Essex, Rutland, and Montgomery,
and possibly among them was a needy and ambitious
scholar named Bacon, who, with an eye to preferment,
maintained their society by secret recourse to the Jews
or to any thing that would put gold for the day in
his purse. Possibly they desired to be unknown, for
the reasons given by Miss Bacon. In what they asked
of him, and what he did for them, he found, at any
rate, his profit. The story goes that the amount
of profit he realized from one of these gentlemen alone
was no less a sum than a thousand pounds. If so—
considering the buying power of pounds in those
days—it is not so wonderful that, at this rate,
William Shakespeare retired with a fortune. Even
at its most and its best, it is an infinitely small
percentum of the world's wealth that finds its
way into the poet's pocket; poetasters are sometimes luckier than poets. That William Shakespeare's fortune came faster than the fortune of his
fellows we do know. This was at once the most secure and the most lucrative use he could have made
of his name. For, as we have seen, owing to the condition of the common law, while he could hardly have
protected himself against any piracy of his name by
injunction, he might have loaned it for value to the
printers, or to any one desirous of employing it, the

risk of piracy to be the borrower's. If these noble gentlemen desired to write political philosophy—as Miss Bacon believed, or belles lettres for their own pleasure—they had their opportunity now; and the NEW THEORY is not inconsistent, either with the Delia Bacon theory or with the Baconian theory proper, as elaborated by Judge Holmes, who recognizes Bacon's pen so constantly throughout the dramas. The same difficulties which those theories meet would still confront us if, as Mr. Boucicault and others have suggested, the plays were offered from lesser sources, and rewritten entirely by William Shakespeare; for we should still be obliged to ask, How did he dare to retain in the plays the material which, unintelligible to him, he must have believed to be unintelligible to his audiences, as calculated to drive them away, rather than to attract them?

Any one of these schemes of assimilated authorship seems at least to tally with the evidence from what we know as the "doubtful plays." In 1600, there appeared in London an anonymous publication—a play entitled "Troilus and Cressida." It was accompanied by a preface addressed, "A never writer to an ever reader," which, in the turgid fashion of the day, set forth the merit and attractions of the play itself. Among its other claims to public favor, this preface asserted the play to be one " never stal'd with the stage, never claperclawed with the palms of the vulgar"—which seems (in English) to mean that it had never been performed in a theater. But, however virgin on its appearance in print, it seems to have very shortly become "staled with the stage," or, at any rate, with a stage name, for, a few months later, a second edition of the play (printed from the same type) appears, minus the preface, but with the announcement on the title-page that this is the play of "Troilus and Cressida, as it was enacted by the King's Majesty his servants at the Globe. *Written by William Shake-speare.*"[1] Now, unless we can imagine William Shakespeare—while operating his theater—writing a play *to be published in print*—and announcing it as entitled to public favor on the ground that it had never been polluted by contact with so unclean and unholy a place as a theater, it is hard to escape the conviction that he was not the "never writer"—in other words, that he was not its author at all—but on its appearance in print, levied on it for his stage, underlined it, produced it, and—it proving a success—either himself announced it, or winked at its announcement by others, as a work of his own.

Again, in 1600, a play was printed in London entitled "Sir John Oldcastle;" in 1605, one entitled "The London Prodigal;" in 1608, one entitled "The Yorkshire Tragedy;" in 1609, one entitled "Pericles, Prince of Tyre;" and, at about the same time, certain others, viz: "The Arraignment of Paris;" "Arden of Feversham" (a very able work, by the way); "Edward III.;" "The Birth of Merlin;" "Fair Em, the Miller's Daughter;" "Mucedorus;" "The Merry Devil of Edmonton;" "The Comedy of George á Green;" and "The Two Noble Kinsmen." All the above purported, and were understood to be, and were sold as being, works of William Shakespeare, except "The Merry Devil of Edmonton," which was announced as

---

[1] Holmes's "Authorship of Shakespeare," third edition, pp. 144-147.

by Shakespeare and Rowley, and "The Two Noble Kinsmen," as by Shakespeare and Fletcher. Now, it is certainly a fact that William Shakespeare, from his box-office at the Globe, or from his country-seat at Stratford, never corroborated the printers by admitting, or contradicted them by denying his authorship of any of the above enumerated plays. The "Hamlet" had been previously published in or about 1603, and the "Lucrece" had made its appearance in 1594. It is certainly a fact that none of these—from "Hamlet" to "Fair Em," from "Lucrece" to "The Merry Devil of Edmonton"—did William Shakespeare ever either deny or claim as progeny of his. He fathered them all as they came, "and no questions asked." And, had Mr. Ireland been on hand with his "Vortigern," it might have gone in with the rest, with no risk of the scrutiny and the scholarship which exploded it so disastrously in 1796. No plays, bearing the name of William Shakespeare on their title-page, now appeared from 1609 to 1622. But in the year 1623, seven years after William Shakespeare's death, a folio of *thirty-six* plays is brought out by Heminges and Condell, entitled "The Works of Mr. William Shakespeare." Of the many plays which had appeared during his life, and been circulated and considered as his, or of which mention can (according to the Shakespeareans) be anywhere found, only twenty-six appeared in this folio, while TEN plays are included which never appear to have been seen or heard of until their presence in this Heminges and Condell collection. The Shakespeareans allow that this is "mysterious," but precisely the same "mystery" would have been discovered in the days of Heminges and Condell themselves, if it had been worth the while of anybody then living to look into the question. Nothing has happened, since the death of William Shakespeare, to make the Shakespeare question any more "mysterious" than he left it himself.

To make this apparent at a glance, let us present the whole in a tabulated statement, only asking the reader to observe that we have in every case given the Shakespeareans the benefit of the doubt, and accepted the mention of a similar name of any play as proof positive of its being the play nowadays attributed to William Shakespeare; and their own chronology everywhere.

The following table shows the plays passing as William Shakespeare's, in London, in the years when he resided in London, as part proprietor and concerned in the management of the Globe and Blackfriars Theaters: the dates of their earliest mention or appearance, and which of them were included in the first folio, edited by Heminges and Condell, in 1623: on the supposition that the plays mentioned by Meres (of which, however, no other traces can be found, during William Shakespeare's life), besides those names in Manningham's and Forman's diaries, and the "Account of the Revels at Court," are the identical plays now included in the Shakespearean drama. The dates are Mr. Grant White's.

PLAYS.	FIRST APPEARANCE OR MENTION.	DATE	FIRST FOLIO OF HEMINGES & CONDELL.	Plays First Appearing in the Folio.
Locrine	Printed.	1595		
Titus Andronicus	First Quarto..	1598	Inserted.	
Love's Labours Lost	Mentioned in Meres' "Palladis Tamia."	1598	Inserted.	
Comedy of Errors	" "	1598	Inserted.	
Taming of a Shrew	" "	1598	Inserted.	• King Henry VI., Pt. I.
Love's Labours Won	" "	1598	Inserted.	• King Henry VI., Pt. II.
The Two Gentlemen of Verona	First Quarto	1598	Inserted.	• King Henry VI., Pt. III.
Richard the Third	Mentioned in Meres' "Palladis Tamia."	1597	Inserted.	• Henry VIII.
Midsummer Night's Dream	" "	1598	Inserted.	• Coriolanus.
The Merchant of Venice	" "	1598	Inserted.	• Julius Cæsar.
Richard the Second	First Quarto..	1597	Inserted.	• Othello. (Entered in the Books of the Stationer's Company in 1621.)
Romeo and Juliet	Mentioned in Meres' "Palladis Tamia."	1598	Inserted.	• All's Well that Ends Well.
King John	First Quarto..	1598	Inserted.	
King Henry the Fourth, Part I.		1598	Inserted.	
King Henry the Fourth, Part II.		1600	Inserted.	
Sir John Oldcastle	Printed.	1600	Inserted.	• Cymbeline.
Thomas Lord Cromwell		1600		• Timon of Athens.
Much Ado About Nothing	First Quarto	1600	Inserted.	
Twelfth Night	Manningham's Diary.	1601	Inserted.	
Henry the Fifth	First Quarto..	1600	Inserted.	
The London Prodigal	Printed.	1605		
As You Like It	Stationer's Register.	1600	Inserted.	
Hamlet	First Quarto..	1603	Inserted.	
Pericles	" "	1609		
Puritan Widow of Watling Street	Printed.	1607		
Yorkshire Tragedy	" "	1608		
Arraignment of Paris		1608		
The Merry Wives of Windsor	First Quarto..	1602	Inserted.	
Measure for Measure	Account of the Revels at Court	1604	Inserted.	
King Lear	Stationer's Register	1607	Inserted.	
Arden of Feversham	Printed.	1608		
Macbeth	Forman's Diary	1610	Inserted.	
The Comedy of George à Green	Printed.	1607		
Troilus and Cressida	First Quarto.	1609	Inserted.*	
Antony and Cleopatra	Stationer's Register.	1608	Inserted.	
The Winter's Tale	Forman's Diary.	1611	Inserted.	
The Tempest	Account of Revels at Court.	1621	Inserted.	
Two Noble Kinsmen	Printed.	1600		
Edward III	" "	1600		
The Birth of Merlin	" "	1600		
Mucedorus	" "	1600		
Merry Devil of Edmonton	" "	1610		

*This play is put in between the 'Histories' and 'Tragedies,' as if received "too late for classification," as the newspapers say. Its pages are not numbered, and so it does not disturb the pagination of the folio.

25

A play called "Duke Humphrey," attributed to Shakespeare, was amongst the dramatic manuscripts destroyed by the carelessness of Warburton's servant, in the early part of the last century, as appears by the list preserved in the British Museum—MS. Lansdowne, 849.

Leaving out these plays mentioned by Meres, we then have twenty-one entirely new plays, which never appeared in William Shakespeare's life, first appearing in Heminges and Condell's edition.

It appearing, then, that, of some forty-two plays credited to William Shakespeare during his lifetime, Heminges and Condell selected only twenty-five, and printed and bound up with those twenty-five nine plays which nobody had ever heard of in print or on the stage or anywhere else, until William Shakespeare had been dead and in his grave seven years, besides the "Othello," which was first heard of five years after his death: it follows either that Heminges and Condell knew that William Shakespeare was in the habit of allowing plays to be called by his name which he never wrote, or that Heminges and Condell's collection of "Mr. William Shakespeare's Comedies, Histories, and Tragedies, published according to the true original copies," is nothing more or less than a collection of plays written prior to the year 1623, and not earlier than the reign of Elizabeth. The Shakespeareans may take either horn of the dilemma they please. "Pericles," one of the plays rejected by Heminges and Condell has since been restored to favor, and no editor now omits it. Surely, under the circumstances, we are justified in asking the question: "If William Shakespeare ever wrote any plays or

poems, which of the above did he write, and which
are 'doubtful?'"

Whether the hand that wrote the "Hamlet" also
composed the "Fair Em;" or the classicist who produced the "Julius Cæsar" and the "Coriolanus" at
about the same time achieved "The Merry Devil"
and "The London Prodigal," is a question lying
within that sacred, peculiar realm of "criticism"
which has "established" and forever "proved" so
many wonderful things about "our Shakespeare"—a
realm beyond our purview in these papers, and
wherein we should be a trespasser. Fortunately,
however, the question has been settled for us by those
to whom criticism is not ultra vires, and may safely be
said to be at rest now and forever. The burden of the
judgment of the whole critical world is of record
that the only true canon of "William Shakespeare"
consists of the plays first brought together in one book
by Heminges and Condell, plus the "Pericles;" and
that certain of the above-mentioned plays, known to
have been published under the name of William
Shakespeare are "spurious;" that, during the lifetime
of William Shakespeare, and in the city where he
dwelt—under his very nose, that is to say—divers and
sundry plays *did* appear from time to time which he
did not write, but which he fathered. Whether, in
pure philanthrophy and charity, he regarded these as
little Japhets in search of a father, and so, pitying
their abandoned and derelict condition, assumed their
paternity, or, whether he took advantage of their bas-
tardy for mere selfish and ill-gotten gain, the critical world find it unprofitable to speculate. But
there can be no reasonable doubt that, in London in

the days of Elizabeth, in the name of "William
Shakespeare" there was much the same sort of common trade-mark as exists, in Cologne, in the days of
Victoria, in the name "Jean Maria Farina"—that it
was at everybody's service. And if William Shakespeare farmed out his name to playwrights, just as the
only original Farina farms out his to makers of
the delectable water of Cologne, wherein shall we
find fault? If, two hundred years after, a lesser Sir
Walter of Abbotsford, be acquitted of moral obliquity
in denying his fatherhood of "Waverly," for the sake
of the offspring, surely the elastic ethics of authorship,
for the sale of the great book, will stretch out far
enough to cover the case of a Shakespeare, who neither
affirmed nor denied, but only held his peace! William
Shakespeare, at least in the days when Lord Coke says
that a play-actor was, in contemplation of law, a vagabond and a tramp,[1] never had to shift for his living.
He always had money to spend, and money to lend,
in the days when we know many of his contemporaries
in the theatrical and dramatic line were " in continued
and utter extremity, willing to barter exertion, name,
and fame for the daily dole that gets the daily dinner."[2]
Of all the co-managers—and, among them, one Burbage was the Booth or Forrest of his day—William
Shakespeare is the only one whose pecuniary success
enables him to retire to become a landed gentleman
with a purchased "Esquire" to his name.

---

[1] " The fatal end," he says, "of these five is beggary—the al-
chemyst, the monopotext, the concealer, the informer, and the
poetaster." A "play-actor," he elsewhere affirms, was a fit subject for the grand jury, as a "vagrant."

[2] "Chambers's Edinburgh Journal," August 7, 1852. p. 88.

No wonder Robert Greene, a well-known contemporary actor, but "who led the skeltering life peculiar to his trade," and who had either divined or
shared the secret of the "Shakespearean" dramas,
raised his voice in warning of the masquerade in borrowed plumes! Was William Shakespeare a shrewd
masquerader, who covered his tracks so well that the
search for a fragment of Shakespearean manuscript or
holograph, which has been as thorough and ardent as
ever was search for the philosopher's stone, has been
unable to unearth them? Certainly no scrap or morsel has been found. The explanation of all this mystery, according to the New Theory, is of very little
value, except in so far as it throws light upon what
otherwise seems inexplicable, namely, that these magnificent philosophical dramas (which are more precious in our libraries as text-book and poems than as
stage shows wherewith to pass an idle evening in our
enlightened day) should have been popular with the
coarse audiences of the times from which they date.
But, if, to conceal their real authors, these magnificent
productions were simply sent out under a name that
was at every body's disposal, the discovery is of exceeding interest. From the lofty masterpiece of the
"Hamlet" to what M. Taine calls "a debauch of imagination . . . which no fair and frail dame in
London should be without"[1]—the "Venus and
Adonis"—it was immaterial what they printed as
his, so this William Shakespeare earned his fee for
his silence. As for young Southampton—then just
turned of nineteen—his part in the covert work of the

---

[1] Crawley, quoted by Taine, "English Literature," book ii.,
chapter iv.

junta might, and, indeed, seems to have been, the accepting of the famous dedication.   That a rustic
butcher-lad should, while holding horses at the door
of a city theater, produce as "the first heir of his invention "—the very first thing he turned his pen to—
so maturely voluptuous a poem as the "Venus and
Adonis," would be a miracle, among all the other
miracles, not to be lost sight of.

We believe that historical and circumstantial evidence alone is adequate to settle or even to disturb
this Shakespearean question ; for it appears to be the
unanimous verdict of criticism that the style of Bacon
and the style of "Shakespeare" are as far apart as
the poles.   Experts have even gone so far as to reduce
both to a "euphonic test," [2] and pronounce it impossible that the two could have been written by the same
hand.   But this is not very valuable as evidence ; for
never, we think, can mere expert evidence be of itself
sufficient as to questions of forgery of authorship any
more than of autograph.   If mere literary style had
been all the evidence accessible, our Shakespeareans
would have been making oath to the Ireland forgeries
to-day as stoutly as when, in the simplicity of their
hearts, they swore the impromptus of a boy of eighteen
surpassed any thing in "Hamlet " or Holy Writ.
Even Mr. Spedding, who ignores any "Baconian
Theory," in writing the life of Bacon, admits that
whenever a literary doubt has to be decided by the
test of style, " the reader must be allowed to judge for
himself."   It was only by just such circumstantial evidence as has been grouped in these papers (such as the

---

[2] Wilkes's "Shakespeare from an American point of view,"
Part III.

Elizabethan orthography and philology—the use of Roman instead of Arabic numerals, etc.) that the Ireland imposture was exploded. Forgery is the imitation of an original, and, if the original be inimitable, there can surely be no forgery. In the case of forgery of a signature, lawyers and experts know that the nearer the imitation, the more easy is it detectable; for no man writes his own name twice precisely alike, and, if two signatures attributed to the same hand are found to be *fac similes*, and, on being superimposed against the light, match each other in every detail, it is irrefutable evidence that one is intentionally simulated.[1] In the case of literary style, however, we are deprived of this safeguard, because, the more nearly exact the counterfeit, the more easily the critic is deceived. Pope was not afraid to entrust whole sections of the paraphrase he called the "Odyssy of Homer," just as Michael Angelo did his frescoes, to journeyworkmen—and not a critic has ever been able to pronounce, or even guess, which was Pope and which was Pope's apprentice; and not only the Chatterton, Ireland, and Macpherson forgeries, but the history of merely sportive imitation and parody prove that literary style is any thing but inimitable; that, in fact, it requires no genius, and very little cleverness to counterfeit it.[2] Nor is—what is incessantly appealed

---

[1] Hunt *versus* Lawless, New York Superior Court, November, 1879. And see, also, Moore *versus* United States, 2 Otto, United States, 270. Criminal Law Journal, Jersey City, N. J., March, 1881. *Art.*, "Calligraphy and the Whittaker Case."

[2] The curious reader is referred to "Supercheries Literaries, Pastiches, etc.," one of the unique labors of the late M. Delapierre. London, Trübner & Co., 1872.

to—"the internal evidence of the plays themselves" of any particular value to the end in view. Were the question before us, "Was the author of these works a poet, statesman, philosopher, lawyer?" etc., etc., this internal evidence would be, indeed, invaluable. But it is not. The question is not *what*, but *who*, was the author. Was his family name "Shakespeare," and was he christened "William"? The Shakespearean has been allowed to confound these questions, and to answer them together, until they have become as inseparable as Demosthenes and his pebble-stones. But, once separated, it is manifest that the internal evidence drawn from the works themselves, however satisfactory as to the one question, is utterly incompetent as to the other, and that it is by purely external—that is to say, by circumstantial evidence, by history, and by the record—that the question before us must be answered, if, indeed, it ever is to be answered at all. And, therefore, it is by circumstantial evidence alone, we think, that literary imposture can be satisfactorily exposed. Neither can we trust to internal evidence alone; for an attempt to write the biography of William Shakespeare by means of the internal evidence of the Shakespearean plays, has inevitably resulted in the questions we have already encountered. Was Shakespeare a lawyer, was Shakespeare a physician—a natural philosopher—a chemist—a botanist—a classical scholar—a student of contemporary life and manners—an historian—a courtier—an aristocrat—a biblicist—a journeyman printer, and the rest!—and in giving us the fairy stories of Mr. Knight and Mr. De Quincy in place of the truth we crave. For we can not close our eyes to the fact that history very decid-

edly negatives the idea that William Shakespeare, of
Stratford, was either a lawyer, a physician, a courtier,
a philosopher, an aristocrat, or a soldier.   Moreover,
while the internal evidence is fatal to the Shakespearean theory, it preponderates in favor of the Baconians:
for, when we should ask these questions concerning
Francis Bacon, surely the answer of history would be,
Yes—yes, indeed; all this was Francis Bacon.   The
minute induction of his new and vast philosophy did
not neglect the analysis of the meanest herb or the
humblest fragment of experimental truth that could
minister to the comfort or the health of man.   And
where else, in the range of letters—except in the
Shakespearean works, where kings and clowns alike
take their figures of speech from the analogies of nature—is the parallel of all this faithful accumulation
of detail and counterfeit handwriting of Nature?   The
great ex-chancellor HAD stooped to watch even the
" red-hipped bumble-bee " and the "small gray-coated
gnat."   Had the busy manager been studying them as
well?   His last act on earth was to alight from his car-
riage to gather handfuls of snow, to ascertain if snow
could be utilized to prevent decomposition of dead
flesh ; and it is related that, in his dying moments—
for the very act precipitated the fever of which he died
—he did not forget to record that the experiment
had succeeded " excellently well."   From these to
lordly music,[1] and in all the range between, no
science had escaped Francis Bacon.   Had the busy

---

[1] Ulrici, p. 248, book ii, Chapter vi., refers to " Two Gentlemen
of Verona," Act 1, Sc. 2. as proving that the author of that play
" possessed in an unusual degree the power of judging and understanding the theory of music."

manager followed or preceded the philosopher's footsteps, step by step, up through them all? And did he pause in his conception or adaptation of a play, pen in hand, to take a trip to Italy, or a run-up into Scotland to get the name of a hostelry or the topography of a highway, to make it an encyclopædia as well as a play as he went along? If the manager alone was the author of these works, there is, we have seen, no refuge from this conviction. But, if, as is the New Theory, those plays were amplified for the press by a learned hand, perhaps, after all, he was the stage manager, actor, and human being that history asserts him to have been. If, as has been conjectured, William Shakespeare sketched the clowns and wenches with which these stately dramas are relieved, it would account for the supposed Warwickshire source of many of them. And if William Shakespeare was pretty familiar with the constabulary along his route between home and theater, so often traveled by himself and jolly coetaneans with heads full of Marian Hackett's ale, and thought some of them good enough to put into a play, his judgment has received the approval of many audiences beside those of the Bankside and Blackfriars. The Shakespearean plays, as now performed in our theaters, are the editions of Cibber, Garrick, Kemble, Kean, Macready, Booth, Irving, and others, and, while preserving still the dialogues which passed, perhaps, through Shakespeare's hands, retain no traces of his industry, once so valuable to the Globe and Blackfriars, but now rejected as unsuited to the exigencies of the modern stage, the "business" inserted in them by William Shakespeare's editorship has long since been rejected. Little as there is of the man of

Stratford in our libraries, there is still less of him in
our theaters in 1881. But the world still retains the
honest Dogberry, who lived at Grendon, in Bucks, on
the road from London to Stratfordtown, and doubtless
many more of the witty manager's master strokes.
At least, the "New Theory" and the "Delia Bacon
Theory" coincide in this, that William Shakespeare
was fortunate in the manuscripts brought to him, and
grew rich in making plays out of them and matching
them to his spectacles.

―――――

Such, briefly sketched, are the theories concerning these glorious transcripts of the age of Elizabeth,
which, while two centuries of literature between is obsolete and moribund, are yet unwithered and unstaled,
and the most priceless of all the treasuries of the age
of Victoria. And yet, there seems to be a feeling that
any exploration after their authorship is a sacrilege,
and that this particular historical question must be
left untouched—as Pythagoras would not eat beans, as
parricidal—that William Shakespeare is William
Shakespeare—and the doggerel curse of Stratford
hangs over and forefends the meddling with his bones.
But no witch's palindrome for long can block the
march of reason and of research. Modern scholarship
is every day dissolving chimera, and, if this Shakespeare story has no basis of truth, it must inevitably be
abolished along with the rest. If this transcendent
literature had come down to us without the name,
would it have been sacrilege to search for its paternity?
And does the mere name of William Shakespeare
make that, which is otherwise expedient, infamous?

Or, is this the meaning of the incantation on the tomb
—that cursed shall he be that seeks to penetrate the
secret of the plays? Such, indeed, was the belief that
drove poor Delia Bacon mad. But we decline to see
any thing but the calm historical question. It seems to
us that, if we are at liberty to dispute as much as we
like as to whether two *a*'s or only one, or three *e*'s or
only two belong of right in the name " Shakespeare,"
surely it can not be debarred us to ask of the Past the
origin of the thousand-souled pages we call by that
name. We believe that, if the existence of these three
theories—as to each of which it is possible to say so
much—proves any thing, it proves that history and circumstantial evidence oppose the possibility of William Shakespeare's authorship of the works called his,
and that there is a reasonable doubt as to whether
any ONE MAN did write, or could have written, either
with or without a Bodleian or an Astor Library at his
elbow, the whole complete canon of the Shakespearean
works.

But is there not a refuge from all these more or less
conflicting theories in the simple canon that human
experience is a safer guide than conjecture or miracle?
In our own day, the astute manager draws from bushels
of manuscript plays, submitted to him by ambitious
amateurs or plodding playwrights, the few morsels
he deems worthy of his stage, and, restringing them
on a thread of his own, or another's. presents the result to his audiences. Can we imagine a reason why
the same process should have been improbable in the
days of Elizabeth and James? And if among these
amateurs and playwrights there happened to be the
same proportion of lawyers, courtiers, politicians,

soldiers, musicians, physicians, naturalists, botanists, and the rest (as well as contributions from the hundreds of learned clerks whom the disestablishment of the monasteries had driven to their wits for support), that we would be likely to find among the corresponding class to-day, it would surely be a less violent explanation of "the myriad-minded Shakespeare," than to conjecture the "Shakespeare" springing, without an interval for preparation, at once into the finished crown and acme of each and all of these. In fact, is it not William Shakespeare the EDITOR, and not the AUTHOR, to whom our veneration and gratitude is due?

It almost seems as if not only the skepticism of the doubter but the criticism of scholarship has all along tended irresistibly to accept this compromise, as all criticism must eventually coincide with history, if it be criticism at all. The closest examination of the Shakespearean plays has revealed to scholars traces of more than one hand. It is past a hundred years since Theobald declared that, "though there are several master strokes in these three plays (viz.: the three parts of 'King Henry VI.'), yet I am almost doubtful whether they were entirely of his (Shakespeare's) writing. And unless they were wrote by him very early, I should rather imagine them to have been brought to him as a director of the stage, and so have received some finishing beauties at his hands. An accurate observer will easily see the diction of them is more obsolete, and the numbers more mean and prosaical than in the generality of his genuine composition."[1] We have elsewhere shown

---

[1] Theobald's Shakespeare (1733). Vol. IV., p. 110.

that Farmer stumbled upon the same difficulty.
Malone "wrote a long dissertation," says Mr. Grant
White, "to show that the three parts of 'King Henry
VI.' were not Shakespeare's, but had only been altered
and enriched by him; and that the first 'part' was
written by another person than the author of the second and third."[1] Drake proposed that the "First
Part of 'King Henry VI.' be excluded from future editions of Shakespeare's Works, because it offers no
trace of any finishing strokes from the master bard."[2]
"It remains to inquire," says Hallam (after a discussion of these plays, which he says Shakespeare remodeled from two old plays "in great part by Marlowe,
though Greene seems to have put in for some share in
their composition"), "who are to claim the credit of
these other plays, so great a portion of which has
passed with the world for the genuine work of Shakespeare."[3] And again, what share he (Shakespeare)
may have had in similar repairs of the many plays he
represented, can not be determined.[4] And Dyce, Halliwell, and all the others follow Mr. Hallam (whose
authority is Greene's well-known complaint about the
"Johannes Factotum, who struts about with his tyger's
heart wrapped in a player's hide;"[5] which allusion to a line in the third part of Henry the Sixth,
locates the particular "steal" which Greene had most
at heart when he complained). Last of all comes Mr.

---

[1] An essay on the authorship of the three parts of King Henry
the Sixth. By Richard Grant White. Riverside Press. H. O.
Houghton & Co., Cambridge, Mass., 1859.
[2] Shakespeare and His Times. Vol. II., p. 297.
[3] Note to Hallam's Literature of Europe. Part II., chap. vi., § 30.
[4] Id., § 35.
[5] "O, tiger's heart wrapped in a woman's hide."—III. Hen. VI.

Grant White, a most profound believer in "Shakespeare, and all that name implies," with "An Essay on the authorship of the Three Parts of King Henry the Sixth,"[1] to prove that William Shakespeare, in plagiarizing from the earlier tragedies, only plagiarized from HIMSELF, he himself having really written all that was worth saving in them! Mr. White labors considerably to fix the exact date at which Marlowe, Peale and Greene—the most eminent playwriters of the day—employed a raw Stratford youth, just truanting in London, to kindly run over, prune, and perfect their manuscripts for them, and to clear Mr. White's Shakespeare from the stigma of what, if true, Mr. White admits to have been a "want of probity on Shakespeare's part, accompanied by a hardly less culpable indifference on the part of his fellows."[2] This "indifference" can not be charged to one sufferer, at least, Robert Greene, who was not silent when he saw his work unblushingly appropriated: thus giving us assurance of one occasion, at least, upon which William Shakespeare posed as editor instead of author.

At any rate, we have seen the circumstantial evidence has been corroborated by the experts (for so, to borrow a figure, let us call them) Aubrey, Cartwright, Digges, Denham, Fuller,[3] and Ben Jonson. All these assure us (Ben Jonson twice, once in writing and once in conversation) that William Shakespeare was a nat-

---

[1] Cambridge, Mass.: H. O. Houghton & Co. Riverside Press, 1859.

[2] Id., p. 100.

[3] See the quotation from his "Worthies of England," in the foot-note, ante, this chapter.

ural wit—a wag in the crude—but that he wanted art. Old Dominie Ward made a note "to read Shakespeare's plays to post him," but even he had heard that he was a wit, but that he wanted art.[1] This testimony may not compel conviction, but it is all we have; we must take it, or go without any testimony at all. At any rate, it sustains and is sustained by the circumstances, and these seven different witnesses, at least, testify, without procurement, collusion, or knowledge of the use to be made of their testimony, and opposed to them all is only the little elegiac rhyme by one of themselves:

> " Yet must I not give nature all thy art,
> My gentle Shakespeare must enjoy a part."

Only one single scrap of mortuary effusion on which to hang the fame of centuries! And if we exclude the circumstantial evidence and the expert testimony as false, and admit the one little rhyme as true, then our reason, judgment, and inner consciousness must accept as the author of the learned, laborious, accurate, eloquent, and majestic Sheakespearean pages, a wag— a funny fellow whose "wit (to quote Jonson again) was in his own power," but not "the rule of it," so much so, "that sometimes it was necessary he should be stopped." Surely it is a much less violent supposition that this funny Mr. Shakespeare—who happened to be employed in the theater where certain masterpieces were taken to be cut up into plays to copy out of them each actor's parts—that this waggish penman, as he wrote out the parts in big, round hand, improved on or interpolated a palpable hit, a merry speech, the

---

[1] Ante, page 68.

last popular song, or sketched entire a role with a name familiar to his boyish ear—the village butt, or sot, or justice of the peace,[1] may be; or, why not some fellow scapegrace of olden times by Avon banks? He did it with a swift touch and a mellow humor that relieved and refreshed the stately speeches, making the play all the more available and the copyist all the more valuable to the management. But, all the same, how this witty Mr. Shakespeare would have roared at a suggestion that the centuries after him should christen by his—the copyist's—name all the might and majesty and splendor, all the philosophy and pathos and poetry, every word that he wrote out, unblotting a line, for the players!

It must be conceded, say the new theorists:

I. That the plays, whether in the shape we now have them or not, are, at least, under the same

---

[1] He had not failed to see Dogberry and Shallow in the little villages of Warwickshire—and the wonderful " Watch." The " Watch " of those days was indeed something to wonder at. In a letter of Lord Burleigh to Sir Francis Walsingham, written in 1586, the writer says that he once saw certain of them standing "so openly in pumps" in a public place, that "no suspected person would come nigh them;" and, on his asking them what they stood there for, they answered that they were put there to apprehend three men, the only description they had of them was that *one of them had a hooked nose*. " If they be no better instructed but to find three persons by one of them having a hooked nose, they may miss thereof," reflects Burghley, with much reason. Mr. Halliwell Phillips, in his "Outline of the Life of William Shakespeare (Brighton, 1881), page 66, thinks that this is unlikely, because the magistrate mentioned by Aubrey would have been too old in 1642, if he had been the model sought.

26

names and with substantially the same dramatis personæ.

II. That William Shakespeare was the stage manager, or stage editor; or, at any rate, touched up the plays for representation.

III. That the acting copies of the plays, put into the hands of the players to learn their parts from, were more or less in the handwriting of William Shakespeare, and that from these acting copies the first folio of 1623 was set up and printed.

At least, the best evidence at hand seems to establish all three of these propositions. This evidence is meager and accidental, but, for that very reason, involuntary, and, therefore, not manufactured; and it establishes the above propositions, as far as it goes, as follows:

I. In a volume, "Poste, with a Packet of Madde-Letters," printed in 1603, a young woman is made to say to her lover: "It is not your hustie rustie can make me afraide of your big lookes, for I saw the plaie of Ancient Pistoll, where a craking coward was well cudgelled for his knavery; your railing is so near the rascall that I am almost ashamed to bestow so good a name as the rogue upon you."

Again, Sharpham, in his "Fleire," printed in 1607, has this piece of dialogue:

"*Kni.*—And how lives he with 'am? .

"*Fle.*—Faith, like THISBE in the play, a' has almost killed himselfe with the scabbard!"

The first author thus makes his young woman to have seen Henry V., and the second alludes to the Midsummer-Night's Dream, where the bumpkin who plays Thisbe is made to kill himself by falling on his

scabbard instead of his sword. Besides, in the imperfect versions of the plays which the printers were able
to make up, from such unauthorized sources as best
served them, it is thought that there are unmistakable evidences that one of the sources was the short-
hand of a listener, who, not catching a word or phrase
distinctly, would put down something that sounded
enough like it to betray the sources and his copy.
For example: In the spring of 1602, a play called
"The Revenge of Hamlet, Prince of Denmark," was
presented at the Globe theater. In 1603, two booksellers, Ling and Trundell, printed a play of that title,
put William Shakespeare's name to it, and sold it.
Now, in this version, we have such errors as "right
done" for "write down" (Act I., Scene ii.); "inven-
om'd speech" for "in venom steeped" (Act I., Scene
i.); "I'll provide for you a grave" for "most secret
and most grave" (Act III., Scene iv.); "a beast devoid
of reason" for "a beast that wants discourse of reason," and the like. Ling and Trundell, somehow or
other, procured better copy, and printed a corrected
edition in the following year; but the errors in their
first edition were precisely such as would result from
an attempt to report the play phonetically, as it was
delivered by the actors on the stage. All the printers
of the day seem to have made common piracy out of
these plays, impelled thereto by their exceeding popularity. (Nash says that the first part of King Henry
VI., especially, had a wonderful run for those days,
being witnessed by at least ten thousand people.[1] Of

---

[1] We take all these references from "Outlines of the Life of
Shakespeare," by I. O. Halliwell Phillips (Brighton. Printed for
the author's friends, for presents only. 1881), page 40, to which
capital volume we acknowledge our exceeding obligation. Mr.

this play a garbled version was put on the market by Millington, who, soon after, did the same thing by the Henry V.)

II. Davenant instructed Betterton how to render the part of Henry VIII., assuring him that he (Davenant) had his own instructions from Lowin, and that Lowin got them from William Shakespeare in person.[1] (We have not accepted Davenant's evidence as likely to be of much value, when assuming to be Shakespeare's son, successor, literary executor, and the like, but this does not appear, on its face, improbable, and is no particular less if untrue.) Ravenscroft, who re-wrote Titus Andronicus in 1687, says, in his preface : " I have been told by some anciently conversant with the stage, that it (this play) was not originally his (Shakespeare's), but brought by a private actor to be acted, and he only gave some master touches to one or two of the principal parts or characters."[2]

"I am assured," says Gildon,[3] "from very good hands, that the person that acted Iago was in much esteem as a comedian, which made Shakespeare put several words and expressions into his part, perhaps not so agreeable to his character, to make the audience laugh, who had not yet learned to endure to be serious a whole play." (But if Shakespeare put them in to "catch the ear of the groundlings," who took

Grant White in the Atlantic Monthly, October 1881, believes that he is able to trace the surreptitious "copy" of this first Hamlet to the actor who took the part of Voltimand. The inference from Mr. White's account of the transaction, is precisely that we have noted in the text.

[1] Id.   [2] Id.

[3] Reflections on Rymer's "Short View of Tragedy," quoted by Mr. Halliwell Phillips, in his work cited in last note.

them out again for the folio of 1623? The Baconians would probably ask: "Did Bacon, after Shakespeare was dead?" And it could not have been a proof-reader; for, if there was any proof-reader, he was the most careless one that ever lived. The folio of 1623 is crowded with typographical errors.) Somebody—necessarily Shakespeare—was in the habit of introducing into these Shakespearean plays the popular songs of the day. For example, the song, "A Lover and His Lass," in "As you Like it," was written by Thomas Morley, and printed in his "First Book of Ayres; or, Little Short Songs," in 1600.[1] And the ballad, "Farewell, Dear Love," in "Twelfth Night," has previously appeared in 1601, in the "Book of Ayres" of Robert Jones.[2] It is probable, however, says Mr. Halliwell Phillips, that William Shakespeare had withdrawn from the management of the Globe; at the date of its destruction during the performance of Henry VIII. (which Mr. Phillips calls the first play on the English stage in which dramatic art was sacrificed to stage effect. It is curious, this being the case, to find the New Shakespeare Society rejecting the Henry VIII. as not Shakespearean on the philological evidence, and assuring us that Wolsey's soliloquy is not Shakespeare's, as did Mr. Spedding so many years before). The story of Queen Elizabeth's order for "Falstaff in Love" first appeared, in 1702, in the

---

[1] In the last issue of the "Transactions of the New Shakespeare Society" is a copy of what purports to be a manuscript respecting the delivery of certain red cloth to Shakespeare, on the occasion of a reception to James I., by the corporation of London, in 1604, unearthed and guaranteed by Mr. Furnivall.

[2] Folio, London, 1601.

preface to John Dennis's "Comicale Gallant," from whom Rowe quoted. Although smacking of the same flavor as the Southampton and King James "yarns"— it is worth noting that this story may possess, perhaps, some vestige of foundation. If these sounding plays, so full of religion, politics, philosophy, and statecraft, were presented at Shakespeare's theater, it is only natural that it should come to Elizabeth's ears. The lion Queen did not care to have her subjects instructed too far. She liked to keep them well in hand, and was only—she and her ministers—too ready to "snuff treason in certain things that went by other's names." The run of comedies at other theaters were harmless enough (an adultery for a plot, and an unsuspecting husband for a butt. This was a comedy; plus a little blood, it was a tragedy). Let the people have their fill of amusement, but it is better not to meddle with philosophy and politics. So there are things more unlikely to have happened than that Elizabeth, through her Lord Chamberlain, should have intimated to manager Shakespeare to give them something more in the run and appetite of the day.[1] The "Merry Wives of Windsor" was, in due time, underlined. But, somehow or other, it was with a would-be adulterer, rather than an injured husband, for a butt; and, somehow or other, Galen and Esculapius and Epicurius had intruded where there was no need of them. The salaciousness Elizabeth wanted (if the story is true) was all there, as well as the transformation scene; but, at the end, there is a re-

---

[1] Collier—"Lives of Shakespeare's Actors, Introduction, page xv."—says that there were at least two, and perhaps three, other William Shakespeares in London in these days.

buke to lechery and to lecherous minds that is not
equivocal in its terms.[1] But that any of this Shakespeare fortune came, by way of gift or otherwise, from
Southampton, there is no ground, except silly and
baseless rumor, for believing. If Southampton had
been the Rothschild of his time—which he was very far
from being—he would not have given a thousand
pounds (a sum we have estimated as equaling $25,000
to-day, but which Mr. Grant White puts at $30,000,
and which Mr. Halliwell Phillips,[2] on account of the
"often fictitious importance attached to cash, arising
from its comparative scarcity in those days," says
ought even be as high as twelve pounds for one) to a
casual acquaintance. The mere passing of such a
sum would seem to involve other relations; and
if Southampton knew Shakespeare, or Shakespeare
Southampton, let it be demonstrated from some auto-
biographical or historical source—from some other
source than the " Biographies of William Shakespeare," written by those slippery rhapsodists, the
Shakespereans. If Damon and Pythias were friends,
let it appear from the biographies of Damon, as well
as from the biographies of Pythias. Let us find it in
some of Southampton's papers, or in the archives or
papers of some of his family, descendants, contemporaries, or acquaintances; in the chronicles of Elizabeth, Raleigh, Cecil, Essex, Rutland, Montgomery,
Camden, Coke, Bacon, Tobie Mathew, Ben Jonson,
or of somebody alive and with open eyes in London

---

[1] Perhaps, if the story were true, a rebuke to Elizabeth personally in the line (Act V., Scene v.), "Our radiant Queen hates
sluts and sluttery."

[2] "Outlines of the Life of Shakespeare," note, page 17.

at about that date, before we yield it historical assent, and make oath to it so solemnly. As a matter of fact, and as the industrious Mr. Lodge confesses,[1] there is no such trace or record. Except from the "biographers" of Shakespeare, no note, hint, or surmise, connecting the two names, can be anywhere unearthed, and they only draw the suggestion on which they build such lofty treatises from a dedication printed in the days when printers helped themselves to any name they wanted without fear of an injunction out of chancery. That any sonnets were ever dedicated to Southampton by anybody, is, we have seen, pure invention.

III. But that the famous First Folio of 1623 was set up from piecemeal parts written for separate actors, and that these were in William Shakespeare's handwriting, there seems to be contemporary circumstantial evidence.

We have seen that, although Ben Jonson has, for two hundred and fifty years, been believed when he said in poetry that William Shakespeare was not only the "Star of Poets" for genius, but that besides he would "sweat and strike the second heat upon the muses's anvil;" when he said in prose that "The players often mentioned it as an honor to Shakespeare that in writing (whatever he wrote) he never blotted out a line," he was supposed to be using a mere figure of speech. But it seems that he was telling the truth. For, in 1623—Shakespeare having been dead seven years—Heminges and Condell—two "players" (i. e.,

---

[1] Portraits, Henry Wreothlesey, Earl of Southampton, Vol. III., page 155, Bohn's edition.

actors), and the same that Shakespeare in his Will calls his "fellows"—publish the first edition of the plays we now call "Shakespeare"—and, on the title-page of that edition, advertise them as "published according to the *true original copies.*" Further on in their preface, they repeat, almost in his very words, Ben Jonson's statement, asserting that "We have scarce received from him (William Shakespeare) a blot in his papers." What papers? What indeed, but "the TRUE ORIGINAL COPIES" of these plays which were in William Shakespeare's handwriting? What else could it have been that "the players" (according to Ben Jonson) saw? Does anybody suppose that the poet's own first draft, untouched of the file and unperfumed of the lamp, went into "the players'" hands, for them to learn their parts from? And, even if *one* player was allowed to study his part from the inspired author's first draft, his fellow "players" must have taken or received a copy or copies of their parts; they could not all study their parts from the same manuscript. The only reasonable supposition, therefore, is, that William Shakespeare made it part of his duties at the theater to *write out* in a fair hand the parts for the different "players" (and no wonder they mentioned it, as "an honor" to him, that he lightened their labors considerably by the legibility of his penmanship, by never blotting out a line) and that, in course of time, these "true original copies" were collected from their fellow-actors by Heminges and Condell, and by them published; they remarking, in turn, upon the excellence of the penmanship so familiar to them. There is only wanted to confirm this supposition, a piece of

27

actual evidence as to what Heminges and Condell *did*
print from.

Now, it happens that, by their own careless proof
reading, Heminges and Condell have actually supplied this piece of missing circumstantial evidence, as
follows: Naturally, in these true original copies of a
particular actors part, the name of the actor assuming
that part would be written in the margin, opposite to
or instead of the name of the character he was to personate; precisely as is done to-day by the theater copyist in copying parts for distribution among the company. It happened that, in setting up the types for
this first edition from these fragmentary actors' copies,
the printers would often accidentaly, from following
" copy " too closely, set up these real names of the actors instead of the names of the characters. And—as
any one taking up a copy or fac-simile of this famous
"first folio " can see for himself—the editors carelessly
overlooked these errors in the proof, and there they
remain to this day : "Jacke Wilson," for " Balthazar ;"
"Andrew" and " Cowley," for "Dogberry;" "Kempe,"
for "Verges," and the like—the names of Shakespeare's
actors—instead of the parts they took in the piece.
It seems superfluous to again suggest that these unblotted " copies " could not have been the author's first
draft of a play, or that an author does not write his
compositions in manifold, or that there had been many
actors to learn their parts in the course of from sixteen to twenty years.

Besides—even if Heminges and Condell had not told
us—it would have still been perfectly evident, from an
inspection of the "first folio," that the " copy " it was
set up from was never completely in their hands, but

was collected piecemeal during the manufacture. For instance, we see where the printers left a space of twenty-nine pages, between "Romeo and Juliet" and "Julius Cæsar," in which to print the "Timon of Athens." But all the copy they could find of the "Timon" only made *eighteen* pages, and so—by huge "head pieces" and "tail pieces," and a "Table of the Actor's Names" (given in no other instance) in coarse capitals—they eked out the "signature;" and, by omitting the whole of the next "signature," carried the pagination over from "98" to "109." The copy for "Troilus and Cressida" seems not to have been received until the volume was in the binder's hands (which is remarkable, too, for that play had been in print for fourteen years). The play is not mentioned in the table of contents, but is tucked in without paging (except that the first five pages are numbered 78, 79, 80, 81, 82, whereas the paging of the volume had already reached 232). "Troilus and Cressida," thus printed, fills two "signatures" lacking one page, and so somebody at hand wrote a "Prologue" in rhyme—setting out the argument—to save the blank page, and the like. Whatever "papers" Heminges and Condell "received from William Shakespeare then, were fair, unblotted copies of the actor parts, made by him for their use. It appears then, that—minute scholarship and the records apart—the foreman of a printing-house would have been at any time in the past two hundred and fifty years, without assistance from the commentators, able to settle the great Shakespearean authorship controversy.

While—from one standpoint—this testimony of the types is strong circumstantial evidence against the Baconian theory, taken from another standpoint it is quite as strongly corroborative. For on the one hand, Bacon was alive when this folio was printed, and the man who rewrote his essays eleven times would scarcely have allowed his plays to go to the public so shiftlessly printed. But on the other hand, if the book was printed without consulting him, that insurmountable barrier—the fact that Bacon never claimed these plays—is swept away at once. We have simply to assume that he always intended, at some convenient season, to acknowledge them : that he was not satisfied with them as they appeared in the Heminges and Condell edition, and proposed revising them himself before claiming them, (we know how difficult he found it to satisfy his own censorship) or that he purposed completing the series, (for which the sketch of the Henry VII may have been placed among his private memoranda) at his leisure. We have then only to imagine that death overtook him suddenly (his death was sudden) before this programme had been completed, and his not acknowledging them ; not leaving them—incomplete as he believed them—to " the next ages," was characteristic of the man.

" If I go, who remains? If I remain, who goes?" said Dante to the Council of Florence. Take the Shakespearean pages away from English literature, and what remains? Retain them, and what departs? And yet are men to believe that the writer of these pages left no impress on the history of his age and no item in the chronicle of his time? that, in the intensest focus of the clear, calm, electric-light of nineteenth century inspection and investigation, their author stands only revealed in the gossip of goodwives or the drivel of a pot-house clientage? Who is it—his reason and judgment once enlisted—who believes this thing?

Columbus discovered the continent we call after the name of another. Where shall we find written the names of the genii whose fruit and fame this Shakespeare has stolen. Having lost "our Shakespeare" both to-day and forever, it will doubtless remain—as it is—the question, " Who wrote the Shakespearean dramas?" The evidence is all in—the testimony is all taken. Perhaps it is a secret that even Time will never tell, that is hidden deep down in the crypt and sacristy of the Past, whose seal shall never more be broken. In the wise land of China it is said that when a man has deserved well of the state, his countrymen honor, with houses and lands and gifts and decorations, not himself, but his father and his mother. Perhaps, learning a lesson from the Celestials, we might rear a shaft to the fathers and the mothers of the Immortality that wrote the Book of Nature, the mighty book which "age can not wither, nor custom stale" and whose infinite variety for three centuries has been and, until Time shall be no more, will be close to the hearts of every age and cycle of men— household words for ever and ever, The Book— thank heaven!—that nothing can divorce from us.

THE END.

INDEX.

A.

C.

N.

O.

P.

U.

Ulrici, opinion of, learning of plays, 221.
Unitary theory, property of Smith and Holmes. See Bacon, Delia, 200.

V.

Vega, Lope de, computed to have written 21,300,000 verses, 184.
Writes " without blotting a line," 184.
Venice, knowledge of, displayed in plays, 219.
Venus and Adonis, argument from that poem alone, 43.
Boldness of assignment to W. S., 275.
Popularity of, 293.
Why not a first production, 294.
Why of doubtful authorship, 41, 218.

W.

Ward, Dominie, hears about Shakespeare, 304.
Testimony as to Shakespeare's acquirements, 265.
Ward, Rev. John, his account of W. S., 68.
Warwickshire, names, use of, in the plays, 248.
Expressions, use of in plays, 248.
" Watch," the, actual curiosities, 305.
Burghley's account of, 305, note.
Werner, anticipated by the plays, 213.
" Wet combats," wit combats were, 268.
Is it a misprint ? 269.
" W. H.," a friend of Thorpe, dedicator or dedicatee ? 278.
Theories as to meaning of, 280–282.
Various translations of, 279.
Who was he ? 109, 279, 280, 282.
White, R. G., admits that managers " kept a poet," 85, note.
His idea of Henry VI., 303.
Opinion of English of plays, 218.
Who wrote Shakespeare ? *Passim.* Question first asked in 1852, 185.
Wilkes, Geo., his "American Point of View," 247.
Will, difficulties of the, explained, 271.